TANTALUS

John Barton is a director and an Advisory Director of the Royal Shakespeare Company (which he helped found in 1959). Barton spent nearly 20 years developing *Tantalus*, which is an extension of his earlier work, *The Greeks* (1980). He has adapted some twenty texts for the theatre and has also had published *The First Stage*, *The Hollow Crown*, *The Wars of the Roses*, *The Greeks*, *La Ronde*, *The Rover* and *Playing Shakespeare*.

John Barton

TANTALUS

An Ancient Myth for a New Millenium

Part I
The Outbreak of War

Part II
The War

Part III
The Homecomings

OBERON BOOKS
LONDON

First published in 2000 by Oberon Books Ltd.
(incorporating Absolute Classics)
521 Caledonian Road, London N7 9RH
Tel: 020 7607 3637 / Fax: 020 7607 3629

e-mail: oberon.books@btinternet.com

A catalogue record for this book is available from the British Library.

ISBN: 1 84002 160 8

Cover design: Jon Morgan

Printed in Great Britain by Alden Press Ltd, Oxford.

Contents

This play cycle can be performed in two formats; on a single day, or on separate days, grouped as follows:

Group 1		Group 2	
	1 Apollo		6 Odysseus
	2 Telephus		7 Cassandra
	3 Iphigenia		8 Hermione
	4 Neoptolemus		9 Helen
	5 Priam		10 Erigone

Introduction

This book goes to press some three months before Peter Hall's production of *Tantalus* opens. There is inevitably a difference between any written text and the playing one, and in this case it is very considerable. This is partly because the original text is so long and covers more material than could ever easily be handled and mastered in rehearsal. This book represents my exploration and shaping of what I find most resonant and rich in the Greek myths on which it is based. The theatre version however has been drastically condensed to provide something more easily accessible in performance. My own vision, however passionate, may not necessarily be welcome in that context, so all I can do is give the production as generous a welcome as I may.

Which is more important about a new play? The author's text or the director who takes it over? A question easy to ask, but not so easy to answer. 'The play's the thing' is a useful yet ambiguous phrase, just as the myths themselves are and always will be. And any interpretation of them in the theatre will always be so too.

John Barton
September 2000

Note

When speech headings are in brackets it means that the speaker has not yet fully become a character in the play or they are only acting a part. In the first play particularly, the characters only gradually become 'real'.

(*) on the right of the page indicates a scene change when a new character enters or some important change takes place.

Characters who speak or who are mentioned in the play

THE HOUSE OF TANTALUS *(Mycenae)*

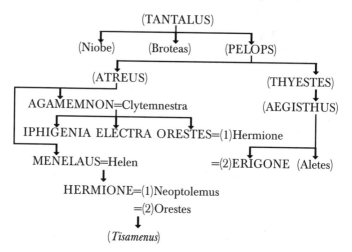

LACEDAEMON *(Sparta)*

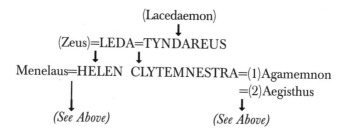

THE ROYAL HOUSE OF TROY

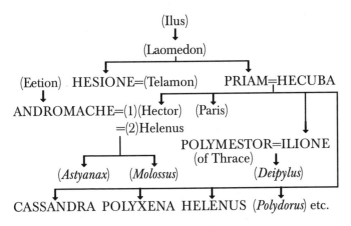

(Ilus)
↓
(Laomedon)

(Eetion) HESIONE=(Telamon) PRIAM=HECUBA

ANDROMACHE=(1)(Hector) (Paris)
=(2)Helenus

POLYMESTOR=ILIONE
(of Thrace) ↓

(*Astyanax*) (*Molossus*) (*Deipylus*)

CASSANDRA POLYXENA HELENUS (*Polydorus*) etc.

PHTHIA *(Thessaly)*

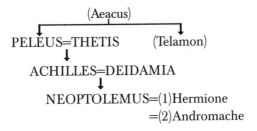

(Aeacus)

PELEUS=THETIS (Telamon)
↓
ACHILLES=DEIDAMIA
↓
NEOPTOLEMUS=(1)Hermione
=(2)Andromache

KEY:
=	married/raped
Brackets	mentioned but do not speak or are children
Italics	for children

Tantalus was first performed at the Denver Center for Performing Arts, on 21 October 2000, with the following cast:

FIRST WOMAN, Ann Mitchell

SECOND WOMAN, Alyssa Bresnahan

THIRD WOMAN, Annalee Jefferies

FOURTH WOMAN, Mia Yoo

FIRST MAN, David Ryall

SECOND MAN, Greg Hicks

THIRD MAN, Alan Dobie

FOURTH MAN, Robert Petkoff

CHORUS, Francesca Carlin, Joy Jones, Tess Lina, Jeanne Paulsen, Christina Pawl, Nicole Poole, Juliet Smith, Mia Tagano, Vickie Tanner, Robin Terry

Other members of the ENSEMBLE, Elijah Alexander, Joshua Coomer, Pierre-Marc Diennet, Morgan Hallet, Steve Hughes, Tif Luckenbill, David McCann, Randy Moore, Matt Pepper

Directors, Edward Hall and Peter Hall

Prologue
ZEUS

A BARREN PLACE

CAST

First Woman	A woman who cooks by the fire
Second Woman	LEDA/THETIS
First Man	a drunken POET/ TYNDAREUS/ PELEUS
Second Man	
Third Man	} STONE MEN
Fourth Man	

CHORUS of NINE WOMEN

(*An empty space with rocks dimly in the
background. Distant sounds of the wind and
sea. An old WOMAN lights a fire, while
TWELVE GIRLS lie on the ground, sleeping.
What they are wearing or not wearing should
suggest no particular period. The scene should
look as spare, simple and ordinary as
possible. A boat horn sounds which could be
either man-made or mythical*)

(CHORUS)	We've missed the boat.
(FIRST WOMAN)	Not again?
(CHORUS)	But I want to know why: Who's to blame?
(FIRST WOMAN)	What's it matter?
(CHORUS)	But I want to know how we missed it.
(FIRST WOMAN)	It will fetch us in the morning. How could it be otherwise?
(CHORUS)	If we're here for the night Someone tell us a story.
(THIRD WOMAN)	What about?
(FIRST WOMAN)	Try the beginning.
(CHORUS)	Of what?
(FIRST WOMAN)	All things and everything. (*)

(*They settle down*)

(CHORUS)	Some say all began in the ocean Which girdles the edge of the world.
–	Don't be silly; everyone knows They began in a great blaze of light.
–	Yes, Mother Earth and all the gods too From some fireball out of nowhere.
–	Nonsense, Eris began it: She rose naked out of Chaos.
–	Some say that out of chaos Harmony is born.

(SECOND WOMAN) No, it all began with a girl
       Called Eurynome. She was lonely
       So she danced and as she danced
       She stirred up a mighty wind;
       And as she danced faster and faster
       It turned into a serpent
       And it twisted with her in a dance
       Which till then had never been seen
       And they twined and twisted till dawn
       And that's how the world began.

(CHORUS)   But these stories can't all be true
   – Why not? – They are only stories.

(FIRST WOMAN) If you want to know the truth
       You could always consult an oracle.

(CHORUS)   They're all lost now or forgotten.

(FIRST WOMAN) Some are nearer than you think
       But it's easy to overlook them.
       Long ago Trophonios the Argonaut
       Made one which is quiet and modest;
       At first it was little more
       Than a hole in the ground or the rock-face…
       And on either side two streams
       Bubbled out from the rock-face.

       (*Two streams begin to trickle*)

       It is said if you drank from the first
       You would quite forget all your sorrows,
       And if you then drank from the second
       You'd remember what you'd never known.
       The first stream is called Lethe.

(CHORUS)   But that is the stream of Death:
       It runs down into Hades.

(FIRST WOMAN) But Lethe in the beginning
       Didn't mean 'death' at all;
       It only meant 'lying hidden'
       Or later to 'slip out of mind':
       These days the world has forgotten
       It means no more than 'forgetting'.

(THIRD WOMAN)   And the second one?

(FIRST WOMAN)   Mnemosyne.

(CHORUS)   But Mnemosyne means Memory.

(FIRST WOMAN)   No, Memory means her:
She is a goddess so ancient
That she may have been here at the start
Or maybe even before it.
Zeus himself used to come here
To refresh and renew himself
By lying with her in a cave.

(*The streams have grown a little*)

(CHORUS)   The streams have come out of that cave
(*To First Woman*)   What's in there?

(FIRST WOMAN)   They say
You'd be sucked down into the darkness
But after a while the water
Would cast you out again.
And if you told what you'd seen
You'd find you could laugh again.

(CHORUS)   But which stream is which?

(FIRST WOMAN)   That's forgotten.

(CHORUS)   You say Zeus himself came here?

(FIRST WOMAN)   Yes, Zeus himself... I remember.   (*)

(*A thunder crack/lightening flash. Some of the rocks crumble and more water spurts from the streams. A ragged MAN appears from the rocks carrying a large leather wine-bag and various props. He brushes dust off himself and drinks from the wine-bag*)

(FIRST MAN)   I heard the name of Zeus...
What have we here?
The three things I love most:
To join in a drinking,
To listen to questions and stories
And to be among beautiful women!

(CHORUS)   Who is this?

(FIRST WOMAN)	It's the Poet.
(CHORUS)	Better be careful; ignore him.
(THIRD WOMAN)	Quiet, there's a sound in the cave: I can hear a baby weeping.
(CHORUS)	In there?
(FIRST MAN)	It is the young Dionysos: I'm his tutor.
(THIRD WOMAN)	Go away, he is drunk.
(CHORUS)	Everyone knows that Dionysos Lived long ago up on Olympus.
(THIRD MAN)	No, he has not gone up yet.
(CHORUS)	Not yet? It's some madman
—	Perhaps he's a god in disguise
—	Excuse us, but are you a god?
(THIRD MAN)	No, I suppose I'm a poet.
(CHORUS)	What were doing in there?
POET	Making things up.
(CHORUS)	You invent things?
POET	No, I put them all together.
(CHORUS)	What?
POET	All the stories.
(CHORUS)	We know them already.
—	Speak for yourself.
POET	But you don't know the lost bits.
(THIRD WOMAN)	How can you is they're lost?
POET	By putting them into a story.
(CHORUS)	What is your story called?
POET	*Kuklos: Epikou cyclou leipsana.*
(CHORUS)	What does that mean?
POET	The lost story Of the Apple Game of Zeus.

(CHORUS) What apple? – He's made it all up.

POET No, many poets made it;
I have merely made up the lost bits.

(CHORUS) You made them up? – That's disgraceful.

POET No, I've merely brought together
The bits that are lost and don't fit.

(CHORUS) We prefer the bits that we know.

POET So you need to know those that you don't:
You shall all take part in mine.

(CHORUS) How till we know what it is?

POET If you were to drink of the streams
You'd forget the moment you live in
And remember all you have lost:
You will find it is sweet in the cave.

(CHORUS) We are not going in there.

(FOURTH WOMAN) What would happen if we did?

POET She told you: you'd be carried
Away in an under-ground stream.

(CHORUS) I don't like the sound of it
– I'd quite like to be carried away.

POET It's only a game: a Zeus game.

(CHORUS) If it's only a game…

POET Why not try it?

(One or two approach the streams)

(CHORUS) I'm going to see what happens.

(A few girls drink tentatively)

– Are there no men in your game?

POET Lots of them.

(CHORUS) Where are they?

POET I will play them myself till it's time,
According to ancient custom.

(CHORUS) The streams taste delicious; come on!

(Music. Over the ensuing lines, the girls go to the streams. THIRD WOMAN doesn't. The POET begins a strange chant)

POET	If you drink the Pierian Spring And close your eyes as you swallow You will find even mortals can sing As sweet and as brave as Apollo.
(THIRD WOMAN)	What are you doing, madman?
POET	Invoking the Muses.
(THIRD WOMAN)	Where are they?
POET	I hear them, I see them! They bathe where no mortals see them In the blessed Peirian Spring, And now they begin to dance And hymn their way up the hill-side To the great throne of Zeus himself! (*)

(Music finishes and the light changes)

	Now begin.
(CHORUS)	Us? How can we?
POET	Say what you remember of this.

(He takes a mask from his bag: it is neutral but numinous)

(CHORUS)	How can we remember What we have never seen?
POET	Each of you take it and touch it: You must tell me what you remember Of how his game first began.
(CHORUS)	May we put it on?
POET	I would not advise it.
(CHORUS)	Is it an image of Zeus?
POET	No more questions: you tell me.

(One by one the CHORUS take the mask. Distant music)

(CHORUS)	I remember... So do I... – It's said he began all things.

17

—	No, he threw down all the gods That had ever been before him.
—	But then he made a harmony Out of chaos.

(THIRD WOMAN)   How did he do that?

(CHORUS)   A balance, a balance in heaven:
Six gods and six goddesses,
Never less and never more.

(THIRD WOMAN)   Till he brought in Dionysos
And Olympus went topsy-turvy.

(CHORUS)   Next he divided the spoils
Of victory with his two brothers;
He made them pick a pebble
Out of his father's old helmet.

(Distant thunder)

POET   Who got to rule Mother Earth?

(CHORUS)   They agreed she was too precious
For a single god to rule her
So she became common to all.

(FIRST WOMAN)   And ever since then she has suffered.

POET   On one glorious day
Zeus came and put his sweet seed
Into some girls just like you
And the Heroes sprang out of their wombs!

(THIRD WOMAN)   Everyone knows that Prometheus
Made mankind and gave us this fire.

(FIRST WOMAN)   Prometheus only made men.

(THIRD WOMAN)   It was not a complete success.

POET   But it gave Zeus the idea
Of doing something better.
Why do you think men are so coarse
And women so luscious and wise?
Because men were made out of clay
By a god who was inferior
And used inferior clay;
But Zeus used only the best clay

| | And the soil of Mother Earth, |
| | And that is how woman began! |

(CHORUS)   I never heard that one.

POET   Zeus is old now;
But at first every girl who was fair
Asked 'When will it be my turn
To unfasten my waist-band to god?'
Zeus himself put his seed
Into so many pretty ones
That it's said all humans thereafter
Are in some sense his relations.

(CHORUS)   You mean we have god-blood in us?

(FIRST WOMAN)   In part.

(CHORUS)   Aphrodite be praised!   (*)

(Much rejoicing and more drinking. SECOND WOMAN comes out of the cave)

(CHORUS)   I wonder what it would feel like
To be taken by a god?

(SECOND WOMAN)   Gorgeous…it is gorgeous…

POET   What is?

(SECOND WOMAN)   Gods…lots of gods…

POET   How do you know that they're gods ?

(SECOND WOMAN) How? By their shapes when they take me,
Lions or eagles or swans.

(SECOND WOMAN begins to imagine she is LEDA)

(CHORUS)   That's how Zeus took Leda!

LEDA   Gorgeous…

POET   Go on and tell us
What happened that day by the river.

LEDA   Where's my husband?

POET   I am your husband.

(CHORUS)   Wait! – Who's Leda? – Where are we?

| | — She was Helen's mother, stupid |
| | — What are you doing, Poet? |

POET   This hat appears to belong
To Tyndareus, King of Sparta.

(*He becomes TYNDAREUS. They act out what follows*)

LEDA   O my Tyndareus…

TYNDAREUS   You seem
Flushed and excited, my dearest.
Speak plainly and tell me your troubles.

LEDA   It happened by a river
Behind a bank of bull-rushes;
I lay there in the sunlight
And there I dreamed soft things.
Suddenly I sneezed:
A feather was tickling me.

TYNDAREUS   On the nose?

LEDA   No, lower down;
I knew at once what it was.

TYNDAREUS   Describe it.

LEDA   I kept my eyes shut
But I knew it was a swan
Because of the tickle of feathers
And because it was dying for love.

TYNDAREUS   How do you know it was dying?

LEDA   It was singing.

TYNDAREUS   Swans do not sing.

LEDA   They do when they are dying.

TYNDAREUS   Swans do not speak language.

LEDA   They do when they are special.

TYNDAREUS   Did it say why it was dying?

LEDA   Of course, for love of me.

(CHORUS)   Can swans really speak?

LEDA   Only if they're special.

POET	Go on.
LEDA	So I cuddled it To make it feel better.
(CHORUS)	Did it?
LEDA	Oh yes, we both felt much better.
POET	You mean that you permitted A common swan to enjoy you?
LEDA	I have often heard you say 'Never resist the gods'.
TYNDAREUS	We are talking about a swan.
LEDA	Yes, he was a god-swan.
TYNDAREUS	Which god was it?
LEDA	Zeus!
TYNDAREUS	Are you certain?
LEDA	Quite certain Because he did it best.
TYNDAREUS	What do you mean by 'best'?
LEDA	I mean he was better than you are.
TYNDAREUS	Young girls should not attempt Invidious comparisons Until they are more experienced.
LEDA	I'm more experienced now.
TYNDAREUS	If it was swan-rape ordinary You will be put to death But if it is a case Of divine intervention We must proceed with care.

(*FIRST WOMAN produces a large egg*)

LEDA	But look what god-swan gave me!
TYNDAREUS	Where did that object come from?
LEDA	Inside me: it was gorgeous! I am going back to the river! (*)

21

(She moves away. POET becomes himself again)

(CHORUS)   What's inside it?

POET   We will find out
Once we really go into it.

(CHORUS)   Wait! That's not how it was.
Everyone knows that Zeus
Begot this egg on Nemesis
And it dropped down from the moon.

(THIRD WOMAN)   If Nemesis is involved
You'd better be careful, old man.

(CHORUS)   Both stories cannot be true;
It must be one or the other.

POET   Why? With all the best stories
Each version may well be the true one.

(Thunder)

(THIRD WOMAN)   More trouble in heaven.

POET   Ignore it.
Zeus' wife Hera is angry
Because of his love-games with mortals.
Poseidon and Apollo
Have joined her but Zeus was warned,
And now he's planning their punishment,
And all is quiet again.   (*)

(CHORUS)   Who warned him?

(SECOND WOMAN becomes THETIS)

THETIS   I did!

(CHORUS)   Who do you think you are?

THETIS   I am Thetis the sea-nymph!
I am the one who saved Zeus.
I was born when the sea was born,
Long before the mountains
And Mother Earth herself.

(CHORUS)   You?

THETIS   Yes, I'm a prophetess,
I know all that is and was
And all that ever will be.
Is it a wonder he loves me?

(CHORUS)   You? – Has Zeus had you too?

THETIS   He wants to, O he craves me!
He has often tried to ravish me;
I was dancing once on the sea-shore
Naked and glistening wet,
But he never caught me
Because I can change my shape
Into anything I want to.

(CHORUS)   You can't.

THETIS   Yes I can!

POET   Don't, you are lovely.

THETIS   I know.

(CHORUS)   She is stream-drunk.

(THIRD WOMAN)   How can you possibly change it?

THETIS   As the sea-shore and the sea can:
I was born when the sea was born,
Long before the mountains
And Mother Earth herself.
The rocks that you sit on
Have changed their shape since then.
You all forget that the shapes
That humans make to fix things
To feel solid and rooted and safe
Are as fixless as the shingle
On the beach at turn of tide.
Pebbles, you're all pebbles.

(CHORUS)   Could Zeus love such a creature?

THETIS   How could he not love me
When I am so tantalising?
But I never let him have me.

(THIRD WOMAN)   How could you have stopped him?

THETIS	Because of what I prophesied:
	That if ever I bore a son
	To him or to any mortal
	That son would become more powerful
	Than his father, and that frightened him.

(*FIRST MAN has put on an old helmet etc., and at once becomes an ancient warrior, PELEUS*)

PELEUS	Then I shall have you instead:
	When I get you with child
	Zeus will feel much safer.
(CHORUS)	Who are you now ? – Tyndareus?

PELEUS (*Looks at helmet*) This helmet is marked 'Peleus'.

I was born in the days of the Heroes;

Heracles was my friend.

THETIS	What have I to do with you?
PELEUS	What will I do *to* you?

(*He snatches at her*)

(CHORUS)	What are you playing at, old man?
PELEUS	I am King Peleus of Phthia.
(CHORUS)	He was the last of the Raptors;
	He only lived to seize
	Gold and horses and women.
THETIS	Peleus the rapist,
	The worst of all the pirates!
PELEUS	Peleus the kindly, Peleus the wise.
	Yes, I am proud to be
	The very last of the Old Ones.
	All my life has been honourable
	And I have had more women
	Than she has danced with dolphins.
	It is the will of Zeus
	That Peleus shall catch you.
THETIS	Then catch me if you can! (*)
PELEUS	And I know when women want it
	And I know when they don't.

(CHORUS)   That's what they always say.

(A chase. She disappears into the cave. PELEUS stumbles after her. Some dust falls from the rock above)

(FIRST WOMAN)   She came ashore by moonlight
Riding on a dolphin
But he grabbed her as she landed
So she turned into a serpent
Then water... Then Air... Then Fire...
Then a cuttle-fish who squirted him
With purple ink all over;
So she vanished into a cave
But he puffed and panted after
And both of them gasped in the darkness
Till Peleus cupped his hands
In some water to refresh himself

(FIRST WOMAN cups her hands in the pool)

And he found that he was holding
A little silver fish,
Wet, tiny, delicate,
Gasping and arching its back
As a loving woman does
And he knew it was her and he stroked it
And she sighed and they wrestled together
Till the dawn broke in the sky.   (*)

(WOMEN applaud. SECOND WOMAN re-enters. She is no longer play-acting. The clothes she had worn before have gone and she has now actually become THETIS. She is naked, but clutching a nymph's dress to herself)

THETIS   He raped me...

(CHORUS)   Yes, we know that.

(Re-enter PELEUS)

PELEUS   Just as Zeus planned it.

THETIS   I am not pretending!

(CHORUS)   Has he really raped her?

(FIRST WOMAN)	She has been, yet she hasn't; That's what it's like in a play.
THETIS	O Zeus, I curse you, Zeus! You told me you'd come yourself And I lay there aching for you.
PELEUS	You ached for whatever could catch you.

(He takes off his helmet and sits down)

(FIRST WOMAN)	Such marital debates should be saved Till after the wedding.
(CHORUS)	What wedding?

(The POET has become himself again)

(FIRST WOMAN)	'The wedding of Peleus and Thetis!' Listen to the Muses And drink again of the streams: The gods themselves have invited you all To join the Wedding Feast.
(CHORUS)	Will there be nectar?
(FIRST WOMAN)	Of course.

*(Some of the CHORUS wash in the streams,
FIRST WOMAN hands THETIS a red dress,
like all the wedding dresses that follow)*

POET	Put this on: Zeus requires it.
THETIS	No, I will go as I am; I will dance for Zeus alone And make him ashamed That he did not dare to take me.
(CHORUS)	See, the streams shimmer with gold! — Let's see what they taste like now.

(They drink again)

O yes, they taste of nectar!

(THIRD WOMAN)	This is all just pretending...

(THIRD WOMAN drinks a little)

THETIS	I am coming, lover-god.
(THIRD WOMAN)	I see no gods and no Muses.

(FIRST WOMAN)	Yet approach them with reverence.
POET	Give us less light, Apollo, Lest the eyes of gazers be tainted.

(THETIS begins very slowly to dance the wedding-dance)

> This may be the very last time
> That the gods will come down to earth
> To meet with human-kind
> And share a feast together
> Close your eyes and you will see them:
> Now tell us what you see.   (*)

(They sit. Sea and wind in the distance. POET plies them with more drink from his wine-bag and FIRST WOMAN gives them food from her cooking-pot. A voice sings in Greek. THETIS goes on dancing)

(FIRST WOMAN)	Everyone's come to the wedding.
(CHORUS)	It's just as I've heard it told of!
–	The Twelve are on golden thrones
–	Hera is raising the wedding-torch
–	Ganymede pours out the nectar
–	The Centaurs are chewing their chaplets
–	Cheiron is giving Peleus A spear of mountain ash
–	And Hephaestus has forged him A suit of golden armour, A gift from all the gods.

(During this nothing is brought except the suit of golden armour. The POET hangs it on the dead tree)

(CHORUS)	But what is our sea-nymph doing?
(FIRST WOMAN)	Dancing all alone, Her head held high and haughty.
(CHORUS)	And Zeus?
POET	Zeus is not there. When he saw her dancing so proudly He could not bear to watch her.

(FIRST WOMAN) So he's slipped down the mountain-side
And is sitting alone on a rock
Listening to the harmony
Which he has made for others.

POET It is the harmony
Which he has never had.

(*Music changes. Singing*)

(CHORUS) All the world is at peace.

(*Thunder*)

(CHORUS) What's that?

(FIRST WOMAN) Zeus is thinking.

(FOURTH WOMAN) Is that what thunder is?

POET It means he is on the verge
Of making some great decision.

(FIRST WOMAN) Zeus knows that no harmony
Can ever last for long;
He knows that a moment
Is nothing but a moment
Which dies as it is known.

POET So he's thought of a plan
To make it a better world.

(*Thunder*)

THETIS (*Quietly*) ... Earth-quakes and sea-quakes,
Star-fire and star-fall,
Flood, famine, pestilence
Are useful but seldom selective,
So he plans that the work
Shall be done by men to men
And by heroes to heroes.

(*More thunder*)

(CHORUS) What is Zeus saying?

THETIS He is saying that the gods
Shall henceforth live apart
From mankind as they first did.

He means to make an end
Of the half-gods and the heroes
In a great game of war
That those born of immortals
And those who think they are,
The mongrels, will all dwindle
And be seen no more on earth.

POET　　　　　　　　It is time to bring Eris in.

　　　　　　　　　　(*A harsh sound of discord for a moment*)

(THIRD WOMAN)　They've invited the Goddess of Discord?

POET　　　　　　　　He has his reasons.

　　　　　　　　　　(*The POET hands FIRST WOMAN a golden apple*)

(FIRST WOMAN)　She too has brought a wedding-gift.　　(*)

　　　　　　　　　　(*She throws down the Apple of Discord. The music becomes sweet again. THETIS sits apart and alone*)

　　　　　　　　　　Apple-day! Apple-day!

POET　　　　　　　　You can open your eyes now.

　　　　　　　　　　(*ALL open their eyes*)

(CHORUS)　　　　　What is it?

POET　　　　　　　　　　　　The Apple of Discord:
　　　　　　　　　　It has fallen from the Tree
　　　　　　　　　　Of Harmony.

(FIRST WOMAN)　　　　　　　…Hesperides

　　　　　　　　　　(*A hint of gold in the streams. The tree becomes an apple tree*)

　　　　　　　　　　Where there grows an apple-tree
　　　　　　　　　　And two streams run beneath it
　　　　　　　　　　And all its fruits are golden.

(CHORUS)　　　　　Is it…the one?
　　—　　　　　　　Is it the Golden One?
　　—　　　　　　　There's writing on it
　　—　　　　　　　What does it say?

—	It says 'To the Fairest'.
—	I want it!

POET   Don't touch it!
It can only be given
By the male to the female.

(CHORUS)   But it's Zeus' gift to Thetis.

THETIS   'Don't want it! I know Zeus' mind:
So long as no one touches it
Time will stand still
And the world will be at peace;
But when the apple is given
The world will be destroyed.

(THETIS screams with pain)

Help me! I'm in pain.

(THETIS' stomach begins to swell)

I am having a child,
A beastly mortal child!

(CHORUS)   If you are you should relax.

THETIS   Zeus, you did this to me!
It was your child I wanted.

POET   Better change your shape again.

THETIS   I can't now, I'm frightened: help me!

(POET becomes PELEUS again)

PELEUS   When a girl is in labour
I find it helps to remind her
Of the labours of Heracles;
It gives them a sense of proportion.

(FIRST WOMAN starts to pull cloth from the cave)

THETIS   O the first one is coming...

(CHORUS)   I thought she had six and burned them.

PELEUS   Not that version today.

(FIRST WOMAN cuts the cloth, and THETIS delivers it)

THETIS	Look, isn't he lovely?
	(*She dips the cloth in the water*)
PELEUS	What do you think you're doing? Don't fiddle around with my boy!
THETIS	I am dipping him in the Styx So as to make him immortal.
(CHORUS) —	She's holding it by the ankle! It is clear that she is quite Inexperienced with babies.
	(*PELEUS retrieves the baby*)
PELEUS	All's well; now suckle the brat.
THETIS	You're his father: give him a name.
PELEUS	Since his mother will not offer Her teat to his lips He shall be called A-chilles.
	(*PELEUS starts to go with the baby*)
(CHORUS)	Where are you taking him to?
PELEUS	Bears up in the mountains.
	(*He takes the baby in*)
(THIRD WOMAN)	His mother tries to drown him; Now his father's feeding him bear's milk.
(CHORUS)	What kind of man will he be?
(FIRST WOMAN)	A warrior.
	(*PELEUS re-enters*)
PELEUS	He will be nourished By the honeycombs on the crags; The marrow of wild boars Will give him strength and courage And the marrow of fawns will help him To outrun a stag or a chariot.
THETIS	In the end what will it matter?
(THIRD WOMAN)	Nothing is more precious Than the life of a child.

THETIS	Those who believe that End up the unhappiest. I know the mind of Zeus.

(Rumbles of thunder far off)

(CHORUS)	Then what is he thinking now?
THETIS	That the gods are good gardeners; It is time for some weeding: It is time to weed the mongrels. Only my son will be spared Because I will protect him.
(THIRD WOMAN)	How can you know that, sea-girl?
THETIS	Because I am a prophetess: I shall go back into the ocean And there I will renew myself.

(She disappears in the sea)

(THIRD WOMAN)	Why should Zeus want war?
(FIRST WOMAN)	Because he loves the earth. (*)
(CHORUS)	But what about our apple?
POET	I told you: it must be given By some male to some female To judge which of you is the fairest.
(FIRST WOMAN)	Yes, they certainly need more men.
(CHORUS)	Look there; I see three men Sleeping beside the cave!
(THIRD WOMAN)	They are drunk and rough and vulgar; Wiser not to wake them.
(CHORUS)	But if they drank and went in…?
POET	Try the Deucalion solution.

(He throws a pebble at the men, who grunt in their sleep)

(CHORUS)	What's that?
POET	I'll tell you later: Throw the bones of Mother Earth Behind you and go on.

(CHORUS)	Why not give it a try?

(They pick up stones)

(FIRST WOMAN)	Be careful where you throw them.
(CHORUS)	Old one, get out of the way! (*)

(CHORUS throw stones. A strange sound. Three tattered men rise from the ground, bewildered from a long sleep. Their clothes are in shreds. The streams are no longer golden)

POET	These are the mongrels.
(FOURTH MAN)	Where am I?
(THIRD MAN)	Who am I?
(SECOND MAN)	Why am I?
	Why have you awaked us?
POET	You must give this beautiful apple
	To the girl you think the fairest.
(THIRD MAN)	We don't play games with girls.
(CHORUS)	We made you, so you'll do
	Exactly what we tell you.
(FIRST WOMAN)	That boy is the prettiest:
	Why not begin with him?

(They present themselves)

HERA	Hera!
ATHENE	Athene!
APHRODITE	And me...!
	I am Aphrodite:
	I was born out of god-foam.
	Look on me well, little boy;
	I am sweeter to the taste
	Than does' milk or wild honey
	Because I am Love itself.
	Lick me if you doubt it
	And give me that nice little apple
	And I will give you a girl
	Who is almost as fair and passionate
	As I am.

(CHORUS)	Answer.
(FOURTH MAN)	Aphrodite makes me nervous.
APHRODITE	Then you're not the man for me.
	(*Two other WOMEN come forward to THIRD MAN*)
(THIRD MAN)	If you are really Athene I will honour you for ever.
	(*He offers her the apple*)
(CHORUS)	He has chosen the wrong one!
–	Better try the third one.
	(*The THREE WOMEN approach SECOND MAN*)
(SECOND MAN)	To choose one and ignore the others Might well lead to evil: So perhaps there is no right answer?
(CHORUS)	But everybody knows it!
POET	Make them drink of the streams.
(CHORUS)	Streams! – Drink! – Get on with it!
–	We made you, stone-men, So we are going to cast you.
POET –	Hurry up and get on with it!
	(*The THREE MEN drink from the streams. The POET throws the apple into the cave*)
(CHORUS)	What are you doing, Poet?
POET	Making them go in and fetch it.
(SECOND MAN)	What's in that cave?
POET	Much fame.
(CHORUS)	Go in and fetch us the apple!
(FIRST WOMAN)	If you go, it will make you more human.
(THIRD MAN)	Then I'll go and I'll do high things!
	(*Music. He goes in*)
(FOURTH MAN)	I'll go and I'll conquer Asia!

(*Distant Trumpet. He goes in*)

POET   You must go too: it will change you.

(SECOND MAN)   I would like to change the world
If I changed it for the better;

(*He goes towards the cave*)

Though it is always possible
It might be a mistake.   (*)

(*He goes in. More trumpets from the CHORUS*)

POET   All in!

(CHORUS)   What a fuss men make;
They always want to change things.
  –   But they'll bring back the apple
And we can get on with our game.

POET   Not till tomorrow morning.

(FIRST WOMAN)   You've all drunk too much nectar
And it's long past your bed-time:
Time for Lethe, children.

(CHORUS)   Where does nectar come from?

(FIRST WOMAN)   Wespero... Hesperides
The Garden of the Evening,
The garden of the West...

(*Music far off. The CHORUS grow drowsy*)

POET   Yes, once upon a time
It is said that all the world
Was filled with golden apples,
Lost now, but still to find.

(*CHORUS hum and begin to fall asleep*)

(CHORUS)   A world of golden apples...

(FOURTH WOMAN)   What's in that cave, Poet?

POET   It's where
Zeus keeps his jars of blessings and pains.

(*She goes towards the cave*)

(THIRD WOMAN)   I can hear a baby weeping.

(CHORUS)   Perhaps it's the young Dionysus.

(THIRD WOMAN)   Better see if it's safe: come on.

(Both WOMEN go in)

(FIRST WOMAN)   So many ages, children;
Silver, Bronze and Brazen...

(CHORUS)   They say we are in the Fifth Age
Where men have lost their way...

   –   But not women – No, not women...

(The CHORUS are all asleep. FIRST WOMAN pokes the fire. POET takes a fresh apple out of his pocket and begins to polish it)

POET   Why do I belong
To the present Age of Men?

(FIRST WOMAN)   Which is that? I have lost count.

POET   So do poets if they're lucky.

(FIRST WOMAN)   Ages are brief to gods.

POET   So are gods but one must not say so.

(The armour clanks again. It rains)

I am of the Age of Iron,
I wish I'd died before it.
When our babies are born
They are thwart things with grey hair.
By day we toil and grieve,
By night we waste and die;
All bonds of kin are broken,
When we're old our children blame us
For all that went wrong in the past;
Men twist and cheapen words
And their voices are harsh and unlovely,
Fame and wealth are abused,
Oaths are broken as twine-twigs
And soon there will be no shame.
That is why the ancient spirits
Of just wrath and reverence

	Have begun to leave the earth And to quit mankind for ever.
(FIRST WOMAN)	So you sing of the past to feel better?
POET	What's past was no better But sometimes, if one's lucky It gives one a sense of proportion. Nothing changes, nothing: Is that why Zeus is angry?
(FIRST WOMAN)	It is told so. Go to sleep. (*)

(*The POET sleeps while FIRST WOMAN
pokes the glowing fire. Music and the Muses
are heard in the distance. The sea sounds*)

PART I
The Outbreak of War

Play 1
APOLLO

A BARREN PLACE

CAST

First Woman	HECUBA/ NURSE
Second Woman	CASSANDRA/ THETIS
Third Woman	CLYTEMNESTRA
Fourth Woman	OENONE/ DEIDAMIA
First Man	POET/ TYNDAREUS/ PELEUS
Second Man	AGAMEMNON
Third Man	ODYSSEUS/ CALCHAS
Fourth Man	ACHILLES

CHORUS of
NINE WOMEN, WAR KINGS
and MYRMIDONS

(Bird-song as it dawns. The POET hangs the golden armour on a tree. It clanks and FIRST WOMAN bangs the gong)

(FIRST WOMAN)   Time to wake up, children.

(CHORUS)   Where are we?

POET *(To First Woman)*   Time to go on.

(He gives her a robe and she goes into the cave. One by one the CHORUS awakes Trojan Music is heard in the distance)

(CHORUS)   Last night I dreamed of Troy
And saw towers as high as heaven.
– I dreamed of shining walls
– Great palaces and temples
– Orchards and fair gardens
– And trees and fruit and flowers
That I never saw in the West.

(A woman's voice is heard singing)

– I hear a woman's voice
Singing across the water.

(The POET puts on PELEUS' helmet)

PELEUS   It's a Trojan song: I first heard it
When the world and I were younger...

(He becomes PELEUS again)

I was sailing once in the Argo
With Heracles and Jason
When we drew near the Hellespont
And saw on the rocks of Tenedos
A naked girl bound to a stake.
When we saw her dress was yellow
We realised at once that we'd stumbled
On some sacrifice situation.

(CHORUS)   You said that she was naked
So how could you see her dress?

PELEUS   It had fallen from her shoulders
As she struggled to be free.

42

(CHORUS)   Yes, free from you and Jason.

PELEUS   No, Apollo had sent a monster
From the sea to devour her.
He and Poseidon were angry:
They had built the walls of Troy
Just as Zeus had commanded
But their father, Laomedon,
Had refused to pay them a penny.
So Apollo sent this monster
To squirt his crops with brine
And devour all his people.
An oracle advised him
To sacrifice his daughter
Or Troy would be destroyed…

(CHORUS)   No father would do that these days.

PELEUS   So I went to Troy with Heracles
And had a word with the Trojan.
As soon as he had agreed
On the going rate for rescues
Heracles killed the monster,
But Laomedon would not pay him
So of course we sacked the city
And enslaved the whole royal family.

(CHORUS)   Of course.

PELEUS   We gave the girl
To my dear brother Telamon.
Then she begged us to free
Her younger brother Priam,
A shrimpling of a boy.
So she sailed away to the West
And ever since Hesione
Has lived happily with my brother,
And Priam is now King of Troy.

(PELEUS takes off his helmet. Thunder)

(CHORUS)   Why is Zeus angry this morning?

POET   He's decided on the punishment
Of Apollo and Poseidon:

	He has made them slaves of toil To rebuild the walls of Troy.
(CHORUS)	Has he not punished Hera?
POET	No, they worked it out in bed.
	(*The sun rises*)
(CHORUS)	Look there across the water I see a great light far off?
POET	It is the light of Apollo: The city is rebuilt and shining!
(CHORUS)	I hear music and laughter And many people dancing.
POET	What else do you hear? Shut your eyes And listen: a great queen is speaking.
	(*FIRST WOMAN re-enters and speaks to the audience*)
HECUBA	Yes, look well on our city: The great tower of Ilion Soars shining up to heaven. Let us give thanks to the gods! Sometimes when a country And its people are destroyed And must grow again from nothing It comes in time to flourish And grow greater than its conquerors Because the gods love best Those people who most honour them. With them to defend and uphold us Troy needs no large army Though our young men are ready And skilled in the arts of war; We have built no war-fleet Lest it seem a threat to others; Our trading ships suffice To make us rich again And bring us those good things We live with and enjoy; I have borne my husband Priam

Many noble children,
Sons to rear as warriors
And daughters for us to marry
Into other royal houses
And forge strong alliances.

Now and then there will of course
Be quarrels with other countries
As is natural among humans;
Yet if we honour the gods,
Should new monsters from the sea
Dare to come again against us
We would laugh at them from our walls
And throw them back in the ocean.

My husband is old now
And he has only one ambition:
To win back his sister Hesione
As he swore to long ago.
Pray with me now to the gods
To send his sister home
To live with us in peace.   (*)

*(FIRST WOMAN becomes herself again.
CHORUS open their eyes. SECOND WOMAN
starts muttering in Greek in the background)*

(SECOND WOMAN) Apollo! Apollo!

(CHORUS)   What is she on about now?

POET   The god is in her again...!
                Cassandra is often like this.

(CHORUS)   But she's Thetis, not Cassandra.

POET   No, she's got into Cassandra.

*(FIRST WOMAN withdraws. SECOND
WOMAN speaks a few lines of CASSANDRA's
speech in 'Troilus and Cressida', overlapping
with the CHORUS' lines)*

CASSANDRA   *'Cry, Trojans, cry! Practice your eyes with tears!*
                Troy must not be...nor goodly Ilion stand;
                Our firebrand brother, Paris, burns us all...!'

(CHORUS)   I remember the story now!
            —   But it hasn't yet happened

| | — | And it won't while we guard the apple
How can she be Cassandra? |

POET In a moment, just as I can. (*)

(*CASSANDRA withdraws. FIRST WOMAN cuts out a piece of cloth and shapes it as a baby*)

(FIRST WOMAN) Look at the new one:
Isn't he beautiful?

(*She sings to the baby*)

(CHORUS) And who do you think you are?

(FIRST WOMAN) The Royal Nurse of Troy.

(CHORUS) But haven't you just been Hecuba?
You cannot be someone else too.

POET It is normal poetic practice;
Once one has gone in
One can be whoever one wants to.

(CHORUS) But she hasn't gone in yet.

POET She came out a long time ago,
So please stop interrupting.
Queen Hecuba has given birth
To another boy.

(*CASSANDRA is heard screaming*)

CASSANDRA Apollo!...
Paris will destroy the city!

NURSE That is why I'm taking him
To the Royal Shepherd on Ida.

(CHORUS) It's a baby, not a sheep.

NURSE Royal shepherds have other duties. (*)

(*She goes. The POET takes down the golden armour and begins to polish it*)

(CHORUS) What are you doing, Poet?

POET Achilles will soon need it.
Time to move on to Mount Ida!

(*Mountain music. FOURTH WOMAN appears as a mountain-nymph. She picks up the cloth baby which the NURSE has left on the rocks above*)

(CHORUS)   What is that girl doing?

(FOURTH WOMAN)   O look what I have found!
I was bathing in a waterfall
And a silly old shepherd left it
On the very top of this mountain.

(CHORUS)   Babies found on mountain-tops
Are better left alone.

(FOURTH WOMAN)   But he's lovely and all shivery.

(CHORUS)   He's a fine boy; you must throw him
Onto the rocks at once.

(FOURTH WOMAN)   Don't you speak to me like that!
I'm the daughter of the River God
And I live here on Mount Ida.

(*She cradles the baby and sings to it softly*)

POET   Oenone, the mountain-nymph.

(CHORUS)   I suppose she's another prophetess.

OENONE   Of course I am.

(CHORUS)   Like Thetis.

OENONE   No, not like Thetis.
Mountain nymphs are wiser
Than the tainted nymphs of the sea;
The water here is snow-fresh
And needs no salt to cleanse it.

(CHORUS)   But if you are a prophetess
You must know about this child.

OENONE   Of course I know: I shall nurse him
And when he has grown up
We are going to have such loving.

(CHORUS)   You may not be happy.

OENONE   I know that I won't be.

(CHORUS)	Then will it be worth it?
OENONE	Yes, for a while.
(CHORUS)	It isn't good for babies To be seduced by nurses.
OENONE	Yet love affairs are always Best on the top of mountains.
(CHORUS)	But do you know his name?
OENONE	I call him Wallet.
(CHORUS)	Why?
OENONE	Because the shepherd took him Out of his satchel or wallet And the Trojan for wallet is 'Paris'.
(CHORUS)	It's begun to happen already.
OENONE	It began to long ago.
(CHORUS) —	But if you can foresee things You surely can prevent them?
OENONE	How could I prevent them?
(CHORUS)	Leave the baby where you found it.
OENONE	Do you believe that one child's death Can prevent what Zeus has planned?
(CHORUS)	But surely to save the world...?
OENONE	That is up to all of you. If you really wanted to save it You and all the world's women Would kill all your babies For the next hundred years; Mother Earth would thank you. If you must have children You must accept the consequences. (*)

(*She disappears with the baby. Music of the West. Many babies are heard squalling. The NURSE comes back, holding four more cloth babies, covered with feathers and pieces of egg-shell*)

48

NURSE

Babies, babies, babies:
Look at all my little ones!

(CHORUS)

More Trojan spawn
To be ditched in the mountains?

NURSE

What are you talking of?
They were born here in the West;
Two boys and two little girls,
All reared in Sparta.

(CHORUS)

How can you be in Sparta
If you're Royal Nurse of Troy?

NURSE

Too many children in Ilion
And all of them wet their beds;
So as good Royal Nurses
Are always in demand
I decided to go to Mycenae
Where they have different problems
And special skills are needed.

(CHORUS)

But you said you were in Sparta.

NURSE

So I was, now is later.
O my arms are aching;
Even with Hecuba
I never had to carry
More than two at once.
Hold these two for me...
Be careful with both of them:
When they grow up they'll be famous.

(*She hands them the infant HELEN and CLYTEMNESTRA*)

(CHORUS)

But this one's covered with feathers
  – Swan-feathers! – It's Helen, the Zeus-child!

(*NURSE hands them the other babies*)

NURSE

Hold these too; my back aches.

(CHORUS)

Are they from Sparta too?

NURSE

                No, Mycenae:
Their father has been murdered

So I've brought them to Sparta
Where Tyndareus of Lacedaemon,
The most powerful man in the West,
Has sworn to restore their fortunes.

(CHORUS)   We do not quite follow you.

POET   These eaglets are descended
From Tantalus himself.

(CHORUS)   Who was he?

POET   Their houses' founder.

NURSE   But these two were born in Sparta:
Helen and Clytemnestra.

(CHORUS)   She's making it all up.

POET   It's well known; check your sources.
All four grew up together.

NURSE   Agamemnon, Menelaus,
Clytemnestra and Helen...
Four lovely, happy children...
O we were all so happy
Till the time came for them to marry.
Ever since they had been children
Clytemnestra had loved Agamemnon
But Tyndareus gave her
To King Broteas of Pisa.

POET   He was Agamemnon's uncle.

(CHORUS)   Never heard of him – Who was he?

NURSE   It is not a nurse's business
To explain genealogies
Of the greatest royal houses
That the West has ever known:
Lacedaemon's descendants at Sparta
And Tantalus' brood from Mycenae.

(POET strikes the gong)

POET   Time to go on.

                  Let's have some music
To take us to Broteas' palace.

NURSE	O they needed me there; When my darling Clytemnestra Was due to be delivered Of her very first child She begged me to go to her. See, another royal baby: Kneel, girls, to the Queen. (*)

(Music. THIRD WOMAN enters with and sings to another cloth-baby)

(CHORUS)	Is that one Clytemnestra?
–	Is the child Orestes?

NURSE	Sh!

CLYTEMNESTRA	Women, look on my first child, The best and the sweetest Ever born to a mortal woman. Men love to search for the First Things As if they were some mystery, But a woman as she suckles Knows what they really are.

(CHORUS)	The child is a fair one.

(War-drums far off)

NURSE	Agamemnon is coming, He means to kill your husband.

CLYTEMNESTRA	He has come to rescue me; I will take the child inside Until the battle is over.

(She goes in. Trumpets and battle-sounds. Smoke)

POET	The battle was a brief one: Agamemnon killed Broteas But he also killed her baby Just as she was feeding him; Then he got drunk and raped her.

(CHORUS)	Is this true? – It can't be.

(As the smoke clears, CLYTEMNESTRA comes out with the dead child)

CLYTEMNESTRA   All you gods, hear me!
Zeus, Hera, hear me!
Look on this child
And grant me blood-vengeance
On the murderer; may he be
As accursed and wretched
As his father and forefathers
Atreus, Pelops, and Tantalus!

(SECOND MAN enters as AGAMEMNON)

I curse you, Agamemnon.

AGAMEMNON   I am ashamed and loathe myself.
What I have done to you
Will haunt me all my life:
Where I meant all gentleness
I have done evil.
It's as if some god had turned me
Into some other creature,
Yet I am still responsible
For what that creature did.

NURSE   Be quiet, never try
To word what is unwordable.

AGAMEMNON   Yes, my words are hateful to me
But I must and will make good.
I will take her to Mycenae
And give her a new life
And make my own a better one.

(CLYTEMNESTRA spits at him)

Yes, you are right to spit at me.

CLYTEMNESTRA   Do not take me there!
I have cursed you and your house.

AGAMEMNON   Our house is cursed already;
We must both learn to bear it.

CLYTEMNESTRA   One day the gods will punish you.

AGAMEMNON   I know the gods are terrible
But I believe that men
Can change and make good.

CLYTEMNESTRA	If you would make good Have done and kill me now.
AGAMEMNON	I love you and I pity you.
CLYTEMNESTRA	Such words have no meaning.
AGAMEMNON	Not now, but when you are home And I have made you my Queen The gods bless your womb again And I will give you new children.
CLYTEMNESTRA	If! I am your slave now But if you give me power I will use it to kill you.
AGAMEMNON	Yes, that is possible And perhaps it would be just, Yet I will take my chance As all must who love women. But first we must both go And make peace with Tyndareus. (*)

(POET becomes TYNDAREUS again.
AGAMEMNON kneels to him)

AGAMEMNON	Father, forgive me; Henceforth I will be gentle To your daughter and yourself And will uphold all your plans.
TYNDAREUS	Don't bother me with trivialities; Something much graver is troubling me. What you've done to Clytemnestra Has been done to Helen too.
(CHORUS)	Has Paris has taken her? — No, the apple's still here.
TYNDAREUS	All of you, be quiet; I am trying to think clearly.
AGAMEMNON	Who has raped Helen, father?
TYNDAREUS	My oldest friend, Theseus.
AGAMEMNON	But he's as old as you are.
TYNDAREUS	I am glad to say he and I Have not lost our vigour.

(CHORUS)   Wasn't it Paris?

NURSE   Sh, later.

TYNDAREUS   My sons of course have rescued her
                 But I fear her belly thickens.
                 Nurse, fetch the child;
                 You know what must be done.

(CHORUS)   What is this?

NURSE   Be patient,
                 This is merely the first time.

                 (*She goes in*)

TYNDAREUS   Of course it's the first time;
                 It's only just happened.

AGAMEMNON   If Helen's safe, all is well.

TYNDAREUS   All is not well:
                 It is bad for the family.
                 One rape is a misfortune
                 But one can learn to live with it
                 As I have done with Leda;
                 Two causes comment
                 And you both should have been more careful;
                 But three is intolerable:
                 It breaks the golden rule,
                 'Nothing in excess'.
                 Take your wife to Mycenae
                 And try to live better.

CLYTEMNESTRA   Don't let me go with him!

TYNDAREUS   What is done is done;
                 You must all make the best of it.

                 (*NURSE returns with another cloth-baby.
                 Music*)

NURSE   Look, she is lovely;
                 She's as fair as Helen herself.

CLYTEMNESTRA   Let me see her, let me hold her:
                 Nurse, what is her name?

TYNDAREUS   We don't give names to rape-brats;
                 Take it up to the mountains.

(*NURSE goes out with the baby*)

CLYTEMNESTRA You shall not take it and kill it!
I too have lost a child
Before I could name it.

TYNDAREUS (*To Agamemnon*) Take your wife to Mycenae.

CLYTEMNESTRA (*To Tyndareus*) My baby was slaughtered
In the smoke of a cruel battle
By a drunken sot in his wrath,
But to kill a child in cold blood
Will make you more contemptible.

TYNDAREUS (*To Agamemnon*) Remove your wife and be silent.

CLYTEMNESTRA Evil, evil, evil!
All the men around me
Are evil –

AGAMEMNON   Come with me.

(*AGAMEMNON takes her away. NURSE
returns without the baby*)

NURSE (*To Tyndareus*) It will take more than this
For a child of Zeus to lose
Her value in the West;
You must send to all the kings
And get her married quickly
To the king who bids the highest.
Pull yourself together;
If there wasn't always trouble
There'd be no need of kings.

(*TYNDAREUS sighs. Music of the War-Kings*)

So they came, all the war-kings!
The palace was a chaos,
There was dancing, feasts and quarrels,
Secret deals and plots;
So I told Tyndareus
I would leave his house at once
If he did not speak to them.   (*)

(*The WAR-KINGS appear, visored.
TYNDAREUS addresses the audience*)

TYNDAREUS   Look at you, what are you?
A heroic chaos.
I want suitors here, not satyrs;
I have not seen such a brawl
Since the Lapiths drank with the Centaurs;
You have bribed me and threatened me
And slept with all my slave-girls.
I had rather hold a party
In a bed of Theban eels.
Be quiet now and listen
To what I have to say.

(*Music changes*)

It is told us that Gaia
The Mother of us all
First rose out of chaos,
And yet from her progeny
The gods and all the riches
Of Mother Earth were born.
So from chaos was bred order;
It is time you should remember this.

(*Music ceases*)

Let me speak of a word
That is still unknown among you;
Unlike the lands around us
We are not yet a country
But prefer to fight each other.
Can you not see that this
Might not be in your interest?
Might it not be wiser
To direct your natural vigour
Against some land far off
In some war which was profitable
And perhaps even just ?
One day you might also
Grow powerful and rich and famous
And even become a country.

Might it not be useful
To try for a while to live

At peace with one another?
But with you, if I chose
One of you as my son-in-law,
The rest would steal my cattle
And burn down my house.
I have received some sound advice
From a cunning king among you,
A red-head with no gold-hoard
Whose realm is small and barren
And who has few ships and warriors;
The people of Ithaca
Are all fishermen or goat-herds:
I fear his name escapes me
But he's given me good counsel.
You shall each swear an oath
That when I choose my son-in-law
You will uphold my choice.
If any man hereafter
Takes Helen from her husband
You will unite and rescue her.
If you do not swear this
Zeus himself must settle it:
Swear it and then go home.

NURSE   And to his surprise they swore it.
So he gave Menelaus Helen
And Penelope to Odysseus
As a well-deserved reward.

POET   And so they all rode home
And the corn that year was golden.   (*)

(*Trumpets and cries. CASSANDRA starts to
scream in the distance and to speak brokenly
in Greek again*)

(CHORUS)   But why are the trumpets sounding?
—   Why is Cassandra screaming again?

(*The POET puts a robe over SECOND
WOMAN. At once she is quiet, and becomes
CASSANDRA's twin brother HELENUS*)

Who is she now? Explain.

57

HELENUS	Women, I must apologise For my sister's behaviour.
(CHORUS)	What are you playing at now?
HELENUS	I am Helenus the priest, Cassandra's twin brother: We are both Apollo's prophets.
(CHORUS)	Do you see the same things?
HELENUS	Mostly.
(CHORUS)	Then why when Cassandra screams Are you so quiet and polite?
HELENUS	I find it more effective.
(CHORUS)	Is she saying that by going in She can even change her sex?
POET	If two snakes once turned Teiresias into a whore Why shouldn't a girl Who has changed her shape already Become her own twin brother?
(CHORUS)	But why is your sister locked up While the rest of Troy believes you?
HELENUS	Because our relationship With Apollo is different.
(THIRD WOMAN)	Because you're a boy?
HELENUS	Not at all. One day when we were little And asleep by the great god's altar Apollo came and promised us We should have the gift of prophecy If we both would lie with him. My sister refused, so he said 'That is sad, but since I love you I will still give you my gift: Open your glorious lips And I'll breathe into your mouth.' She did and the god spat into it

And said, 'Now you have what you long for;
But since you have given me
Nothing in return
When you try to prophesy
No one will believe you
And you will be mocked and hated.'

(CHORUS)   That is sad.

HELENUS   Yes, it is sad.

(CHORUS)   And what did you do, Helenus?

HELENUS   Closed my eyes and did what he wanted
And became a sound prophet at once.

(CHORUS)   But which of you speaks the truest?

HELENUS   Neither one nor the other.

(CHORUS)   But it does not make sense.

HELENUS   Why do you think that it should?

(CHORUS)   Then tell us what's going to happen.

HELENUS   Apollo will uphold
Our city for a while,
So I shall serve my city
And in time command its army;
Beyond that, Apollo
Has as yet shed no light.

(CHORUS)   Then you would betray your city
If a god commanded it?

HELENUS   No one can ever be certain
What a god will command;
But supposing that our city
Should in time betray itself
Then things might be otherwise...   (*)

*(He goes. CASSANDRA screams again.
POET bangs the shield-gong)*

POET   Paris has come home again.

(CHORUS)   Where is the apple?
    − Who had it? − You did
    − I think our Poet had it.

(*HELENUS re-enters with HECUBA*)

HECUBA

Helenus, what is it now?
What is your sister saying?

HELENUS

Paris has come home again.

HECUBA

But I sent him to die on Ida:
How can he be home?

HELENUS

Hesione shall come home also:
He who is found shall redeem her.

HECUBA

How is that possible?

HELENUS

This is Apollo's plan:
Let Paris seize some woman
Who is precious to the West
And bring her to Troy as a hostage.

HECUBA

The god-plan is a good one;
I shall go and greet my son.

HELENUS

The plan is rash; it offends
Against all nations' guest-laws.

HECUBA

It is no offence to use
Sharp means to mend a crime.

HELENUS

There are more ways than one
Of offending against guest-laws.

HECUBA

If he dotes on a fountain-nymph
He will look at no other woman.

HELENUS

Such a plan may anger Zeus
Since Helen is his daughter.

HECUBA

That will put up her value
When it's time to negotiate.

HELENUS

We are not a violent people;
It could lead to a general war.

HECUBA

The kingdoms of the West
Are always slow to act.

HELENUS

I am not easy, Mother:
We must speak of this with Priam.

HECUBA

Do you wish to offend
The god who built our city?

HELENUS
My sister has warned us
That Paris will destroy it.

HECUBA
Then we must consult with Calchas.

HELENUS
Calchas has gone to the West.

HECUBA
To consult with the god at Delphi?

HELENUS
Apollo has commanded him
Henceforth to serve the war-kings.

HECUBA
What is the traitor telling them?

HELENUS
He is saying that a war-game
Is pleasing to the High Ones.

HECUBA
So I hold: it provides
Much matter for the Muses.

HELENUS
Apollo does not know yet
All that's in his father's mind.
But while gods smite at mortals
And sometimes at other gods,
Zeus will live the quieter
High on the Holy Mountain.

HECUBA
We shall have busy battle-plains.

HELENUS
Mother, tread carefully
Lest our city should die again.

HECUBA
All cities, my son,
That ever were or will be
Die sooner or later,
But the time and the means of death
Lives alone in the mind of Zeus.
We that live in Asia
Honour the gods more truly
Than the lout-lords of the West
And we will win back Hesione.
What have we to fear?
Those who cling to peace
Are those who soonest lose it;
If a city does not grow
Either by trade or conquest
It will soon lose its power

Over other eager kingdoms.
To be revenged on pirates
Such as Telamon and Heracles
Is to uphold a moral law
Which rules all the world.

HELENUS   My father believes Cassandra.

HECUBA   He won't when I've spoken to him.

HELENUS   What moral law do you speak of?

HECUBA   Revenge: let us speak with Priam.   (*)

*(They go. A great flash of light. The POET
strikes the war-gong, puts on PELEUS' helmet
and takes down the armour)*

PELEUS   Your apple-game is over
And Zeus' has begun!

(CHORUS)   Has Paris taken her?

PELEUS   No, she's taken him:
I warned Menelaus
What would happen if he left her
And went away to Crete.

(CHORUS)   You warned him about Paris?

PELEUS   No, I warned him about Helen.
I must take this to my son.

*(Trumpets sound. He throws stones over his
shoulder)*

I must summon up the Myrmidons
That fought for me long ago.
Time to arm, ant-men!

*(The MYRMIDONS rise from the earth; they
are visored)*

Agamemnon is summoning
The thousand ships to Aulis!

*(He goes with the armour. FIRST WOMAN
returns and CALCHAS appears masked on the
rocks and prophesies in Greek)*

(CHORUS)   Who is that?

(FIRST WOMAN)	The prophet Calchas: In ten years Troy will die.
(CHORUS)	He said that? – What about Helen?
(FIRST WOMAN)	Helen was not mentioned.
(CHORUS)	Did the army believe him?
(FIRST WOMAN)	All armies believe their prophets; That is why the General Has summoned all the War-Kings. (*)

(CALCHAS goes. PELEUS strikes the war-gong a third time. Trumpets etc. AGAMEMNON enters and speaks to the audience and the WAR-KINGS)

AGAMEMNON   Do not listen to traitors' prophesies.
There is as yet no question
Of going to war at all,
Let alone of sacking a city.
Our aim is a simple one,
To fulfil the oaths you swore.
My own oath is different;
I was not Helen's suitor
Since I had a wife already
And a marriage which is a happy one,
For the sake of all the West
I have sworn to lead you
Till we bring our Helen home.

Some say that she went willingly
But there is as yet no proof of it.
I believe that Priam is testing us
To see what he can get away with.
For many years the Trojans
Have been seizing our women
To increase their small work-force.
We have never responded
Because we are divided
While they have grown richer
Through trade and shrewd alliances;
But they have no standing army
To uphold their pirate actions,

So if we act swiftly and sensibly
Priam will soon give way.

Tyndareus once told us
That the West would know no quiet
Till we learned to act together.
That is why I have agreed
To serve as your General;
Not because I am
A great or proud commander
But because I love my brother
And because we have as yet
No common name to bind us.
We are called the Men of the West
Because our forefathers came here
From Asia which is the source
Of our culture and our wisdom.
I say this to remind you
That we are not savages
And our purpose here is honourable.

Yet some of our Kings are absent;
They wish to avoid their duty.
Where is Odysseus?
It is said he loves his wife
Better than his honour,
So I and Palamedes
Will leave at once to fetch him.
Calchas has also told us
We cannot set sail for Troy
Till we have fetched Achilles.
If we hold together
We shall all be home by winter
And earn ourselves the right
To call ourselves a nation.   (*)

(*He goes, and the WAR-KINGS disappear.*
Trumpets rise and fade. FOURTH MAN
comes out of the cave as ACHILLES)

ACHILLES   What is that sound?

POET   The war-song of the West.

ACHILLES

It is glorious! It is time
To say good-bye to Cheiron.

(THETIS comes back from the sea)

THETIS

Achilles, don't listen, my darling !

ACHILLES

Who are you? You're all wet.

THETIS

Don't you know your own mother?

ACHILLES

No, I have never seen her
Since the day that I was born.

THETIS

But you are in great danger
So I have come to hide you.

ACHILLES

Go away.

THETIS

       I'm so afraid.

ACHILLES

Of what?

THETIS

       If you go to the war
You will get what you long for,
Fame, honour, riches,
But you will die young;
Yet if you stay at home
Quietly and obscurely
You will live a long life
And you will be happy.

ACHILLES

Why did you tell me that?
If it's true it will poison
The rest of my life.

THETIS

       It is true.

ACHILLES

Then it would have been better
If you had never born me.

THETIS

That is what I thought too.

ACHILLES

Then why did you give yourself
To Peleus in the sea-cave?

THETIS

How can you say I gave myself?
Everyone knows he raped me.

ACHILLES

You provoked my father
By dancing obscenely.

(CHORUS)	Tell the truth, sea-nymph
—	Tell us how it was.
THETIS	Hot and brief and sandy.
ACHILLES	Girls who are decent Don't dance naked on beaches.
THETIS	It is nicer dancing on sand Than on lobster-pots or coral.
ACHILLES	So you rode ashore on a dolphin And offered yourself to the world.
THETIS	How can my own son speak to me So cruelly and coarsely? When you were little We were happy and I fed you On the umbles of young bears.
ACHILLES	You never came near me; you drowned me And left me with a Centaur.
THETIS	Because he could teach you Things that I couldn't.
ACHILLES	No, it was because You could not bear to suckle me.
THETIS	I tried to but you bit me And made my nipples bleed.
ACHILLES	So you got a bear to feed me; No wonder I am coarse.
THETIS	It would have been better If you had been a girl.
ACHILLES	No, it would be better If I were as you are…
THETIS	That's what I am saying; That is why I've come.
ACHILLES	Make me immortal, Mother.
THETIS	I tried to, my darling…

(Enter PELEUS with the golden armour)

PELEUS	For a man to become immortal He needs a good suit of armour.

THETIS	Don't listen to him: If you go you will die!
PELEUS	Go, all the world will honour you: Think of the glory, the prizes And most of all, think of the women.
ACHILLES	What women?
PELEUS	The women That you will win in the war.
ACHILLES	Yes, I would like that But I have no experience; There are no girls on Pelion.
THETIS	Then you'll have to practise.
PELEUS	You are right, he needs practice.
THETIS	I will take you to Scyros.
PELEUS	Why should he go to Scyros?
THETIS	There are many fair girls In the court of King Lycomedes.
PELEUS	Girls are hard to get there; He always locks them up.
THETIS	But I shall get him in By changing my darling's shape.
PELEUS	You can change yours, sea-girl, But not other people's.
THETIS	Yes, I shall change him Into a lovely girl.
ACHILLES	Then I am going with Peleus.
PELEUS	Wait, it is true that sometimes It's the best way to get in.
ACHILLES	To get into what?
PELEUS	Into the women's quarters. Many boys have done it; In the old days they used To call it rites of passage.

(THETIS offers a dress)

THETIS	Put this on, my darling; What are you afraid of?
ACHILLES	Anything that's shameful.
PELEUS	To be a girl is shameful But to act one shows skill.
ACHILLES	What is 'acting'?
(FIRST WOMAN)	Taking part.
ACHILLES	I will not.
THETIS	Don't be sulky.
PELEUS	Go with her but take that armour; Then however the Fates decide it You'll enjoy it either way.
ACHILLES *(To Thetis)*	Do you think I will ever Forget what you have told me? Your words will never leave me, They will haunt me all my life.
THETIS	I love you, my son. (*)

(Trumpets sound. ACHILLES goes into the cave. PELEUS goes elsewhere)

(To Chorus)	You and I can stop this war; They can't leave without him.
(CHORUS)	We don't want to stop it — We want to see what happens.
THETIS	Then you must go to Scyros.

(A ball rolls out of the cave)

(CHORUS)	Where did that come from?
THETIS	From the women's quarters in Scyros: Deidamia, the King's daughter, Is dressing him already.
(CHORUS)	What can we do, sea-thing?
THETIS	Help hide him among you So nobody will find him.

(FIRST WOMAN brings dresses out of the cave)

(FIRST WOMAN)   Put these on and paint your faces
And you'll be as fair as he is.

THETIS   Quickly, while I raise a storm
To stop the fleet from sailing.   (*)

(She goes. CHORUS retire. THIRD MAN enters as ODYSSEUS in Ithaca)

ODYSSEUS   I will not leave my wife
To rescue some lecherous woman;
If any man seized Penelope
I would summon no armada
But I would rescue her myself.

(FIRST WOMAN)   You will have to go, Odysseus,
Just like the rest of them.
See, the General is coming
And Palamedes too.
You swore an oath, it binds you.

(ODYSSEUS cries out)

Go into the house;
You must not receive them
Till you have composed yourself.

ODYSSEUS   Tell him I am sick.

(He goes in. Enter AGAMEMNON and POET for PALAMEDES. He is carrying various devices)

AGAMEMNON   Where is the Lord of Ithaca?

(FIRST WOMAN)   In the house.

AGAMEMNON   Then fetch him.

(FIRST WOMAN)   I fear he is not yet himself.

(Wild cries from within)

He has a strange sickness.

AGAMEMNON   Sick? Some are home-sick
Before they leave their homes.

(ODYSSEUS comes out with a plough and sower's pouch. He is wearing a conical cap)

POET What is Odysseus doing?

(FIRST WOMAN) Ploughing winter wheat.

AGAMEMNON Those that sow salt
Seldom reap a harvest.

POET He is mad.

AGAMEMNON No, he's playing with us.

POET Where is his son Telemachus?

(FIRST WOMAN hands the POET another baby. He puts it in front of the plough. ODYSSEUS avoids it)

AGAMEMNON You do not plough straight, ploughman.

(FIRST WOMAN) Mad ploughmen seldom do.

AGAMEMNON Stop this, Odysseus,
It is unworthy of you.
Palamedes invents things
And has brought you much that is useful
To while away the hours
While Priam and I negotiate.

PALAMEDES This is a discus:
These are drafts and dice
And these are scales to weigh things.

AGAMEMNON Weigh it well, Odysseus.

(ODYSSEUS hugs the baby and weeps)

It gives me no pleasure
To see a good man caught
In a net of his own making.
You persuaded Tyndareus
To impose the war-kings' oaths
So he'd give you your Penelope.
I love my wife as you do
So I understand your feelings,
But you must put your wits
To a better use than this

> Or men will say 'He loved his wife
> More than he loved the high things.'

ODYSSEUS
> I'm ashamed: I will go with you.
> I who love peace
> Will serve and uphold you
> Better than you deserve
> And better than the kings
> Who have more ships than I.
> Though I will never like you
> I will serve you faithfully
> Till all is done as it must be.
> When your mind is cloudy
> I will make you resolute
> And when you wish to end it
> I will make you go on.
> I am stronger than you are
> Because Athene is with me
> And I will never leave you
> Until we take the city.

AGAMEMNON
> All I ask is your help
> To rescue my sister Helen.

ODYSSEUS
> And you shall have it, my General;
> But for your Palamedes
> I never will forgive him.

AGAMEMNON
> Go now and fetch Achilles
> And bring him quickly to Aulis;
> It's reported that his mother
> Means to hide him on Scyros.

ODYSSEUS
> I will fetch him, my lord.

(*He goes. POET follows*)

(FIRST WOMAN)
> No goodbyes, Odysseus,
> To your wife or your children?

AGAMEMNON
> I understand him;
> He does not wish to show
> His pain in front of others.

(FIRST WOMAN)
> He is rightly punished; nobody
> Should play games with their own babies.

(AGAMEMNON going)

AGAMEMNON

Take the child and tell Penelope
I am sorry to have taken her husband.
Let her make the house fair
For a swift and safe homecoming.
The soil is not good here;
She must look to the vineyards.   (*)

(He goes. All the CHORUS come forward, their faces painted, some finely dressed and some only half-dressed)

(CHORUS)

Here we are in Scyros!
— Did you see what was happening
  In there with Deidamia?
— No, it was too dark
— What do you think it would be like
  To lie with Achilles?
— I should think it would be dreadful;
  He has had no experience
  Except for watching bears.

(Cries and noises within)

— Was that him or her?
— It sounds to me as if
  He is teaching her his war-cry
— No, she's teaching him.

(FIRST WOMAN)

Perhaps Aphrodite
Is teaching both of them.

(FOURTH WOMAN comes out of the cave as DEIDAMIA)

(CHORUS)

Speak to us, Deidamia.

DEIDAMIA

He raped me.

(CHORUS)

                    You too?
— Was it terrible or sweet?

DEIDAMIA

It was hateful.

(CHORUS)

                        Was he rough?

DEIDAMIA

Yes.

(CHORUS)	But was he tender?
DEIDAMIA	Both. I hate myself: I had sworn I would be A priestess of Artemis.
(FIRST WOMAN)	And you shall be.
DEIDAMIA	No, not now, There's a living child inside me...
(CHORUS)	How can you be certain?
DEIDAMIA	Apollo speaks within me: The child will be a cruel one. I see beacons in the night And the hearth-fires are all out; Only camp-fires and battle-fires And the funeral pyres of warriors.
(FIRST WOMAN)	But now you must name Achilles.
(CHORUS)	What about Aissa?
–	Or Cercysera?
DEIDAMIA	No, We shall call him 'Pyrrha'.
(CHORUS)	But that means 'rage'.
DEIDAMIA	I know. (*)

(*Trumpet sounds*)

(FIRST WOMAN)	Odysseus is coming And Peleus is with him.
(CHORUS)	We can handle Odysseus. But can we handle Peleus?

(*Enter ODYSSEUS and PELEUS*)

DEIDAMIA	Son of Laertes, I am a royal princess: How dare you enter my quarters And with that foul old man?
(CHORUS)	Get out, both of you.
ODYSSEUS	We will when we've got what we came for.
(CHORUS)	Shame on you, Odysseus.

DEIDAMIA   What would Penelope say
            If she saw you watching them dressing?

ODYSSEUS   You know why we've come.

PELEUS   Which of you is my son?

(CHORUS)   Only girls here.

DEIDAMIA   Are you suggesting
            That one of my women's a boy?

PELEUS   I think he may be this one.

(CHORUS)   How dare you call me a boy?

PELEUS   You must let me inspect you.

(CHORUS)   Dirty old man – Try me,
            I might be Achilles.

ODYSSEUS   This foolishness must stop.

PELEUS   All of you, take your clothes off.

ODYSSEUS   We are guests in Scyros, Peleus.

PELEUS   Guests have their privileges.

ODYSSEUS   Let me deal with this.

(FIRST WOMAN) Three versions are told here,
            Try them.

ODYSSEUS   Look in this bag;
            They are all kinds of weapons:

            (*He empties soldiers' gear on the ground*)

            Each of you must pick one.

(CHORUS)   Do you want us in your army?

DEIDAMIA   Only a man would know
            A good sword from a bad one.

(CHORUS)   Girls know the difference
            Between men's weapons, Peleus.

PELEUS   That's him, the one with the spear!
            Come with me, Achilles.

(CHORUS)   Anywhere you want to.

            (*Reveals herself to ODYSSEUS*)

PELEUS	O you are delicious!
ODYSSEUS	Try the second plan: The apple, where is the apple?

(FIRST WOMAN hands the apple to ODYSSEUS)

All of you, sit down
And see if you can catch it.

(Throws the apple at one of them)

(CHORUS)	Ugh, it's half-eaten
—	If you want us to eat apples At least bring ones that are fresh.
ODYSSEUS	Peleus, more apples.

(PELEUS and ODYSSEUS throw apples to each of them. All catch them in their skirts)

PELEUS	Strange, that should have worked.
(CHORUS)	What are you trying to do?
DEIDAMIA	Men use their hands for catching But women use their skirts.
PELEUS	These girls have taught him well.
ODYSSEUS	We are wasting time, Peleus. Which of you is Achilles?
ALL	I am! – I am! – I am!
ODYSSEUS	This pretence is unworthy, Achilles; The thousand ships are waiting.
DEIDAMIA	Didn't you pretend When they came to fetch you, Odysseus?
ODYSSEUS	I am ashamed that I did so As Achilles should be now.
(FIRST WOMAN)	If the war's to last ten years What is the hurry, Odysseus?
ODYSSEUS	Try the third version.

(PELEUS collects a musical instrument)

(FIRST WOMAN)	Truth Is often revealed in music.
(CHORUS)	Very good, we'll sing to you. (*They do so*)
ODYSSEUS	Sound the war-drums, Peleus, The cymbals and the trumpets. (*A great bray of war-sounds*)
(CHORUS)	What's this? – Is it pirates? – No, the Trojans are attacking! – Save us, Achilles! (*ACHILLES' war-cry is heard within*)
DEIDAMIA	Don't come out! (*)
	(*Thunder and war-music. ACHILLES utters his war-cry and comes out from the cave, monstrous. He is visored and in his father's armour. He begins to dance a war-dance. MYRMIDONS appear and join him. The fire blazes. THETIS rushes in*)
THETIS	Wait! All the world wait! Why have you chosen The wrong shape, my darling?
ODYSSEUS	It is too late, sea-nymph, To change what is unchangeable.
THETIS	You must not go, Achilles! (*ACHILLES and ODYSSEUS go, PELEUS follows*) Zeus, do not let him die!
DEIDAMIA	Since it's told you have already Made six sons immortal To ask for more is greedy.
THETIS	Zeus, spare my child! (*She runs out. Waves break over the crest of the ambience. CALCHAS appears on the crags above and speaks again in Greek over the speech which follows*)

(CHORUS)	How does Zeus answer, old one?
(FIRST WOMAN)	He says it is not he Who will triumph in this war But his prophet son Apollo, The Healer who destroys.

(CHORUS sing under what follows)

(CHORUS)	Who is to blame for this?
–	What is the truth of it?
(FIRST WOMAN)	How could it be otherwise?

(POET comes back)

POET

He who began this story
Will in time be forgot,
And win a lesser glory
Than he who shapes the plot.
Mark the Lord of Light
And how he works his way:
The plan may be the father's
But Apollo makes the play.

(ALL go. Detritus falls from above)

Play 2
TELEPHUS

AT MYCENAE

CAST

First Woman	NURSE
Second Woman	(–)
Third Woman	CLYTEMNESTRA
Fourth Woman	ELECTRA
First Man	POET/ PELEUS/ TELEPHUS
Second Man	AGAMEMNON
Third Man	(–)
Fourth Man	ACHILLES/ AEGISTHUS
	CHORUS of WAR-KINGS in background

(*The ambience is now green and friendly, and over the entrance of the cave there is a suggestion of the Lion Gate. Music is heard within. The NURSE is tending the fire. The POET is wearing a mask and quoting in Greek from Aeschylus' Agamemnon, based on the words at line 40. The CHORUS enter. They are not part of the household*)

(CHORUS)   What's our Poet doing now?
               — He's telling another story.

POET   'Ten long years since the sons of Atreus
                  Put forth with their thousand ships
                  To bring the wanton home...'

(CHORUS)   Will it really take so long?

(*POET takes off mask. Music stops*)

POET   It's the way it will be told of.

(CHORUS)   — It won't be ten years, it can't be
               — Ten years in cold beds
               — Supposing that it's twenty?
               — We will all be old hags by then
               — Where are we now?
               — What is this house?

NURSE   The home of Agamemnon
                  And his wife Clytemnestra.

(CHORUS)   Mycenae?

NURSE   Where else?

(CHORUS)   We have heard dreadful things
                  Of this place and those who lived there
               — We have heard the names of the criminals
               — Pelops — Thyestes — Atreus.

NURSE   Has your Poet not yet told you
                  Of the Founder?

(CHORUS)   The Founder?

POET   The founder of this house.
                  Look up into the sky:

He is chained beneath that rock
Forever...

(CHORUS)   I see nothing.

POET   ... For ever and for ever.
                Yet not so long ago
                The gods loved him so much
                That Zeus invited Tantalus
                To dinner on Olympus;
                And after they'd drunk and feasted
                Zeus opened up his heart
                And told him all the secrets
                Of his own divine nature.

(CHORUS)   All?

NURSE   All that matter.

POET   So when the gods were asleep
            Or drunk or at their lovings,
            Tantalus stole some nectar
            And a pot of ambrosia too,
            Slipped away down the mountain-side
            And at once began to share it
            With his friends and his children.
            When Zeus woke up in the morning
            He was angry with the night-thief
            And gave him a punishment
            More terrible than any
            Human-kind till then had known.

(CHORUS)   What was it? – Tell us.   (*)

            (*The POET puts on the mask of Zeus*)

POET   'Listen with reverence,
            Children of Tantalus,
            Earth-girls and clay-stuff'...

            (*Takes off the mask, looks at them and the
            audience and drinks*)

            I will tell you what he said.
            You all have sipped my nectar
            So in part you are immortal;
            You hope to become god-like

Without first understanding
What it is to be human.
That is dangerous, so I must bind you
Like Prometheus before you;
I shall set a rock above you
Tied with ropes to the sky
And you will never know
The season, year or day
When I or some other
May unloose the bonds of heaven.

(*CHORUS look up at the rock for the first time*)

Yet if you are lucky
And if there is time
You may learn many things
That you do not yet know,
Perhaps about the gods
Or the ocean and the sky
Or even about yourselves.
Of course you may learn wrongly
Or even discover things
You do not want to know.
Sometimes you will feel
That you have become wiser
And sometimes you will get
The sense of making sense
Of something strange and deep,
But when you wake up in the morning
It will make sense no longer
Nor fit as well as you thought it did.
Sometimes you will feel
You have left something out
And will wonder if it's lost
Or whether yet to find.'

(*Drinks*)

Finish the story, old one.

(FIRST WOMAN)   'This work will make you thirsty
So I'll set you in a pool
Of fresh refreshful water

But when you try to drink
It will ebb and shrink and dry.
This work will make you hungry,
So I will set a fruit-tree
By the pool with golden branches,
Luscious, thick and loaded
With all the fruits of the world;
When you grope to reach them
You may feel the bloom of a peach
With the tip of your finger,
But the Four Winds will be watching
And when you grunt and grasp
They will swing it from your clutch.

POET   Yet take heart, one night of nectar
Lasts long in human bellies.
But since the truth that's told
The morning after a drinking
Is apt to be garbled
Your children may be tantalised
And you will not know why.'

(CHORUS) Will the rock ever fall?
      – Will the rock fall on us?

NURSE   Not unless you're underneath it.

POET   We are all underneath it.   (*)

*(POET goes. CLYTEMNESTRA comes out of
the house with libations. She is singing softly to
herself)*

Every day the Queen offers
Libations to Apollo
For her husband's safe return.

(CHORUS) How can she do that
After what he did to her?
      – If a woman is to survive
She may have to pretend
And hide what's in her heart.

NURSE   She is not pretending;
She has loved Agamemnon
Since both of them were children.

(CHORUS)　　　　But when he killed her child
　　　　　　　　She swore to revenge it.

NURSE　　　　　When women are wretched
　　　　　　　　They swear foolish things.

(CHORUS)　　　　But when women swear revenge
　　　　　　　　They mean it.

NURSE　　　　　　　　Not always;
　　　　　　　　When they bring forth new children
　　　　　　　　It can bring a kind of healing;
　　　　　　　　When she bore Agamemnon
　　　　　　　　Three new ones, full of life,
　　　　　　　　She did become happy
　　　　　　　　Just as he foretold.

(CHORUS)　　　　They say that dead babies
　　　　　　　　Are heard screaming here at night.

NURSE　　　　　Babies don't need reasons
　　　　　　　　To make them scream and weep.
　　　　　　　　Night-creaks or nightmares
　　　　　　　　Fratricide or flatulence,
　　　　　　　　It all comes out the same.

(CHORUS)　　　　But we've heard how the blood
　　　　　　　　Is still wet on the walls,
　　　　　　　　All because of Tantalus.

　　　　　　　　(*CLYTEMNESTRA rises*)

CLYTEMNESTRA　How often have I told you
　　　　　　　　That I will not have that name
　　　　　　　　Nor that of other criminals
　　　　　　　　Mentioned in this house?
　　　　　　　　You are an experienced nurse
　　　　　　　　And should know that evil stories
　　　　　　　　Work evil on small children.
　　　　　　　　You frightened me and my sister
　　　　　　　　When both of us were little;
　　　　　　　　Now you do it to Orestes,
　　　　　　　　I have heard you; go and fetch him.

　　　　　　　　(*NURSE goes in*)

	Strangers, go in with her. Travellers are welcome here.
(CHORUS)	Lady, forgive us; We can help you with the harvest, But we dare not go in.
CLYTEMNESTRA	Because of the stories?
(CHORUS)	The curse; is it true?
CLYTEMNESTRA	Curses are not bred By what is done in palaces But by what is told afterwards By women such as you. If you will all come in You will find no curse within; Decent people live here Doing the best they can. I have made this palace finer Than any in the West;

(NURSE brings in the baby ORESTES and gives him to CLYTEMNESTRA)

	When my husband comes back He will bring me silks from Asia And tapestries with pictures Of the great tales of the past And the house will be even fairer. See, my son is not crying; Isn't he beautiful?
(CHORUS)	The boy is a fair one — But there's something we must ask you.
CLYTEMNESTRA	Ask it.
(CHORUS)	It is personal.
CLYTEMNESTRA	Then ask me!
(CHORUS)	Is it true That you came out of an egg?
CLYTEMNESTRA	Of course not, it's a story Put out by my father To make him feel important.

(CHORUS)   Was Zeus your father?

CLYTEMNESTRA   Tyndareus was my father.

(CHORUS)   But your sister?

CLYTEMNESTRA   She was an egg-child.

(CHORUS)   Was Helen really raped?
         —   Or did she go willingly?

                  (*Pause*)

CLYTEMNESTRA   When a woman is brutalised
                  Why does the world assume
                  It's her who is the guilty one?
                  Helen is as faithful
                  To her lord as I to mine.
                  You all know how it is:
                  When a woman is insecure
                  She needs to put on a show
                  And wear too many jewels
                  And paint herself too much.

(CHORUS)   Insecure?

CLYTEMNESTRA   Wouldn't you be
                  If you had had two fathers?
                  Would you know for certain
                  Who you really were?
                  Wouldn't you try to invent yourself
                  So as to feel stronger?
                  Wouldn't you feel safer
                  At home with your husband?
                  She is just like poor Penelope!
                  She hates having visitors.
                  When Paris came to Sparta
                  Helen begged Menelaus
                  Not to leave her alone with him:
                  Poor darling unlucky Helen.

(CHORUS)   Unlucky? – You pity her?

CLYTEMNESTRA   I pity her beauty;
                  It won't make her happy.

(CHORUS)   And you? Are you happy?

CLYTEMNESTRA	More than any living woman.
(CHORUS)	That is strange – We are glad of it.
CLYTEMNESTRA	Women have to learn Not to let the past torment them.
(CHORUS)	If I lost a child I never could forget it.
CLYTEMNESTRA	When something is lost That can never be found again It is best to forget it.
(CHORUS)	I could not – Nor I.
CLYTEMNESTRA	Then you are stupid girls. When a man does something terrible It can change him for ever As it has changed my husband. (*)

(PELEUS enters)

	Agamemnon has sworn To make good; that is why He has gone to rescue my sister.
(CHORUS)	The aim is a noble one.
PELEUS	Zeus, save me from noble aims, They always bring disaster.
CLYTEMNESTRA	What are you doing here, Peleus? I forbade you to come here. You tell lies about my sister, You try to grope my women And now you insult my husband.
PELEUS	I have come to get news of the army.
CLYTEMNESTRA	None yet.
PELEUS	None yet, she says! Heracles and I and Telamon Went to Troy with eight ships only And we sacked it in a week. Of course one must allow For your husband's incompetence But even he should manage

With a thousand ships as back-up
To bring Helen home by winter.

CLYTEMNESTRA   That is what we all pray for.

PELEUS   Once the whole point of a war
Was to get hold of women
And to get and give them pleasure.
If we did want to rescue them
We didn't make moral speeches,
We got on with the job.
Why go to war for a woman
Who as clear as the day-sky
Doesn't want to be rescued?

CLYTEMNESTRA   Get out of my house.

PELEUS   I was there in Sparta:
I saw how it happened.

CLYTEMNESTRA   It happened in your mind,
Your filthy senile mind.

(CHORUS)   Dirty old goat
—   He should have been castrated.

PELEUS   Why make all this fuss
About what Helen did
Or didn't do or might have done?
Now the war's begun
Why give moral reasons
For something that's enjoyable
And worth-while in itself?

CLYTEMNESTRA   You're not sane; go away.

PELEUS   A good war refreshes everyone,
Men, gods and Mother Earth.

(*CLYTEMNESTRA is suckling ORESTES*)

If there were no wars
Life would be impossible.
How could we breed warriors
If they get no experience?
How could kings test their chariots
Or their new Thracian horses

Till they've used them in the field?
How can poets sing great deeds done
If none are done to sing of? (*)

(*Trumpets sound, then bright music*)

CLYTEMNESTRA	That's my husband's trumpet!
PELEUS	It can't be, not yet.
(CHORUS)	Look, lady, someone's lit The beacon on the watch-tower.
CLYTEMNESTRA	That is only to be lit When a signal comes from Troy. What does it mean? Who lit it?

(*ELECTRA enters*)

ELECTRA	I did!
CLYTEMNESTRA	And the beacon?
ELECTRA	I lit it!
CLYTEMNESTRA	Why, Electra?
PELEUS	What's the point of lighting beacons When it is high noon?
NURSE	What have you been up to this time?
CLYTEMNESTRA	You went into the watch-tower Though I told you not to go there. Go to your room and lie down; I will come and speak to you later.
ELECTRA	My mother is a fool: I was taking some drink to the watchman When I saw their armour shining And flashing in the sun.
(CHORUS)	Whose?
ELECTRA	All the War-Kings! When I saw my father with them I told him to light the beacon So that all the West might know That my father has come home again.

PELEUS   Praised be the gods!
                  Tonight there will be feasting!

CLYTEMNESTRA   This cannot be true, Electra.

ELECTRA   Go and see for yourself.

(CHORUS)   Zeus, we praise and thank you:
                  It is over, all over!

                  *(CLYTEMNESTRA gives ORESTES back to
                  the NURSE who continues to suckle him)*

                  Helen has come home again!   (*)

                  *(Enter AGAMEMNON. CLYTEMNESTRA
                  embraces him)*

CLYTEMNESTRA   O my love, you have come home
                  And the victory was easy!
                  I have been so afraid
                  Because of Calchas' prophecy.
                  Every night I have wept
                  And dreamed of dreadful things,
                  Of ten years of waiting
                  And sitting here alone,
                  Of hearing daily rumours
                  That you were dead or wounded,
                  Of dreaming you lay beside me
                  And waking to find the bed empty,
                  And I became like Niobe
                  Still weeping, but stone-hard.
                  But now my tears are bubbling
                  As these streams do when they welcome
                  All travellers who are thirsty,
                  Except it is I
                  Who am thirsty for you.

AGAMEMNON   You weep for the wrong things;
                  Weep for your sister Helen.

CLYTEMNESTRA   She is dead?

AGAMEMNON   No, she flourishes.

CLYTEMNESTRA   But –

AGAMEMNON   The war is not over:
                  It has not yet begun.

CLYTEMNESTRA   What are you saying?

ELECTRA   Did you not land and attack them?

AGAMEMNON   O yes, we landed
But in the wrong place.

CLYTEMNESTRA   How is that possible?

AGAMEMNON   Some say it was the work
Of Poseidon and Apollo
Because they are guarding Troy.

PELEUS   Do you mean to say you managed
To get lost with a thousand ships?

AGAMEMNON   We set sail so quickly
That we did not take a pilot.

PELEUS   Only idiots need pilots
To find their way to Asia.

ELECTRA   Where did you land?

AGAMEMNON   In Mysia.

PELEUS   Mysia! In Mysia?
That's a hundred miles from Troy.
Heracles, Jason and I
Sailed there in three days
And sacked it in a week.
You a general? If you tried
To take a herd of cattle
From here down to Argos
It would take you ten years
And you'd end up in Sicily.

AGAMEMNON   I did not guide the fleet;
Your son was our Admiral.

PELEUS   You made Achilles Admiral?
A boy who has spent his life
On Mount Pelion? Who till now
Has never seen the sea?

AGAMEMNON   The title was only honorary.
We expected no difficulties
But he said he would not join us

	Unless I made him Admiral;
	Calchas agreed with him
	And so did all the Council.
PELEUS	I do not believe this.
AGAMEMNON	Go in and ask him.
	He has come with the rest of the kings;
	When they have washed and rested
	We shall feast in his honour.
CLYTEMNESTRA	We shall have no feasting here
	Till Helen's back in Sparta.
	Nevertheless it's our duty
	To refresh weary travellers.
	Come in with me, Electra;
	We must wash and change and greet them.
(*To Chorus*)	Now will you come in?

(She goes in with the CHORUS.
AGAMEMNON calls after her)

AGAMEMNON	Don't take too long:
	The War-Kings are thirsty.
	Go in with her, Electra.
ELECTRA	Let her change her dress,
	I want to be with you.
AGAMEMNON	Go in and change yours too.
ELECTRA	I swore I would never change it
	Till you came back victorious.
AGAMEMNON	Do it.
ELECTRA	If you wish me to.
AGAMEMNON	You must fill Achilles' wine-cup;
	If he saw you like this
	He would take it as a rebuke
	For his mistake when he landed.
ELECTRA	Must I fill his cup?
AGAMEMNON	To the brim; go and change
	And show the boy honour.
	Some scent would help also. (*)

(ELECTRA goes in)

PELEUS

Before you give him honour
You should send him to Nauplius,
Palamedes' father,
To learn navigation.
A war that never was,
It is shameful.

AGAMEMNON

We'll go back
As soon as we find a pilot.

PELEUS

With you in command
The war will be a filthy one.

AGAMEMNON

Not a war, Peleus.

PELEUS

No, a 'rescue operation'!
What needs rescuing here
Is our war-fleet's reputation.

AGAMEMNON

Go in and greet your son.

PELEUS

It could have been a good war
But the Trojans are warned now
And no one will enjoy it.

AGAMEMNON

You should try to understand
The difference between
A good war and a just one.

PELEUS

What is that?

AGAMEMNON

Have you never
Heard of the word 'Justice'?

PELEUS

Yes, it belongs to Zeus.

AGAMEMNON

And to all who rule men.

PELEUS

That's where there's a problem.

AGAMEMNON

Yes, to men like you.

PELEUS

No, to men like you
Who love to use high words
To justify their actions.
It is always those big words
That breed the big disasters.

AGAMEMNON   It's because of men like you
                    That we need such words, Peleus;
                    I mean to rid the world
                    Of your kind for ever.

PELEUS   That is what I'm saying;
                    It's always the good men
                    Who are the real destroyers.
                    I will go in to your Admiral;
                    If you ever get to Troy
                    Try not to put the cavalry
                    In charge of a tortoise.   (*)

                    (*Goes*)

AGAMEMNON (*To Nurse*) Give me the child to hold.
                    Why can one never tell
                    Why a baby's crying?

NURSE   He is crying because he's hungry.

                    (*Takes the baby*)

AGAMEMNON   Little noble child,
                    Little king, little warrior,
                    It is lawful to weep now
                    When you do not know why;
                    But when you are a king
                    You must learn to hide your tears
                    To endure through times of trouble.

                    (*CLYTEMNESTRA comes back finely
                    dressed*)

CLYTEMNESTRA   Give him to me, my darling,
                    And come into the house.

AGAMEMNON   Let me hold him for a while;
                    There are things I must tell you.

CLYTEMNESTRA   What things?

AGAMEMNON   It may take
                    Rather longer than I'd hoped
                    Before I see the boy again.

CLYTEMNESTRA   What are you saying?

(Gives the baby to the NURSE, who goes in)

AGAMEMNON   Palamedes is back from Troy.
                He confirms that Helen is there
                And has said she wishes to stay there
                As a suppliant.

CLYTEMNESTRA   A suppliant?
                It's not possible.

AGAMEMNON   Priam told him
                He is bound to protect her
                Because she's in love with Paris.

CLYTEMNESTRA   How can she love a man
                Who seized her and raped her?

AGAMEMNON   There are precedents.

CLYTEMNESTRA   Not Helen.

AGAMEMNON   Some of the kings are saying
                That if she went willingly
                Their oaths would not be binding.

CLYTEMNESTRA   If they choose to break their oaths
                You must go on without them.

AGAMEMNON   I do not believe that Priam
                Wants war any more than I do.
                He wants to win his sister back
                By some exchange of hostages
                And thinks he can get away with it
                Because we are not united;
                But a show of force is often
                The best means of persuasion.

CLYTEMNESTRA   It will not persuade Hecuba.

(Angry voices are heard within)

AGAMEMNON   That is Achilles' voice.

CLYTEMNESTRA   Wine cheers seasoned warriors
                But it's apt to make boys quarrel;
                We had better go in.

AGAMEMNON   No, wait.
                I am wondering why Palamedes

                            Sailed to Troy in a single ship
                            While a thousand landed in Mysia:
                            It may be some warning
                            That the war's not meant to happen.

CLYTEMNESTRA   You swore to rescue Helen.

AGAMEMNON   I will, in my own way.

CLYTEMNESTRA   What does that mean, Agamemnon?

AGAMEMNON   Calchas' prophecy, ten years…

CLYTEMNESTRA   It's not possible.

AGAMEMNON   Of course not,
When they've sacked Dardania
And enjoyed one good battle
They will come home happy
And weighed down with prizes
Long before it's winter.
That is not why I am going.

CLYTEMNESTRA   Calchas has confused them
With his talk of a ten-year war.
He is dangerous, Agamemnon;
You must get rid of him.

AGAMEMNON   I cannot, they honour him.

CLYTEMNESTRA   But you? Do you believe him?

AGAMEMNON   I do not need a prophet
To know that the walls of Troy
Are too high for men to scale
And too thick for any engine
Yet designed by men to crack them.

CLYTEMNESTRA   No walls built by men
Have ever stopped men breaking them.

AGAMEMNON   Troy's walls were built by gods.

CLYTEMNESTRA   Then gods can destroy them.

AGAMEMNON   But why should Apollo's Oracle
Speak prophecies against
A city built by Apollo?

CLYTEMNESTRA	One can never be sure that the gods Are on the side one thinks.
AGAMEMNON	Yet all that Delphi prophesies Has always turned out true.
CLYTEMNESTRA	That's because we only hear Of an oracle's successes.

(More noises and shouting within)

Achilles is drunk.

AGAMEMNON	They all love to quarrel.
CLYTEMNESTRA	The sooner you find a pilot And set sail with the lot of them The better for this house.
AGAMEMNON	I will wait till Menelaus Has spoken in Troy with Priam: Patient negotiation Often reconciles great kings.
CLYTEMNESTRA	If you trust in negotiation Then the war will take ten years.
AGAMEMNON	You and I worked things out.
CLYTEMNESTRA	It is easier to reconcile Families than kingdoms.
AGAMEMNON	I am thinking too of families: How can we win wars When there is a blood-feud In our own house? That is why I have sent for Aegisthus.
CLYTEMNESTRA	Why?
AGAMEMNON	To be reconciled.
CLYTEMNESTRA	You'd be mad to bring back someone Whose brothers were murdered here And who killed your own father.
AGAMEMNON	He has done no wrong to me Nor I to him.
CLYTEMNESTRA	Don't do it; He is dangerous.

AGAMEMNON   No, he's weak,
                        He's a sick man and he's frightened.
                        All he wants is to feel safe;
                        While I'm gone he shall stay here.

CLYTEMNESTRA   For ten years? I'll not have it.

AGAMEMNON   It won't be ten years.

CLYTEMNESTRA   It might, I couldn't bear that.

AGAMEMNON   Nor could I.

CLYTEMNESTRA   You say that
                        But sooner or later
                        You would take some other woman.

AGAMEMNON   I wish for no other
                        Than the one I have already.

CLYTEMNESTRA   Swear it.

AGAMEMNON   I swear it.

CLYTEMNESTRA   And swear not to sack the city.

AGAMEMNON   That's an easy oath: I swear it.

CLYTEMNESTRA   Maybe, but I know you:
                        Sometimes you see too much
                        And so you lose your way;
                        Sometimes you forget
                        The meaning of your name,
                        'Very resolute'.

AGAMEMNON   So I am.

(*More shouting heard within*)

CLYTEMNESTRA   You must prove it to me.

AGAMEMNON   I am not a god;
                        I will do what is possible.

CLYTEMNESTRA   If you wish to prove forever
                        You are not the man you were
                        And that all your high resolves
                        Are not mere words to please me
                        You will go on, Agamemnon,
                        Till you bring my sister home.
                        But you will not harm the city

Or its people: if you avoid that
I will give you such love
As you have never known;
If you don't, I will know
You're unfit to be my husband.

AGAMEMNON Don't scold me, my darling.
When Priam sees our tents,
Our spears and our chariots
It will not be so hard
To bring our Helen home.

CLYTEMNESTRA Now you are my Agamemnon.

AGAMEMNON And you are lovely to me.   (*)

(Enter ELECTRA)

ELECTRA You must come in quickly, Father.

CLYTEMNESTRA What is the matter?

ELECTRA Achilles is angry;
The kings are insulting him.

CLYTEMNESTRA Then you shouldn't have filled
His wine-bowl so often.

ELECTRA Father told me to honour him
But he's kicking over benches
And scattering the wine-cups
And saying he'll kill the kings.

AGAMEMNON Why?

ELECTRA   Because none of them
Are giving him the honour
You told him he deserves.

AGAMEMNON One has to say such things.

ELECTRA But he's angriest with you.

AGAMEMNON Me?

ELECTRA   Because you blamed him
For landing in Mysia.

AGAMEMNON I never said so,
Not to his face.

ELECTRA	You said so here to us.
CLYTEMNESTRA	And you went and told him?
ELECTRA	Yes, and so I told him That I would never marry him.
AGAMEMNON	You said that to Achilles?
CLYTEMNESTRA	She says it to every man.
AGAMEMNON	I must go into the house; I do not want trouble At a feast in his honour. The whole army knows He will be a great warrior, But if he quarrels here How shall I handle him If we ever get to Troy?

(*Goes in*)   (*)

CLYTEMNESTRA	Why did you tell Achilles You didn't want to marry him?
ELECTRA	Because I don't and won't.
CLYTEMNESTRA	Just because he excites you Like all the other girls –
ELECTRA	He does not excite me And I don't want to marry him.
CLYTEMNESTRA	Who said you should?
ELECTRA	You did, to my father; You said it was the best way To get me out of the house.
CLYTEMNESTRA	That was a joke.
ELECTRA	Not funny, Mother.
CLYTEMNESTRA	Why are you so stupid? How often have I told you Not to insult our guests?
ELECTRA	Why do you always try To put me in the wrong?
CLYTEMNESTRA	Why are you rude to everyone?

ELECTRA   I speak my mind.

CLYTEMNESTRA   I know;
                 But it's time that you learned
                 To keep your tedious malice
                 And jealousy to yourself.

ELECTRA   Who am I jealous of?

CLYTEMNESTRA   O Electra, everyone
                 Knows that a daughter
                 Loves her father too much
                 And her mother too little.
                 It is natural but it need not
                 Turn into a sickness.
                 Do you think the way you treat me
                 Makes your father love you better?

ELECTRA   He loves me most of all.

CLYTEMNESTRA   Then why make him angry
                 By saying stupid things?

ELECTRA   What things?

CLYTEMNESTRA   By telling him
                 A child is created
                 By the man's seed alone
                 And that the mother's womb
                 Is only a vessel.

ELECTRA   It is true.

CLYTEMNESTRA   O Electra,
                 Long before the gods
                 Came to Olympus
                 People said such things;
                 They even said that women
                 Do not conceive at all
                 By making love with men
                 But because the wind blows through them
                 Or because they bathe in rivers.
                 If you don't stop this silliness
                 You will spoil your father's homecoming.
                 Don't let us argue
                 On such a day as this.

ELECTRA	Then don't put me down.
CLYTEMNESTRA	Then let us each promise Not to put the other down. Now go back and apologise To Achilles and your father.
ELECTRA	I will never marry.
CLYTEMNESTRA	Probably you are right; If you do not change Nobody will have you. Now go and help your sister To entertain our guests.
ELECTRA	She isn't there.
CLYTEMNESTRA	Where is she?
ELECTRA	She is praying at some altar To Artemis or Apollo.
CLYTEMNESTRA	Find her; Achilles Would like her to sing to him.
ELECTRA	I can sing as well as she does.
CLYTEMNESTRA	When you do you wake the Furies. (*)

(ELECTRA goes in. NURSE returns with ORESTES who is crying and the CHORUS)

NURSE	You should both be ashamed; Every time you quarrel You start Orestes weeping.
CLYTEMNESTRA	The noise in the house has frightened him: I must go in to my husband. Take the child from me; Pray for my husband's victory And for glory to our country. But remember, no stories.

(CLYTEMNESTRA goes. Music begins in the house)

(CHORUS)	What is a country? The word is strange to me. I know what a home is,

Or a kingdom or a citadel,
But a country...did I ever
Know one? I've forgotten
— Have you ever lived in one?

— I might have. I've forgotten.

— I don't remember clearly.

— Isn't it to do with boundaries?

— Or language?

    — Or is it blood,
The blood we were born with?

— I remember, it's what gives one
A sense of being in the right.

— What does that mean?

    — If we know
What country we belong to,
We know that in any quarrel
With some other land or people,
That our country is in the right
And theirs is in the wrong.

— That is useful — Don't be stupid;
Where we're born is blind chance.

— Now you're being stupid;
It depends on our parents.

— But what does that depend on?
— On the gods, stupid.   (*)

(*Distant thunder. A RAGGED MAN staggers in*)

Who is this? No beggars here.

NURSE   Not when there's a feast on.

(CHORUS)   Go away, you stink
— Wait, something's wrong with him.

(*The MAN falls to the ground, writhing*)

— We'd better get rid of him
Before the General sees him

— We ought to wash him first
— I am not going near him

(*The MAN cries out and makes wild sounds*)

— What is he saying?
— Clearly he's a foreigner
— This is not language.

(*Re-enter CLYTEMNESTRA*)

CLYTEMNESTRA Women, what is happening?

(CHORUS) This man is mad or dangerous.

CLYTEMNESTRA No he's not, he's in pain.
Tell us who you are;
You need not be afraid of us.

MAN I am...my pain...
Don't come near me, no one
Can bear the stench of my wound;
It is dangerous to touch me.

CLYTEMNESTRA Then tell us what you want of us?

MAN I want to be healed.

CLYTEMNESTRA Drink this and tell us your name.

MAN Telephus.

NURSE 'Thele Alaphos':
That means suckled by a doe.

(CHORUS) Another abandoned baby
— Were you found by shepherds too?

CLYTEMNESTRA Fetch a cloak or a blanket,
Some wine and some bandages.
Drink this... What is it?

(*TELEPHUS lets out a long, agonized cry.
Then he drinks*)

TELEPHUS It is over for a little.
Once every minute
The poison-pangs burn me
And then I lose language.

(CHORUS) Then tell us your story
Before it comes again.

CLYTEMNESTRA   Tell us, if you can.

TELEPHUS   Once upon a time
There was a king of Mysia,
A fair land and fertile,
But one morning the black ships
Came out of the west
And a warrior leaped ashore
In shining golden armour.
When the king went to greet him
The warrior cried out
A war-cry more terrible
Than the roar of the Minotaur;
So he ran and he ran
Just as the deer had taught him
But the warrior ran faster
And thrust his spear of ash
Deep in the sad king's side.
Very soon the wound festered
And stank so that his people
Exiled him out of fear
That their land would be polluted.
So he went to the oracle
Of Apollo, God of Healing,
Who told him that the wound
Would still bleed and fester
Till Achilles, son of Peleus,
Had searched the wound himself
And touched it with the rust
On the spear which had made it.

(*TELEPHUS cries out again*)

CLYTEMNESTRA   And you are the man?

TELEPHUS   Is Achilles here?

CLYTEMNESTRA   He is in the house
With my husband Agamemnon.

TELEPHUS   Take me to him.

CLYTEMNESTRA   No,
The War-Kings would kill you.

TELEPHUS   But I am a suppliant.

CLYTEMNESTRA	We must find a better way.
TELEPHUS	Find it quickly or I'll die.
CLYTEMNESTRA	I have it: some goddess Must have put it in my mind. Women, lay Orestes On the ground beside him And one of you fetch an axe.
(*To Telephus*)	You must lift it over the child And I'll scream until Achilles comes; Then you must say you will kill my child If he does not heal you.
(CHORUS)	But how can you trust him?

(*One of them brings AGAMEMNON's axe*)

CLYTEMNESTRA	Here's the axe, take it: When I cry out, do the same.
TELEPHUS	You are a good woman.
CLYTEMNESTRA	One must try to be so. All of you, let's begin.

(*TELEPHUS cries out again*)

Achilles, Achilles!

(CHORUS)	Come quickly, Achilles!	(*)

(*AGAMEMNON enters*)

AGAMEMNON	Women, be quiet; Why are you screaming?
CLYTEMNESTRA	This man will kill Orestes If Achilles does not heal him.
AGAMEMNON	Why should he heal this beggar?
CLYTEMNESTRA	He's a king. Apollo's oracle Has said that the spear which wounded him Will make him whole again.
AGAMEMNON	The boy will not heal Trojans.
TELEPHUS	I am not a Trojan.
CLYTEMNESTRA	Fetch Achilles quickly.

AGAMEMNON   This kind of thing saddens me
But it has grown too common;
Powerless men seek power
By punishing the innocent.
If we give way to him
We will regret it later.
Stranger, be sensible;
You must know that your threats
Will not work on a king
Much more powerful than you are.

TELEPHUS   Don't talk to me, heal me.

CLYTEMNESTRA (*To Agamemnon*) He will do it, I know it,
He is desperate with pain.

(*TELEPHUS begins to scream again*)

AGAMEMNON   Think clearly, beggar-king.
In this house we welcome suppliants,
Not those who use violence.
If you kill the child you'll die;
What's the point of that?

CLYTEMNESTRA   Don't you see how he's suffering?

AGAMEMNON   If the spear is poisoned
Either Achilles is at fault
Or some god has punished him
For some crime that's not our business.

CLYTEMNESTRA   Have you no pity?

AGAMEMNON   Yes,
But the pity of the moment
Can lead to problems later.

TELEPHUS   Don't debate me, heal me.

(*Another long scream of pain*)

AGAMEMNON   If you want to live, stranger,
Give the child back to its mother.

TELEPHUS   No one understands pain
Till they themselves feel it.
If you don't fetch Achilles
Then I *will* kill your child.

CLYTEMNESTRA   But you promised not to harm him
                When I put him beside you!

AGAMEMNON   You gave the child to him?
                You gave him your own child?

TELEPHUS   I don't want to kill him
                But I will unless you fetch him.

AGAMEMNON   How can we be sure
                That you're telling us the truth?

TELEPHUS   My wound is my truth.

AGAMEMNON   Achilles will not do it;
                When he's drunk he's dangerous.

TELEPHUS   Achilles! Achilles! Achilles!   (*)

                (*CHORUS join in TELEPHUS' cries. ACHILLES
                enters, drunk*)

ACHILLES   Be silent, all of you!
                Who is this beggar
                Who dares call for Achilles?

CLYTEMNESTRA   You must heal him with your spear
                Or he will kill Orestes.

ACHILLES   If he does, I will kill him.

CLYTEMNESTRA   Don't! He's a King.

AGAMEMNON   He is also a suppliant.

CLYTEMNESTRA   He was poisoned by your spear
                And it alone can heal him.

ACHILLES   How dare you accuse me
                Of using a poisoned spear?

AGAMEMNON   An oracle has foretold
                That you alone can heal him.

ACHILLES   But I know him, he attacked me;
                Why should I heal an enemy?

CLYTEMNESTRA   He is not an enemy;
                When you landed in Mysia
                You attacked him by mistake.

ACHILLES   I am leaving this house.
                Your husband invited me

Saying he meant to honour me
For winning a great battle;
But as soon as I came here
Everyone has insulted me
And said I made mistakes.

CLYTEMNESTRA Don't be angry, not now.

ACHILLES I have cause.

AGAMEMNON You have cause;
But if you heal this man
You will win much fame and honour.

(*TELEPHUS screams*)

All the world will know Achilles
Has the godlike power of healing,
And they will honour you
More than they do already.

ACHILLES I am going.

CLYTEMNESTRA Achilles…

AGAMEMNON Quiet! Time to bargain:
If you heal him, Achilles,
I will give you my own daughter
As your wife.

ACHILLES Which daughter?

CLYTEMNESTRA Electra, we will give you
Electra.

AGAMEMNON Yes, Electra.

ACHILLES I would not take her
For one night, Agamemnon,
Let alone a lifetime;
Give me Iphigenia.

AGAMEMNON That is not possible:
She is to be a priestess.

ACHILLES Not when I have married her.

CLYTEMNESTRA Agamemnon, let him have her.

AGAMEMNON No, I love her best
Of all my children.

CLYTEMNESTRA   Yes,
                  I know it. Let him have her.

AGAMEMNON   Very well, but heal him.

ACHILLES   What dowry?

AGAMEMNON   Three talents.

ACHILLES   And four, no, seven horses
                  And three bronze cauldrons.

CLYTEMNESTRA   Stop this!

AGAMEMNON   No problem's ever solved
                  Without negotiation.
                  You, Telephus, must also
                  Offer something in return.

TELEPHUS   What do you want most?

CLYTEMNESTRA He wants to find a pilot
                  To guide the fleet to Troy.

TELEPHUS   Agreed, I am skilled
                  In all the arts that are needed
                  To outwit the god Poseidon.

AGAMEMNON   Swear it.

TELEPHUS   I swear it.

ACHILLES   By which god?

TELEPHUS   By Apollo.

ACHILLES   Men in pain swear anything;
                  If I heal him he will say
                  That a forced oath is not binding.

CLYTEMNESTRA What does it matter?

AGAMEMNON   Achilles,
                  The bargain is a fair one
                  And I'll make this man fulfil it.

ACHILLES   I accept it: fetch my spear.

TELEPHUS   No, take me into the house:
                  My pain will be greatest
                  When the spear is in the wound.
                  I do not want women

	To watch my shame and agony;
(To Agamemnon)	You will have to hold me down
	When his spear is inside me.

AGAMEMNON   I will take you in, come with me.

CLYTEMNESTRA   Give Orestes to me.

ACHILLES   You are learning, Agamemnon,
That you will only thrive
Through the spear of Achilles.   (*)

(CLYTEMNESTRA takes ORESTES, and the three men go in)

(CHORUS)   Lord of light, Apollo,
Take away his pain
And from all those who are suffering
—   Take off the pollution,
Apollo, we beseech you.

NURSE   See, the baby is quiet now.

(CHORUS)   It is silent in the house.

(Cry within)

What was that?

NURSE   It was the voice
Of Apollo the Healer.

(CHORUS)   See, Orestes is smiling.

CLYTEMNESTRA   Praised be Apollo!

(CHORUS)   Apollo! Apollo!

(They all begin to laugh and celebrate)

CLYTEMNESTRA *(To Orestes)* That is how the world is:
Learn from this, little one,
However much one suffers
In the end the gods are kind.

(TELEPHUS and AGAMEMNON come back)

TELEPHUS   It's gone, it's clean gone!
I can move without pain.

(CHORUS)   The foul stench is gone
And all the air is sweet again.

NURSE   Praised be Apollo!

                 (*Music. TELEPHUS dances. ACHILLES comes back*)

CLYTEMNESTRA   Achilles, I love you.

AGAMEMNON   And I.

CLYTEMNESTRA   All is well.

                 (*ACHILLES vomits*)

                 What's the matter with Achilles?

AGAMEMNON   He was closest to the poison;

NURSE   He needs some food and wine.

CLYTEMNESTRA   Come in and feast with us.

TELEPHUS   No, not in the house again,
                 Not among the War-Kings.

CLYTEMNESTRA   Then sit here and drink with us.

                 (*CHORUS fetch wine*)

                 Sit with us, Achilles:
                 You must drink and cleanse your throat.

ACHILLES   I will not drink with him.

CLYTEMNESTRA   But we are friends again.

                 (*ACHILLES starts to retch again*)

                 What's the matter?

ACHILLES   Death:
                 I looked on death, I saw it,
                 I saw it when I healed him.

AGAMEMNON   It is true he would have died
                 If you had not healed him.

ACHILLES   Not his death, I saw mine;
                 The poison that I breathed
                 Was not his but my mother's.

CLYTEMNESTRA   What are you talking of?

ACHILLES   A prophecy my mother made.

                 (*ACHILLES makes to go*)

CLYTEMNESTRA	Where are you going?
ACHILLES	To summon the army.
AGAMEMNON	That's my task, not yours; Sit with us and be easy.
CLYTEMNESTRA	We have much to celebrate.

(*ACHILLES pauses*)

ACHILLES	I should be happy, lady, If I live till the war is won To sit here with you both And with my Iphigenia, In peace by your hearth fire Which is as dear and lovely To me as your daughter is. I am glad to have helped you And saved your little boy; But now I must go to Aulis. Once we've sacked the city There will be time for drinking.
AGAMEMNON	That's not our aim, Achilles.
ACHILLES	So you say, it is the army's.
CLYTEMNESTRA	Let us have no more arguments.
NURSE	You were sick because you've drunk too much.
CLYTEMNESTRA	Stay with us a little Till Iphigenia joins us.
ACHILLES	When her wedding-dress is ready Send her to me at Aulis. (*)

(*He goes. They start to eat and drink*)

TELEPHUS	Young warriors are eager.
CLYTEMNESTRA	You must forgive him; His parents abandoned him As yours did. You were lucky To have had does to nurse you; He had bears to suckle him.
AGAMEMNON	Qualities that make a warrior Effective in a battle

Are not always helpful
In between the fighting.

CLYTEMNESTRA But he will be a great one.

TELEPHUS I have no doubt of that;
But his victory was not
Quite as he has told it.

AGAMEMNON He made a mistake
And we all did, I admit it.
I am sorry.

TELEPHUS   The real mistake
Was after he had landed.

CLYTEMNESTRA The battle on the sea-shore?

TELEPHUS There was no battle.
I went there to welcome him
To tell him where he was
And how we were neutral
And friendly to the West.
I offered him a drink
And told him where he'd landed;
When I did so, he struck me.
My mistake was to tell him
That he'd made a mistake;
It is never wise to argue
With a war-man in his wrath.
So I ran but he ran faster;
As we hurtled, I tripped
And so he pierced my thigh.
Then his Myrmidons slew my men,
Set fire to our crops
And began to rape our women
And to do as is natural
To warriors in all places.
It was all a misunderstanding;
I of course understand
How you have had to report it.

AGAMEMNON All you say is true.

CLYTEMNESTRA And you are a great king
And lord of many people?

TELEPHUS	I am a son of Heracles.
AGAMEMNON	They are always welcome here.
CLYTEMNESTRA	And your wife?
TELEPHUS	Laodice.
CLYTEMNESTRA	A daughter of Priam!
AGAMEMNON	Then you must be his ally?
TELEPHUS	His friend but not his ally.
CLYTEMNESTRA	If you wanted to stay out of it So far you've been unlucky.
AGAMEMNON	Sail with us to Troy And help me talk sense into Priam.
TELEPHUS	Priam does not understand Why you think that your envoys Will persuade him to release Helen Till you have returned Hesione.
AGAMEMNON	Telamon her master Refuses to release her; He has sent his son Ajax To fight for us instead.
CLYTEMNESTRA	We don't understand why something Priam swore fifty years ago Is any justification For seizing my sister now.
TELEPHUS	Questions of right and wrong In dealings between kingdoms Are often hard to fathom: Much depends on the starting-point.
CLYTEMNESTRA	What is the starting-point? (*TELEPHUS drinks*)
TELEPHUS	Whenever a child is born It is taught or it assumes That its birthplace and its hearth-fire Is the centre of the world.
AGAMEMNON	That is natural enough.

CLYTEMNESTRA It is natural.

TELEPHUS   Quite natural.

AGAMEMNON Are you speaking of Mycenae?

TELEPHUS But suppose that your starting-point
Is in some way tainted?

AGAMEMNON Are you speaking of Mycenae?

TELEPHUS I am speaking of all homes
And so of all hearth-fires
Now burning in the world.

CLYTEMNESTRA Do not speak ill of the hearth.

TELEPHUS I do not, there is nothing
More holy than a hearth-fire;
But if one destroys other hearths
For the sake of one hearth only
Could that not be dangerous?

AGAMEMNON The hearths of Troy and Mysia
Are as sacred as ours are.

TELEPHUS Though of course not so dear.

AGAMEMNON That is natural.

TELEPHUS   That is natural.

AGAMEMNON But I fear one must not say so
In front of one's own army.

CLYTEMNESTRA Clever words, Telephus,
But this war is just.

TELEPHUS Of course, all wars are held so
In the place where they begin.

AGAMEMNON I know that and I fear it.
Of course we all want to live
At peace in the land
Our fathers won and lived in
And so we forget that they won it
By war-fire and bloodshed,
And feel it is right and virtuous
To shed more blood to keep it:

It will always be so.
Let us leave this; only Zeus
Can wipe out human folly.
Till he does so I believe
That wars between kingdoms
May be needful and lawful
For quite another reason.

TELEPHUS   I should be glad to know it.

AGAMEMNON   When some great anger grows,
Some fear or some frustration
Or some excess of energy,
A king with restless warriors
Will be wise to give it vent
If the cause is a good one.

TELEPHUS   Vent? You mean channelled
And put somewhere else?

CLYTEMNESTRA   My husband did not say that.

TELEPHUS   He did and he is right;
If we want to draw out poison
It must go somewhere else.

AGAMEMNON   Poison? What do you mean?

TELEPHUS   The poison that was in me
Is in you now, not me.

CLYTEMNESTRA   What are you saying?

TELEPHUS   I was told by Apollo's oracle
That all whom I touched
Would in time be polluted.
A little drop of pus
Has touched each one of you;
I regret it deeply
But no one is to blame.

AGAMEMNON   Why did you not tell us?

TELEPHUS   Pain blurs explanations.

CLYTEMNESTRA   My baby, tell me,
Is it on my baby?

TELEPHUS On him most of all;
I held him the longest.

CLYTEMNESTRA You are evil.

TELEPHUS Yes, I think
That suffering is evil.

(*CLYTEMNESTRA puts ORESTES down on the ground*)

AGAMEMNON This pollution, will it come
Suddenly or slowly?

TELEPHUS It will take some time;
I am sorry.

CLYTEMNESTRA Kill him,
Kill him, Agamemnon!

AGAMEMNON Quiet: a guest is sacred.

CLYTEMNESTRA Get out of our house!

TELEPHUS So I will; Agamemnon,
If you come to Aulis quickly,
I will guide the fleet to Troy
And then return to my people
And try to your mistake.

AGAMEMNON Maybe that is all
Any king can hope for,
To undo mistakes.

TELEPHUS Maybe what has happened
Is the will of Apollo.
The god who is a healer,
Like his sister Artemis
Loves at times to destroy.
But we must remember too
How all men hold that Delphi
Is the centre of the world,
So perhaps it is the starting-point.
It may be so or not so:
No one is to blame.   (*)

(*He goes. ORESTES begins to cry again*)

NURSE   Sh, sh, my little one,
         It's time to go to bed.

AGAMEMNON Take him into the house.

         (*CLYTEMNESTRA doesn't move*)

NURSE   I will take him in.

         (*Goes in with ORESTES*)

AGAMEMNON If we had not done as we did
         We would not have been human.

CLYTEMNESTRA Yes, we have been human;
         Perhaps that is the mistake.

         (*Pause*)

         Go after him and kill him.

AGAMEMNON Then we may not get to Troy.

CLYTEMNESTRA But he has polluted our child!

AGAMEMNON Why did you let him hold the baby?

CLYTEMNESTRA I wanted to help heal him!

AGAMEMNON We must both mend our mistakes
         As quickly as we can.
         You must look after Orestes
         And I must go now to Aulis.

CLYTEMNESTRA But you've only just come home;
         Be with me tonight.

AGAMEMNON He who sets sail quickest
         Comes home the soonest;
         You must rule here while I'm gone.

         (*Re-enter NURSE*)

AGAMEMNON Is he here?

NURSE   Yes, he is here.

CLYTEMNESTRA Who?

AGAMEMNON   Bring him to me.

CLYTEMNESTRA No! I will not have
         Aegisthus in my house.

AGAMEMNON   It's his house as much as mine;
            We must help to heal him too.

CLYTEMNESTRA   Not at my expense.

AGAMEMNON   He has rights here in Mycenae.

CLYTEMNESTRA   No, Agamemnon, no!

AGAMEMNON   You must give your time and love
            To your children while Aegisthus
            Rules the affairs of the citadel.

CLYTEMNESTRA   I will not have him here.

AGAMEMNON   I have given way to you
            In what concerns the war
            So give way to me in this:
(To Nurse)   Fetch him from the house.

NURSE   He is not inside the house,
        He says he will not enter it.

AGAMEMNON   Then find him and bring him.

(*NURSE goes*)

CLYTEMNESTRA   You cannot go to Aulis
               Till you've told Iphigenia
               Who is to be her husband,
               And Electra will be angry
               If you don't say goodbye.

AGAMEMNON   Electra will be angry
            Whatever I say or don't say;
            She is very like Achilles.

CLYTEMNESTRA   They'd have made a better match.

AGAMEMNON   Yes, I would have preferred it.
            When you've prepared her wedding-dress
            Bring Iphigenia to Aulis.
            Each day we delay
            The Trojans will grow stronger.   (*)

(*NURSE brings in AEGISTHUS*)

NURSE *(To Aegisthus)*   Don't be afraid, my duckling,
                         The king means much good to you;
                         But you should have put on better clothes

When you visit your own cousin.
You must both be gentle to him.

AGAMEMNON   Aegisthus, you are welcome,
There's nothing now to fear.

CLYTEMNESTRA   Why is he so dirty?

NURSE   He is as he's always been.

AGAMEMNON   Drink with us, Aegisthus.

AEGISTHUS   Drink first.

CLYTEMNESTRA   Don't be childish;
Afraid of poisoned wine?

AEGISTHUS   Why have you brought me here?

AGAMEMNON   That we may be reconciled.

AEGISTHUS   Such words are meaningless.

NURSE   Always the surly one.
Do as your cousin bids you;
A good drink will refresh you
And make you less repulsive.
Before the evils came
You were a gentle child.

AGAMEMNON   Those days are gone, Aegisthus.

AEGISTHUS   They will never go away.

CLYTEMNESTRA   Then there's no point in your coming here.

AGAMEMNON   Aegisthus, I drink to you.

(*NURSE gives AEGISTHUS drink. He pours it on the earth*)

AEGISTHUS   There's drink for my brothers
Whom your father sent down to Asphodel.

AGAMEMNON   It is fitting that we honour them.

(*AGAMEMNON does the same*)

AEGISTHUS   How can you honour those
Whom your own father murdered?

CLYTEMNESTRA   How can you say that
When you murdered his?

NURSE	Children, stop this.
AEGISTHUS	I am going.
AGAMEMNON	First hear what I have to say to you.
NURSE	Listen to him, child.
AEGISTHUS	Then fill my cup again.
AGAMEMNON	Our fathers did cruel things here,
	Each hoping to be King.
	In my view my father Atreus
	Did the greater evil
	When he murdered your brothers,
	So I have brought you here
	To atone and to honour you
	That the dead may live in peace.
AEGISTHUS	They don't sleep, they're listening.
AGAMEMNON	Let what is done be done with.
AEGISTHUS	I killed your father.
AGAMEMNON	That seems to trouble you
	More than it does me;
	What you did was just
	And I have never reproached you.
	It is time for our family
	To stop this endless blood-feud:
	Give me your hand, Aegisthus.
AEGISTHUS	Let me go, Agamemnon.
NURSE	It's the house he fears, not you.
AEGISTHUS	From the time of Tantalus
	It has always bred evil.
AGAMEMNON	It is men, not houses,
	That breed evil, Aegisthus.
CLYTEMNESTRA	I'm tired; forgive and forget.
AEGISTHUS	Yes, let us all forget!
	Your father never butchered
	My brothers when we were babies;
	I did not kill your father,

You did not kill her child,
Neither she nor I
Swore oaths to avenge it!

CLYTEMNESTRA   When one is wretched
One says foolish things.

NURSE   And when one is happy
One does much the same.
Your cousin's words are good ones
So don't try to twist them.

AEGISTHUS   Good words come easy,
Good deeds are rarer.

CLYTEMNESTRA   I do not understand him;
Why cling to old evils?

NURSE   He is afraid of kindness.

AEGISTHUS   I don't want your kindness.

NURSE   Yes he does, this is the way
He has always tried to get it.
Why are you so scruffy?
Drink this, you big baby.
All my babies, drink
And be friends.

AGAMEMNON   I drink to you.
We must all learn to live
In harmony together.

NURSE   Drink, Aegisthus.

(*AEGISTHUS and AGAMEMNON drink*)

AGAMEMNON   While I am gone
You shall rule here with my wife;
It is your right, Aegisthus.

AEGISTHUS   It will all begin again.

CLYTEMNESTRA   He is right, Agamemnon.

AGAMEMNON   Enough. I have work to do;
Take him in and bring
Iphigenia to Aulis.   (*)

(He goes)

AEGISTHUS	It won't go away.
CLYTEMNESTRA	'It'? What does 'it' mean?
AEGISTHUS	Do you need me to say it again?
CLYTEMNESTRA	It will go if you want it to But it's hard work, Aegisthus. Take him in and wash him And when you have bathed him And given him clean clothes, I will show him that this house Is no longer the one His sick memory feeds on. If you then still reject What my husband has offered I will know you are not only A bad man but a stupid one.
AEGISTHUS	Don't pretend; you hate me.
CLYTEMNESTRA	Why should I hate you? We have both suffered. It is true you are not Very likeable, that's different. Take my cloak, you are shivering.
AEGISTHUS	This kindness is false.
CLYTEMNESTRA	To reject it is a sickness.
AEGISTHUS	And you mean to heal me?
NURSE	Yes, as Achilles did.
AEGISTHUS	Achilles used a spear.
CLYTEMNESTRA	That will not be necessary.
AEGISTHUS	If you wish to heal me It will take you some time.
CLYTEMNESTRA	We have time; go in And do as I tell you.
NURSE	I'll prepare you a nice bath To comfort and refresh you.

124

CLYTEMNESTRA	Take him in and scrub him.
	I must speak to my daughters.

(AEGISTHUS starts to go)

AEGISTHUS	Babies crying... Can't you hear them...?
CLYTEMNESTRA	I hear nothing. Take him in
	And fetch me my wedding-dress. (*)

(NURSE goes in with AEGISTHUS)

How ugly he is.

NURSE	Lady,
	Why do you want your wedding-dress?
CLYTEMNESTRA	There's no time to make a new one;
	I will alter it a little
	And Iphigenia shall wear it.
(CHORUS)	They say to remake a wedding-dress
	Is displeasing to Hymen.
CLYTEMNESTRA	Some thread and a little needle
	Will change the shape of anything
	If it's fair in the first place.

(The NURSE returns with the wedding-dress. It is red)

NURSE	Orestes is quiet now.
CLYTEMNESTRA	I will go in and sing to him.

(She kneels)

You gods, bless our hearth-fire
Till my husband comes home.
Hera, bless this marriage
As you have blessed mine,
And Artemis, Protectress
Of children, bless my son,
And Hermes, stone-god,
Protector of travellers,
Bring my lord safe home.

(She goes in with the wedding-dress)

(CHORUS)	She's a good lady.

NURSE   Maybe,
                 But she should not have been
                 So reckless with her child.

(CHORUS)   —   Now she's gone, let's have a story.   (*)

                 (*AEGISTHUS returns, grotesquely masked
                 and drunk*)

AEGISTHUS   You want to hear a story?
                 A tale of blood at bed-time?

(CHORUS)   Who is this? – He frightens me.

NURSE   Take it off, Aegisthus.

                 (*AEGISTHUS takes off the mask*)

AEGISTHUS   I found it in the house;
                 It belonged to my brothers
                 Whom I loved until that day...

                 (*He weeps*)

                 Give me some more drink
                 And I'll tell you how it was.

(CHORUS)   No, we are going.

AEGISTHUS   Where to?

(CHORUS)   To Aulis to see the ships.
            —   We are going to count them.

AEGISTHUS   Why?

(CHORUS)   They say there's a thousand.

AEGISTHUS   Don't believe what people tell you.

(CHORUS)   We shall know when we've counted.
            —   Better go then – Better go.

                 (*The CHORUS go*)

NURSE   Go to bed.
AEGISTHUS   I'm frightened;
                 I won't be able to sleep
                 Until you have told me a story.

NURSE   Why are you crying, little one?
                 It's yourself you hear weeping.

Come to bed and I'll tuck you in;
And if you're very good
I will tell you a new one.
Come into the house.

(*They go in. CLYTEMNESTRA is singing within*)

Play 3
IPHIGENIA

THE SEA-SHORE AT AULIS

CAST

First Woman	NURSE
Second Woman	(–)
Third Woman	CLYTEMNESTRA
Fourth Woman	HERMIONE/ ELECTRA/ IPHIGENIA
First Man	PELEUS/ PALAMEDES
Second Man	AGAMEMNON
Third Man	ODYSSEUS
Fourth Man	ACHILLES

CHORUS and MYRMIDONS

(The cave is now the shrine of Artemis in her sacred grove at Aulis. The fire is smoking, and the FIRST WOMAN stokes it. A dead stag lies by it, and the helmets of Achilles' Myrmidons are watching over the brow of the rocks. As the CHORUS enter, FIRST WOMAN goes into the cave)

(CHORUS)   Here we are at Aulis!
- We've come to see the ships!
- We've come to see the wedding!
- We've come to say goodbye!
- But look, nothing's happening
- It's all still and silent
- Why's the air so close and thick?
- The smell here is horrible
- It always smells in war-camps
- But this is the grove of Artemis.

(CALCHAS is heard speaking in Greek. He is quoting from Aeschylus or Euripides)

- What is that sound?
- It is the voice of Calchas
- What is he saying?
- Are they some words of Apollo's?

(NURSE enters from the cave)

NURSE   No, he's speaking for his sister;
He is speaking for Artemis.

(CHORUS)   But what are those eyes watching us?

(NURSE sits poking the fire)

NURSE   Myrmidons. They were ants once;
They're waiting for it to happen.
When it's done they will rise up
And turn into warriors.

(CHORUS)   What d'you mean? Why are you here?

NURSE   Iphigenia begged me to help her
To persuade Agamemnon
Not to marry her to Achilles.

I've been feeding my darling
To build up her strength.
She wants to be a priestess;
Now in a way she will be.

(CHORUS)   Where's her mother?

NURSE   Coming soon
When the wedding-dress is ready.   (*)

(*PELEUS enters*)

PELEUS   It's her mother who is to blame
For the whole situation.

(CHORUS)   What situation, Peleus?

PELEUS   If she'd brought the dress at once
We would be in Troy by now.

(CHORUS)   We do not understand you.

PELEUS   How could my son Achilles
Let his own wife be sacrificed
Until they'd danced the wedding-dance?

(CHORUS)   Why should she be sacrificed?

PELEUS   Why? Because of the stag.

(CHORUS)   Take us with you, Peleus.

PELEUS   It is not fair on my son,
Nor on me. I am old now;
It's the last time I shall see him,
So I've come to say farewell
And to try to make the General
Face his responsibilities.

(CHORUS)   What are you talking of, Peleus?

NURSE   The command of the Goddess.

PELEUS   The price to be paid for the stag.

(CHORUS)   What price?

PELEUS   To get rid of the stench.

(CHORUS)   What is it?

PELEUS   The sacred stag
Killed by that idiot general.

	Everybody knows That hunting is forbidden In the grove of a great goddess.
NURSE	He rode here by mistake.
PELEUS	The man makes too many And now he must pay for it; Artemis is very reasonable And demands compensation.
(CHORUS)	That is fair.
PELEUS	Of course it's fair; She has simply stopped the wind Till the General makes amends At the goddess' sacred altar.
(CHORUS)	It sounds fair and reasonable.
PELEUS	It *is* fair and reasonable But the General refuses.

(*Sounds inside the cave*)

	He is with her in the shrine; He thinks he can protect Iphigenia from the army. The Myrmidons are guarding her: That is why Achilles' armour Is hanging outside the cave; While it's there no-one will touch her.
(CHORUS)	Can you mean what we think you mean? You speak dreadful words.
PELEUS	The goddess will not raise the wind Till the girl has been sacrificed: Is that clear enough for you? (*)

(*AGAMEMNON enters from the cave*)

AGAMEMNON	Speak more quietly, Peleus; You're upsetting my daughter.
PELEUS	You're upsetting my son.
AGAMEMNON	Your son is acting honourably.

PELEUS	Of course he's acting honourably; But your stubbornness has put him In a false and foul position.
AGAMEMNON	Since he's marrying my daughter He is bound to defend her.
PELEUS	Not when the army Have begun to throw stones at him.
AGAMEMNON	I regret that.
PELEUS	You regret that? Is that all? He regrets it! You gather an army, good, But then you don't set sail; Not so good. There's nothing worse Than inconsistent generals. To delay such a sacrifice For a week would be proper But a month will do no good To the army's morale; It is mere self-indulgence.
AGAMEMNON	Does no one understand yet What I've said to all the kings?
PELEUS	No, they don't understand. All the goddess asks of you Is fair compensation For a serious offence: One girl, only one. The gods have required fathers To do worse things in the past. Sometimes it worked out well And sometimes not so well, Just like a battle. Get it over with, it's kinder.
AGAMEMNON	Kinder?
PELEUS	To the girl. These things are best done quickly As any soldier finds When he has to kill his prisoners; The prisoners prefer it.

AGAMEMNON	Nothing is more precious –
PELEUS	'Than the life of a child.' Yes, I said that to my wife once And she was killing seven. All Artemis asks is one, But your power to think clearly Has been blurred by the smell of stag-rot. This is not a moral question But a military matter Of simple sanitation.
AGAMEMNON	If you don't like the smell Get out of the sanctuary.
PELEUS	War, Agamemnon, Is like making love; Once it is embarked on It is never satisfactory To break off in the middle. There's a phrase for it in Sicily: *Bellus interruptus.* Is it true that you've sworn To lie with no woman Until the war is over?
AGAMEMNON	That is my business.
PELEUS	Ten years, Ten years without a woman; Have you really sworn that?
AGAMEMNON	It won't last ten years.
PELEUS	It will now, Agamemnon.
AGAMEMNON	The fleet will not set sail Till my brother's back from Troy; He may bring Helen with him.
PELEUS	He won't because he hasn't.
AGAMEMNON	He is back?
PELEUS	Last night.
AGAMEMNON	Why has he not come to me?
PELEUS	Because he is asleep.

AGAMEMNON   Then we don't yet know what's happened.

PELEUS   We do, we saw his face;
            Now you must get on with it;
            When it's done you will feel much better.
            You must learn, Agamemnon,
            To show the gods reverence:
            They never let one off.   (*)

            (*He goes*)

AGAMEMNON   How can I show them reverence
            Till I understand why Artemis,
            Protectress of young girls,
            Demands this of me?

            Moon-goddess, silver, pure,
            It is right that you have punished me;
            I have grieved many weeks
            And offered compensation
            But to ask for human blood
            To pay for a single beast
            However sacred and noble:
            I will never do that!

(CHORUS)   You're a good man, Agamemnon
         — Men are mad to think
            That to swear to do a thing
            Makes it right to do it.
         — Only weak men need oaths
            Because they do not trust themselves
            To do what's right without them.

            (*Enter ODYSSEUS*)

ODYSSEUS   Agamemnon, do you still
            Wish to lead the army?

AGAMEMNON   You know my mind, leave me.

ODYSSEUS   I have come with a message
            From the Council of the Kings:
            If you do not obey Artemis
            By dawn tomorrow morning
            They will choose another general.

AGAMEMNON	Palamedes?
ODYSSEUS	It is possible.
AGAMEMNON	By the time they've agreed my replacement The wind will have changed anyway.
ODYSSEUS	Now your brother is back There can be no more delay. If we do not sail tomorrow All the army will go home.
AGAMEMNON	Have you still not learned That nobody can pressure me?
ODYSSEUS	You and I have still to learn Whose will is the stronger.
AGAMEMNON	Artemis requires Me alone to order the sacrifice.
ODYSSEUS	Forgive me, but the Kings Might respect you more highly If you were to speak to them Instead of sending messages.
AGAMEMNON	You know if I left this grove They would come and seize my daughter.
ODYSSEUS	I sympathise, Agamemnon, Since I too am a father But I do not quite believe You're as certain as you say; If you were so, by now You would either have resigned Or disbanded the army.
AGAMEMNON	I am certain.
ODYSSEUS	It would seem so, But I suspect that secretly You are wrestling with what seems to you Some kind of moral problem. But there are times in war When right answers matter less Than making a decision. When kings try to solve things In terms of right and wrong

They are apt to grow confused
And lose touch with their sense
Of what is and is not possible.
I understand of course
You fear that when you do it
You will find that your humanity
Will in some way be diminished,
But a King who dare not choose
Is unfit to govern men.
In one way or other
Like all who are human
You and I must be corrupted.

AGAMEMNON I read you, Odysseus:
You are trying to confuse me.
Since you would not kill you own child
You should understand me
Better than the rest.

ODYSSEUS And I do; it was you who showed me
I was wrong to break my oath;
Now it's my turn to remind you
Of your own oath to lead us.

AGAMEMNON Would you kill your son Telemachus
If a god told you to do it?

ODYSSEUS Listen, Agamemnon;
In spite of what has happened
I and all the kings
Still want you as our general.
If you do what must be done
The army will respect you
For making a hard choice.
If you don't they will despise you
And you will lose control.

(Sounds of weeping in the cave)

AGAMEMNON You keep speaking of choices
As if I had not made one.
Send my brother to me,
And tell your fellow Kings
I will only speak to him.

ODYSSEUS   I will tell them you are still
Confused; I am sorry.   (*)

(He goes. AGAMEMNON calls after him as CALCHAS' voice is heard again in the distance)

AGAMEMNON   I will not kill my child
If all the winds of the world
Were stopped by the gods forever!

(He goes back into the cave)

(CHORUS)   But suppose, just suppose
That the words of the goddess
Are not as Calchas speaks them?
   – Priests don't hear words
They read a bird's entrails
   – But supposing they misread them?
   – Or suppose they distort them
For some purpose of their own?
   – Improbable – Impossible,
Prophets never lie
   – A stag dies, the wind dies;
There need be no connection
   – But the goddess says 'If';
She gives him no commands,
So what answer does she want?

   – I do not believe
That what is happening here
Is Artemis' doing at all
   – Then why does Calchas say so?
   – Because her brother Apollo
Has sworn to fight for the Trojans;
He is the one behind it
   – You should appeal to Delphi.

NURSE   Why trust in Delphi
Any more than Calchas?

(CHORUS)   Because Delphi never lies.

NURSE   Delphi may change as the wind may;
It depends on who controls it.

(CHORUS)	It's the centre of the world, So how could it change?　　　　(*)

(HERMIONE enters)

HERMIONE	Where is my uncle?
(CHORUS)	Who is your uncle?
HERMIONE	The General of course.
(CHORUS)	It's Menelaus' daughter, Hermione of Sparta – Why are you here?
HERMIONE	I wish I wasn't here; I shall be sick if I stay. I only came to Aulis To say goodbye to my father.
(CHORUS)	Your uncle is in there With his daughter.
HERMIONE	Go and fetch him.
(CHORUS)	You must wait – And while you wait You can tell us about it.
HERMIONE	My message is for my uncle.
(CHORUS)	Never mind him, Hermione, Tell us about *it* – Tell us what really happened When the Trojan came to Sparta.
HERMIONE	Don't ask.
(CHORUS)	You were there When your father sailed to Crete: When he left them alone, what happened?
HERMIONE	Don't ask, it's not your business.
(CHORUS)	But we all want to know.
HERMIONE	Would you like other people To know what goes on In your own home?
(CHORUS)	That's irrelevant – Go on, Hermione, tell us – We have a right to know.

| HERMIONE | People such as you |
| | Have no right to know anything. |

(CHORUS)	Yes, we have the right
	To know all the stories
	That belong to all people
—	We need to know.

| HERMIONE | Why? |

(CHORUS)	Because if we didn't
	Our lives would be unbearable
—	What would it be like
	If we didn't know the secrets
	Of all the kings and queens?

| HERMIONE | It would be much better. |

(CHORUS)	But we want to know the truth
—	There are so many versions
—	You can tell us which is the true one.

| HERMIONE | I could, but I won't. |

(CHORUS)	But we know so much already
	About your family's secrets
—	Your great-uncle Thyestes
	Slept with his own daughter
—	And he ate his own sons
	Which his brother had cooked for him
—	What we want to know
	Is much more straightforward.

HERMIONE	You are disgusting women;
	If everyone knew everything
	That went on in royal palaces
	Our lives would be impossible.

| (CHORUS) | But we want to know the truth. |

HERMIONE	That is what's disgusting;
	Because your lives are little
	You want to feel important
	By thinking that you know things.
	But you don't know what it's like
	To be a royal princess:
	It is horrible, disgusting. (*)

(AGAMEMNON enters from the cave)

AGAMEMNON   Hermione, why are you weeping?
Where's your father?

HERMIONE   In his tent.

AGAMEMNON   But I sent for him; fetch him.

HERMIONE   He sent me here instead.

AGAMEMNON   I want him, not you.

HERMIONE   He says you must go to him.

AGAMEMNON   I cannot leave this grove;
He must know that.

HERMIONE   He is sick.

AGAMEMNON   Sea-sick or shame-sick?

HERMIONE   He's unhappy and confused.

AGAMEMNON   So it's true that your mother
Went with Paris willingly?

HERMIONE   I don't know.

AGAMEMNON   But he knows;
He saw her in Troy.

HERMIONE   No, he didn't really see her.

AGAMEMNON   Not?

HERMIONE   And yet he did.

AGAMEMNON   He did and didn't see her?
Try to speak more clearly.

(HERMIONE starts to cry again)

HERMIONE   He said it was as if
He spoke to some other woman.

AGAMEMNON   He must know his own wife.

HERMIONE   He never did.

AGAMEMNON   But you,
You were there when Paris came.

HERMIONE   Don't ask me, don't ask me!
I didn't want to come here
But he sent me with a message.

141

AGAMEMNON	Then dry your eyes and tell me.
HERMIONE	He wishes to be loyal To you and the army.
AGAMEMNON	What does that mean, Hermione? Does he want the sacrifice?
HERMIONE	Of course he doesn't want it.
AGAMEMNON	Then he must either come to me So that we may act together Or speak his will to the Council.
HERMIONE	He would like to come to you.
AGAMEMNON	You said that he couldn't.
HERMIONE	He wants to, but he can't.
AGAMEMNON	Why not?
HERMIONE	Because of the spitting.
AGAMEMNON	Hermione –
HERMIONE	How would you like it If you were to come home After a painful meeting And a beastly choppy sea-voyage And have a whole army Spit at you?
AGAMEMNON	All of them?
HERMIONE	Some of the soldiers winked at him, Others laughed openly; They all read his face. But the worst thing of all Is the songs.
AGAMEMNON	The songs?
HERMIONE	The foul songs They have made up while they've waited.
AGAMEMNON	What songs?
HERMIONE	Don't be stupid; The songs about *them*: Filthy, horrid songs.

AGAMEMNON	I am sorry.
HERMIONE	I'm ashamed To belong to such a family.
AGAMEMNON	You should not say that.
HERMIONE	I do, they are right: I spit at us too.
AGAMEMNON	Try to control yourself And answer me one question: Will he go to the Council And speak against the sacrifice?
HERMIONE	He is not a good speaker.
AGAMEMNON	You mean he is a coward.
HERMIONE	You've no right to say that! And don't treat me as a child.
AGAMEMNON	Then do not behave like one.
HERMIONE	How can you think my father Would want you to kill my cousin? He wants to rescue mother But not at your expense.
AGAMEMNON	Does he still love her Or does he wish to punish her?
HERMIONE	Yes, I think so, both.
AGAMEMNON	But will he speak to the Council?
HERMIONE	I think that he thinks The best way is silence. He does not believe The kings will dare to act Against the wish of both of you. And I think he thinks…
AGAMEMNON	Go on.
HERMIONE	That it would be wisest To disband the fleet and the army Till some oracle has made The goddess' mind more clear.

AGAMEMNON	So he leaves it to me And sends you to say sorry. Have you no more messages?
HERMIONE	Yes, something horrible.
AGAMEMNON	Go on.
HERMIONE	More horrible Than the stench of this stag.

(She begins to weep again)

AGAMEMNON	Stop this and tell me.
HERMIONE	He told me to promise you That whatever way it goes He will give me to your baby.
AGAMEMNON	To my baby? Hermione –
HERMIONE	When your son grows up He will give me to Orestes.
AGAMEMNON	Why is that so terrible?
HERMIONE	By the time he's a man I shall be an old woman.
AGAMEMNON	The offer is a fair one.
HERMIONE	Fair? I spit at 'fair'! There is only one thing Either of you care about.
AGAMEMNON	Of course we both care about What's best for our family.
HERMIONE	Don't say that word!
AGAMEMNON	What word?
HERMIONE	It's the cause Of everything that's happening. All both of you ever think of Is how to make your family Richer and more powerful, So you treat all your daughters As if we were ingots To trade with from your gold-hoards.

AGAMEMNON   That is not true.

HERMIONE   It is!
Tyndareus says my mother
Chose my father, but she didn't.
If she'd chosen for herself
None of this would have happened.
You chose to give Achilles
To my cousin who detests him,
And now you want to give me
To a baby who's been poisoned.

AGAMEMNON   This self-pity is irrelevant.
Go and tell your father
That before I make bargains
He must speak to me himself.
If he will release
The kings from their oaths
I promise my son Orestes
Shall In time be your husband
Whatever happens here.

HERMIONE   I will not be a part of it.
When I marry it will be
With the man I choose myself.
I don't know who he'll be,
But one thing is certain:
He will not be a member
Of the house of the sons of Atreus.

(She goes)

NURSE   Best not to see your brother;
When each of you is troubled
It always leads to quarrels.
You must eat a little, child,
To keep up your strength.

(She puts food in front of him)

AGAMEMNON   I will take it in to my daughter:
I must keep her strength up too.   (*)

*(He goes into the cave again. A sound of birds
high in the sky)*

145

(CHORUS)   Listen; do you hear that?
        —   It is only the cawing of cranes
                Flying south for winter
        —   And look, there's Palamedes.

                (*PALAMEDES appears, joyful above them*)

NURSE   The flight of the cranes has helped him
                To finish the alphabet!

(CHORUS)   What is an alphabet?
        —   Some beast? — Some engine of war?

NURSE   It is something Old Cadmus began.

(CHORUS)   But what's it to do with cranes?

NURSE   They have shown him the missing letters.

(CHORUS)   What is a letter?

                (*PALAMEDES stretches his arms out
                upwards*)

PALAMEDES   A lineary:
                And this is the letter that's missing:
                Till now it has never been seen.
                Now the scribes of the West
                Will be able to keep records
                Of all our supplies and armaments;
                And no story will be lost now
                But will live on for ever and ever
                Till Time itself turns mortal.

(CHORUS)   Is that good?

PALAMEDES   It is good for poets.

NURSE   But less good for Palamedes.

(CHORUS)   But what is the missing letter?

PALAMEDES   'Y', I am showing you 'Y'.
                It is time for that to be written.

                (*Music*)

(CHORUS)   Look, the Queen is coming
        —   She will give you strength
        —   And we shall see the wedding-dress!   (*)

(ELECTRA runs on as AGAMEMNON returns)

ELECTRA   Father, we are here:
                 All will be well now!

(CLYTEMNESTRA follows with the baby ORESTES and with her wedding-dress in a basket)

CLYTEMNESTRA   O my love, we've heard it all;
                 You have been brave and strong.

AGAMEMNON   You should have come sooner.

CLYTEMNESTRA   Orestes was sick when you left us.
                 Nurse, take the child.

AGAMEMNON   Why did you not come sooner?

ELECTRA   She thought it was the poison,
                 So she doesn't dare to hold him
                 But I am not afraid.

CLYTEMNESTRA   Monstrous things are being told
                 About my sister's suffering.

AGAMEMNON   It's our daughter who is suffering.

CLYTEMNESTRA   Yes, she must be frightened
                 But of course there is no danger.

ELECTRA   If the gods want a sacrifice
                 Why not start with Calchas?

AGAMEMNON   There is great danger.

CLYTEMNESTRA   Where is she?

AGAMEMNON   In there.
                 This grove is sacred;
                 No one will dare to touch her
                 As long as I stay here.

CLYTEMNESTRA   And when she is married
                 No one will dare either.

AGAMEMNON   That is not certain
                 And that is why I'm armed.

CLYTEMNESTRA   But you are their General.

AGAMEMNON
: The Council are meeting
And planning to replace me.

CLYTEMNESTRA
: You must go to them at once
And speak to all the War-Kings.
Take this dress in, Electra;
She must put it on at once
To bind Achilles to her.

ELECTRA
: You brought it, take it to her.

CLYTEMNESTRA
: Has Achilles spoken to her?

AGAMEMNON
: Yes, and more than that.

CLYTEMNESTRA
: Her beauty will work on him.

AGAMEMNON
: I believe that it did.

CLYTEMNESTRA
: He has lain with her already?

AGAMEMNON
: In the sacred shrine.

CLYTEMNESTRA
: Good, that will bind him.

AGAMEMNON
: She begged me to keep him away from her.

CLYTEMNESTRA
: Young girls always say that.

ELECTRA
: Yes, she would say that.

CLYTEMNESTRA
: Where is Achilles?

AGAMEMNON
: At the Council of the Kings.

CLYTEMNESTRA
: I will go at once and speak to him.

AGAMEMNON
: Be careful what you say.

CLYTEMNESTRA
: I know how to handle him...

AGAMEMNON
: Don't tell him what to do.

CLYTEMNESTRA
: I will tell him how you've suffered.

AGAMEMNON
: Let me see the boy.

CLYTEMNESTRA
: Be careful.

ELECTRA
: Let me take him.

AGAMEMNON
: Take the dress in to your sister.

ELECTRA
: If they wanted a sacrifice
The gods should have chosen me

| | Or even Hermione |
| | Who shares her mother's blood. |

CLYTEMNESTRA   No one understands the gods' ways;
But once I've found Achilles
And they've danced the wedding dance
The army won't dare touch her.   (*)

(She goes. IPHIGENIA is heard weeping again)

ELECTRA   She is not fit to be sacrificed;
Artemis does not love cowards.

AGAMEMNON   Go in and comfort her
And take the dress with you.

ELECTRA   But I want to see the ships
And the horses and the warriors.

AGAMEMNON   Give it to me, I'll take it.

ELECTRA   It is I who should be wearing it;
I'd not hide in some cave.

AGAMEMNON   Go and look at the ships.
When I'm back from Troy
I will give you to some warrior
Who knows how to rule you.

ELECTRA   There is only one man
Whom I will ever love.

AGAMEMNON   If you go on thinking that
It will destroy your life.
Leave the dress but take the child.   (*)

(She goes with ORESTES. AGAMEMNON takes the dress towards the cave. A buzzing of flies. CALCHAS repeats the words of ARTEMIS)

(CHORUS)   That girl has courage
— But why didn't she go in
And speak to her sister?
— Why didn't her mother?
— Both of them are reckless
— Much care is needed here.

AGAMEMNON   *Talas Talantatos*!
So many voices,
Warriors, women, gods
And the buzzing of the ant-men.
You Myrmidons were better creatures,
Busy, restless, useful
When you built your little ant-heaps
Before you put on helmets;
Why do you want
To destroy a great city?   (*)

(*ACHILLES enters*)

ACHILLES   Agamemnon you have shamed me
In front of all the army.

AGAMEMNON   What has made you angry now?

ACHILLES   You sent your wife to plead with me
In front of all the Council.

AGAMEMNON   I advised her not to go;
It was her choice, not mine.

ACHILLES   Her husband advised her!
You've humiliated both of us.

AGAMEMNON   I am sorry you should think so;
We must hold together now
For Iphigenia's sake.

ACHILLES   You may need my friendship
But I have no need of yours.
Of course I am sorry
That the girl has to die;
For weeks I have defended you
But I should have realised
When your wife was slow in coming
That you and Palamedes
Were plotting to stop the war.

AGAMEMNON   That's not true; you have been hoping
I would order the sacrifice
So that you could avoid making
A hard choice yourself.

ACHILLES   It's for husbands, not fathers,
                      To make choices for their women.

AGAMEMNON   You speak of your wife
                      As if she was a war-prize.

ACHILLES   You gave her to me as a bargain;
                      It must be kept as oaths must.
                      Make her put on the wedding-dress,
                      And when we've danced together
                      I will lead her to the altar.
                      I at least have the courage
                      To obey a god's command.

AGAMEMNON   If you won't protect your own wife
                      You're not human.

ACHILLES   Don't say that.

AGAMEMNON   I am sorry, I forgot
                      That you are half divine.

ACHILLES   You dare say to my face
                      What others say in secret.

AGAMEMNON   What?

ACHILLES   That I lack courage.

AGAMEMNON   Why should they say that?

ACHILLES   Because they know the prophecy.

AGAMEMNON   That the war will last ten years?

ACHILLES   No, my mother's prophecy.

AGAMEMNON   I wish to hear no more
                      Of prophecies and prophets.

ACHILLES   She called it a prophecy
                      But to me it is a curse.

AGAMEMNON   What is it that troubles you?

ACHILLES   Every time Calchas speaks
                      It is her words I hear.

AGAMEMNON   Gently now; tell me.

ACHILLES (*Closing his eyes*) 'You will either live a long life
                      Happy but unknown

Or you will become more famous
Than any other warrior
But die while you are young.'

AGAMEMNON   Is that so terrible?
That's how it is with all warriors.
Why are you weeping?

ACHILLES   Did you not realise
When your wife bade me sit
By your fire-side in Mycenae
With the girl who I loved
That I longed to stay with you?
When I left you I knew then
I had chosen for ever.

AGAMEMNON   To be famous, and you will be.

ACHILLES   I have already learned
That our deeds matter less
Than the way others tell of them.

AGAMEMNON   That's the nature of fame.

ACHILLES   'Fame': the sneers of little men.

AGAMEMNON   I was thinking of the poets.

ACHILLES   What poets?

AGAMEMNON   Those to come
Who will sing of your deeds
And perhaps of mine also
If we have earned their songs.

ACHILLES   Yes, I wish to earn them
That the West may remember me.

AGAMEMNON   Well said; but I wonder
What the poets will say of you
If you lead your own wife
To a sacrifice of blood?
You want to be honoured
Like the heroes of the past,
And today we need heroes,
And honest poets too
To disturb us and remind us
Of what is and is not noble.

(Some of the CHORUS make music quietly)

ACHILLES
I know what the poets sing of:
Of what happens afterwards
When we lie beneath the earth
In the meadows of Asphodel,
Grey, bloodless wraiths,
Cold, listless, lifeless.
They say there are no songs
Nor joy nor laughter there.
What's it worth, Agamemnon?

AGAMEMNON
We do not know, Achilles.

ACHILLES
No, we do not know…
It seems to me as if
Beyond this life there's nothing
But one thing is certain:
There is nothing fairer
Than the sun up there, shining.
Only madmen want to die.

AGAMEMNON
That is well said: it is how
Your wife feels now in the shrine.
It is natural that the resentment
Of the army should confuse you
But the two of us together
Can bring our Persephone
Back into the light.
Think deeper now, feel deeper.

ACHILLES
Yes…
The girl is fair and pleasing
But her mind is on holy things;
She neither knows nor cares
How to give or take pleasure.
There are many fair women
But fewer great warriors;
It is said that in Troy
There are many luscious girls
To be won without bargaining.

AGAMEMNON
I do not wish such warriors
To serve in my army.

ACHILLES	You cannot do without me.
AGAMEMNON	You have yet to prove, Achilles, You're a warrior at all. What is it to the poets That you have won a skirmish Which you please to call a battle?
ACHILLES	If you go on insulting me I shall leave your army.
AGAMEMNON	If you love your own life Better than my daughter's Then go back to the mountains; I have no need of bear-whelps. Live long and be happy.

(*ACHILLES takes his armour from the tree where it is hanging. CLYTEMNESTRA enters*)

ACHILLES	This man is contemptible! If you dare not obey the goddess I will order my Myrmidons To drag your precious daughter To the altar tomorrow morning And launch the ships myself. You must learn, Agamemnon, What belongs to the gods And what to Achilles. (*)

(*He goes and his MYRMIDONS follow*)

CLYTEMNESTRA	O my love, I am sorry.
AGAMEMNON	Go back to Mycenae!
CLYTEMNESTRA	Don't be angry with me, I was trying to help you.
AGAMEMNON	You are a foolish woman.
CLYTEMNESTRA	Yes, I made a mistake But they cannot set sail without you.
AGAMEMNON	They'll replace me tomorrow.
CLYTEMNESTRA	Achilles will not let them; He'll soon get over his anger.

AGAMEMNON   He has already dared to enter
             A sacred place and defile
             Our daughter.

CLYTEMNESTRA   That was natural;
             He had waited long enough.

AGAMEMNON   How can you say that?
             He raped her, Clytemnestra.
             All that we feared
             And all that we swore to change
             Has already begun to happen.

CLYTEMNESTRA   Gently now, my darling,
             You will find a way
             To bring our Helen back.
             I will give you strength.

AGAMEMNON   Our daughter needs your strength;
             Why have you not seen her?

CLYTEMNESTRA   You are angry now and tired
             So you cannot think clearly;
             Be quiet now for a while
             And drink a little with me.

             (*She gives him drink and sits beside him*)

             I've heard how the poet Orpheus
             Could charm a stone with singing;
             Let me sing to you as he did
             And I'll ease and charm you now.

             (*Pause. CLYTEMNESTRA sings*)

AGAMEMNON   Listen to the sea:
             It gets inside mens' hearts
             Like a grey shifting ghost
             And steals them from their homes,
             Their women and their children.
             When we are on Troy's beaches
             We will hear the same sound
             And we'll weep too in secret.

             (*The sea sounds. Pause*)

CLYTEMNESTRA   You know you can't save both of them.

AGAMEMNON | I must.

CLYTEMNESTRA | Are you as sure
Or as clear as you're pretending?

AGAMEMNON | What are you trying to say to me?

CLYTEMNESTRA | It is said that Zeus himself
When he's made some great decision
Sometimes doubts if he's chosen rightly.

(She picks up AGAMEMNON'S helmet)

Remember how he divided
Earth and heaven with his brothers:
He took his father's helmet
And put three pebbles in it,
And bade his brothers pick one.

AGAMEMNON | It is told so.

CLYTEMNESTRA | He was wise:
Poseidon's was purplish grey
So he won the sea for his empire,
The one whom we do not name
Took the black and without a word
Went down to his dark kingdom,
But Zeus took out a white one
And so became Lord of the Sky.

AGAMEMNON | That's no way to rule the world.
What are you trying to tell me?

CLYTEMNESTRA | Zeus knows that all who are certain
They are right in their choosings
End up as fools or madmen
For the Fates are stronger than he is.

AGAMEMNON | Go in now to our daughter.

CLYTEMNESTRA | You love her too much, my darling.

AGAMEMNON | I love her as a father
Should love his daughter.

CLYTEMNESTRA | Yes,
But when the war-drums sound
Father and mothers too
Have to make sacrifices.

156

AGAMEMNON   Of their sons, not their daughters.

CLYTEMNESTRA   Mothers find losing daughters
Easier than losing sons:
Remember I have experience.
If something's to be gained
Something else must be given up;
Maybe that's what Artemis
Is trying now to teach you.

AGAMEMNON   Maybe you do not love her
As a mother should.

CLYTEMNESTRA   I love her
But not as I love you,
Nor I think as you love her.

AGAMEMNON   Leave this and go to her.

CLYTEMNESTRA   It would be a kind of Justice...

AGAMEMNON   Justice?

CLYTEMNESTRA   Yes, my darling;
Remember what our father
Tyndareus used to say:
'Keep it in the family'.

AGAMEMNON   I do not understand you.

CLYTEMNESTRA   It's better that you don't,
Not before these women.

AGAMEMNON   Then why do you speak of it?

CLYTEMNESTRA   Because Helen herself might agree;
She has a daughter too.
If your brother wants his wife back
Let him offer her to Artemis.

AGAMEMNON   What's this? What are you saying?

CLYTEMNESTRA   I think that the poets might call it
Just their kind of Justice.

AGAMEMNON   What have the poets
Or Helen to do with it?

CLYTEMNESTRA   It all began with her.

AGAMEMNON   I know that.

CLYTEMNESTRA   No, before that,
Long ago when she was little;
You were there when Tyndareus
Sent a baby to the mountains.

AGAMEMNON   What are these riddles?
If you can speak such words
You no longer deserve the name
Of mother to my daughter.

(CLYTEMNESTRA laughs)

If we let her die tomorrow
What will be in your heart
When you sit by our hearth-fire
And stare at her empty chair?
What god will you pray to?
Go back to Mycenae
And leave me to protect her.

CLYTEMNESTRA Very well, Agamemnon.

(She puts three pebbles in his helmet, starts to go and stops)

Women know better than men do
How it feels to lose a child,
Whether in child-birth
Or perhaps some other way.
They learn as I had to
They will get other children
If they're lucky. Agamemnon,
You are going to have to do it
For the sake of all those women
Whom men like Achilles
Have had their brutal way with.

AGAMEMNON   What you say is terrible.

CLYTEMNESTRA Yes, an oath is terrible.
You swore to lead the army,
You swore it at Mycenae.
Men talk of Fate
When things go against them

But women use another word
Which we learn from bearing children:
The word is Necessity.

AGAMEMNON   Yes, I know that word.

CLYTEMNESTRA   O yes, you know it
But women understand it;
By the time men have decided
That something can't be done
Women will have done it.

AGAMEMNON   Leave me! Tell my brother
I will disband the army
If he will release the kings
From their oaths to Tyndareus.

CLYTEMNESTRA   I will tell Menelaus
To trust in Helen's innocence
And hold them to their oaths.
You're a good man, Agamemnon,
And if the gods exist
They will reward your choice.
If they don't, what does it matter?   (*)

(*She goes. The sea sounds*)

(CHORUS)   I understand the Queen.
I have lost two children
And wept for them and suffered
But the next one gave me strength
And so I went on.

—   When a boy is killed in war
We grieve and yet we honour him
Because he died for his country.
If there's to be a sacrifice
Why should there be a difference
Between a girl and a boy?

—   Some of us have endured
The pain of bearing children
And perhaps for a while
A little joy till we lost them;
But we know that if they'd lived

159

They would still have suffered
In some other way.

AGAMEMNON You want this, you all do!

NURSE No, they only want
To see what's going to happen.
I have suckled more babies
Than I can remember;
Some of them died so soon
That there was no time to name them,
Others died soon after
And some of them later on
Which is not very long
In the eyes of the High Ones.

AGAMEMNON You know what would happen
If I killed another child
Of the family of Tantalus.

NURSE Sooner or later
Bits of the rock will tumble
On the heads of all my babies,
Great ones and little ones.

AGAMEMNON That doesn't mean
That we should tug the rock down.

NURSE You will never stop men trying to.

(*Pause*)

Let it out, my child.
When you were little
And frightened or unhappy
You would scream and kick and weep
And then you'd let me wipe your tears
And beg me for a story;
And as soon as I began one
You would fall asleep
And wake strong and fresh again.
Let it out: time to weep.

(CHORUS) Let it out, Agamemnon.

AGAMEMNON I must not.

| (CHORUS) | He cannot |
| | –   That is bad, he'll suffer more. |

AGAMEMNON If I am to lead the army
I must show I am the strongest.

NURSE Weep, or you'll lose your way.

AGAMEMNON I'll not weep till I find it.
What you all say is true
But I cannot and will not do it.
Speak to me, Artemis:
Why? Tell me why? (*)

(*Wind sounds far off. A voice speaks from within*)

VOICE I will tell you why.

NURSE Let the Goddess herself
Show you your way.

VOICE Can't you see? Look seaward.

AGAMEMNON I can see nothing
But the ship-masts on the beaches.

VOICE Helen's waiting, Agamemnon;
Soon it will be dawn
And the great walls will be shining.

(*IPHIGENIA comes from the cave in a yellow dress of sacrifice*)

AGAMEMNON Iphigenia…go back!
Where did you find that dress?

IPHIGENIA Artemis gave it to me.

AGAMEMNON You must take it off, go in
And put on your wedding-dress.

IPHIGENIA This is now my wedding-dress.

(*She picks up the red dress and throws it on the fire*)

I have danced with Achilles already.

AGAMEMNON That is why you must marry him.

IPHIGENIA	How can you say that?
AGAMEMNON	Iphigenia…
IPHIGENIA	Be silent: I have heard all the arguments And I have read your heart.
AGAMEMNON	Go in and take it off!
IPHIGENIA	Not till you yourself Have led me to the altar.
(CHORUS)	Either she is mad Or some god is inside her.
IPHIGENIA	Yes, I am god-cast: She's inside me, Agamemnon.
AGAMEMNON	I will not let you do it!
IPHIGENIA (*To Chorus*)	Gently now, you're trembling. Fill up my father's cup; He is tired and he is shivering. Come, sit now beside me; Look into the fire And you will see more clearly.

(*CHORUS put more logs on the fire*)

AGAMEMNON	I will never show you Naked to the army.
IPHIGENIA	Are you ashamed Of the body that you gave me? You should be proud, you made it. You told me when I was little That when some doomsday threatens us And no more can be done, Then, if we are brave enough We shall find that we are blessed. Now let us drink together.

(*Sits by him*)

You have taught me many things;
A just war is one of them
And all your aims are noble
Because you yourself are noble.

AGAMEMNON   It won't work, my darling;
             Only a virgin
             Is acceptable to Artemis;
             If she holds you impure
             She will send us no wind.

IPHIGENIA   She has purified me
             So that I may bless you;
             She and I have chosen.

AGAMEMNON   How can you want to die?

IPHIGENIA   Can you offer me a better life
             Than I have at this moment?
             Would you like me to linger
             Till my breasts sag and my hair
             Is grey from bearing children?
             What do you think my mother meant
             When she spoke of Poetic Justice?

AGAMEMNON   Her words were not clear to me;

IPHIGENIA   I know what they mean.
             Do you fear death, Agamemnon?

AGAMEMNON   No, but I fear to die
             Before I have done
             What I believe I was born for.

IPHIGENIA   Do you know what it is?

AGAMEMNON   Not yet.

IPHIGENIA   Then I must help you;
             I have found what I have searched for.

AGAMEMNON   What is it?

IPHIGENIA   I have learned
             What the gods want of humans.

AGAMEMNON   They want us to suffer.

IPHIGENIA   No, they only want us
             To give them a little pleasure.
             Do you know what they do
             While they're feasting on Olympus?
             While I wept in the cave
             Artemis came to me

And told me how they love
To talk of what we do,
To laugh at us and sing of it
Not because they are evil,
Though some of them are,
But because they enjoy us.
We make so much of things,
Forgetting that our pains,
Our hopes and our fears
Are only tiny bits
Of a story shaped by Zeus
Ten thousand years ago.
We are all bits of cloth
Cut up by his dark daughters
Whom he begot on Night:
One who weaves and spins us,
One who with her measure
Fixes our human span
And one who cuts the cloth
When our time is appointed.

AGAMEMNON   Even if it's true
That the Fates begin and end us
What we make of our lives
Is our own and no god-game.

IPHIGENIA   Yes, beginnings and endings
Are tedious to the gods
Because they already know them.
What they love best
Is the middle of a story;
It is open and its ours.
Can't you hear them laughing
Because you are still trying
To stop a beginning
That already has begun?

AGAMEMNON   I have heard all the voices,
I have heard all the arguments
And my mind is worn down
Like the pebbles on the shingle.
Yet at first I was as clear

As the day-sky and I *knew*
That I was acting rightly:
Pride? Delusion? Ignorance?
Is our sin to think
We are clear when in reality
We are lost in a labyrinth?
I have always felt compassion
For poor Oedipus of Thebes;
Maybe the gods now punish me
For believing that mankind
Can ever heal mankind.
But this is my truth:
I *cannot* do it.

IPHIGENIA   Then I must do it for you.
Put your hand now in your helmet:
If you draw out the white
You shall send me home,
If the grey you will stay stubborn
Till the War Kings replace you,
But if it's black you will do
As Artemis commands you.

AGAMEMNON   Let be!

IPHIGENIA   Yes, I'm letting you
Be what you were born for:
I am your instrument,
Your sail and your sea-road,
Your wind and your way.

(*She rises and moves round him as he holds
the pebbles*)

Do you see how light my dress is?
Can't you feel on your cheek
A little whisk of air?
Soon it will be a breeze
Tickling your ship-sails
And then it will become
The freshest, fairest wind
That ever filled a ship-sail.

AGAMEMNON   No, I cannot do it.

IPHIGENIA   Don't you remember
            A story we were told
            When all of us were little?
            Long, long ago
            Before the world began
            A girl began to dance...

            (*The CHORUS start to play and sing, as
            IPHIGENIA begins to dance*)

(CHORUS) (*Quietly*)   And as soon as she began
                       She felt free and full of joy
            –   And so she danced faster
                       Till she stirred a little breeze
            –   And it started to dance with her...

IPHIGENIA   ... And that is how the world began
            And how it will again.
            Look at me, my love;
            I am your bride of war.
            Nurse, go on and tell him
            How that breeze became a wind
            That blew through all the Universe.

            (*A slight breeze begins*)

NURSE   It turned into a serpent
            And it loved her and they danced
            And exactly nine months later
            She laid a silver egg.

(CHORUS)   That is how it's told.

            (*AGAMEMNON weeps*)

NURSE   Put your hand now into the helmet
            And you'll find Poetic Justice.

            (*He takes out the black pebble as if under a
            spell*)

IPHIGENIA   See, Artemis has chosen:
            It was all so easy.
            Take your helmet, my darling,
            And summon all the army.
            I will light the beacon
            To tell them all in Ilion

That Agamemnon's coming
With the Men from the West.

(*It begins to dawn. She takes fire from the
hearth and lights the beacon*)

NURSE (*To Agamemnon*) Don't forget, my child,
To take the other pebbles out
When you put your helmet on.

(*IPHIGENIA strikes the battle-gong. A breeze
begins to grow*)

IPHIGENIA   Time to sound the trumpets!
Time to wake the West!   (*)

(*Trumpets. EVERYONE including the
MYRMIDONS re-enter, armed.
CLYTEMNESTRA is carrying ORESTES*)

ODYSSEUS   Who has summoned the army?

ACHILLES   Where is your wedding-dress?

IPHIGENIA   In the fire, Achilles.

PELEUS   In the fire? A wedding-dress?

IPHIGENIA   Yes, it's time for fire!

CLYTEMNESTRA   What is she doing?
Speak, Agamemnon.

IPHIGENIA   No, I will speak for him!
Prometheus gave us fire
For men to use wisely.
As flames change their shape
So humans change their purposes:
There is torch-fire for marriages
That Hymen delights in,
There is beacon-fire for messages
That wing across the water,
And when the gods will it
There must also be war-fire
When wicked men grow proud
So that when our own come home again
They may enjoy the hearth-fire
That human-kind loves best.

167

PELEUS	That is well said.
ODYSSEUS	But what is she saying? Agamemnon, tell us.
AGAMEMNON	I have no more words.
IPHIGENIA	My father has chosen To make a noble sacrifice For the sake of all those women Who suffer on this earth At the hands of such men As I see here among you. But when you've brought our Helen Home to her hearth-fire All the world will know the West Punishes those who break The just and holy laws That should and must rule humans.
PELEUS	She speaks like a god.
NURSE	She is over-excited.
(CHORUS)	Let us all honour her.
NURSE	But whether she is right Is perhaps another question.
ACHILLES (*To Iphigenia*)	I am ashamed Of the evil words I spoke; You have won fame and honour But I have yet to earn it.
CLYTEMNESTRA	Let all the army honour Their General: he has chosen.
IPHIGENIA	Yes, you must honour him. When we are at the altar He himself will take the knife.
PELEUS	No, that is Calchas' task.
IPHIGENIA	You are weeping, Odysseus; What is your trouble?
ODYSSEUS	I am weeping because your face Shines like Athene's.

IPHIGENIA   No, you weep for your wife
And your own child.
Don't you want what I give you?

ODYSSEUS   I want it less than any
Whose lives will now be wasted.

IPHIGENIA   But it's you more than any
Who will make it all happen.

ODYSSEUS   Only for my oath's sake.
I could not do what your father's doing;
I could not kill my child.

IPHIGENIA
(*To Peleus*)
Then you should kneel before him.
Weeping too, old man? Be happy:
Your son will win much fame.

PELEUS   We should not kill girls
When they are so lovely;
We should just listen
And look at them for ever.

IPHIGENIA   We must do what we're here for:
Mother, you must promise
Never to reproach
My father for his choice.

CLYTEMNESTRA   I promise you, my darling;
He is doing as he must.

IPHIGENIA   Let me hold my brother
And say good bye to him.

(*CLYTEMNESTRA gives ORESTES to IPHIGENIA*)

IPHIGENIA (*To Orestes*) Sh…listen to me.
You will never know me
But when you hear my story
You must know that it's a happy one;
And when you come to be
High King of Mycenae
You must tell it to your children.
Look he's smiling, he has promised;
Take him and cherish him.

(Gives ORESTES back to CLYTEMNESTRA)

Weeping too, Mother?
You have often told me
Men and women must endure:
The words are worn and ancient
But they are still fresh.
Nothing's new or changes
But each of us, like children,
Must learn it all anew.
I am happy, dying;
Life is brief and brutish
But by how we live we give it
A meaning and a brightness:
So our light braves the darkness.
Mother... and you, my father,
I love you very much!

ODYSSEUS

Before she goes to the altar
We must bind her and hood her;
And when you are there your father
Must tear your dress from you
According to the custom.

AGAMEMNON

No! I forbid that.

ODYSSEUS

Agamemnon, Lord of the Ships,
Have you not yet learned
That when a god speaks plainly
It's unwise to disobey?

PELEUS

The rite is an ancient one
And pleasing to the gods.

ACHILLES

You are right; it is time to bind her.

*(AGAMEMNON takes the torch and
ODYSSEUS binds her)*

CLYTEMNESTRA

Let us sing to Artemis
Virgin and Healer,
Protector of travellers
And of the army, waiting
Raise the torch, Agamemnon.

*(AGAMEMNON lifts the torch and looks at
IPHIGENIA. The CHORUS sing in Greek from*

Euripides' 'Iphigenia in Aulis' e.g. lines 1505-1509, while she speaks her English translation)

IPHIGENIA

O Zeus of the day-sky
Hold high the flame of dawn...

(Speaks the next two lines in Greek. The breeze grows)

'Hail and farewell,
Sunlight that I love'.   (*)

(ODYSSEUS hoods her and ACHILLES leads her towards the sea. AGAMEMNON drops the other pebbles in the fire; they are both black. The fire blazes high. All follow except CLYTEMNESTRA and the CHORUS. The singing fades. The sea sounds and the wind grows great. ORESTES starts to cry)

CLYTEMNESTRA

Don't be frightened, baby.
Are you weeping for your sister?
You need not, she is happy:
Or do you weep for me?

NURSE

Don't ask stupid questions.

CLYTEMNESTRA

I know why he's weeping;
He's weeping for his father
And the world I've pushed him into.
Those who try to do what's right
As you will have to, baby,
Never find it easy.

(All weep and begin keening. The sound of many birds rising. The wind grows in strength and the sea sounds louder. ELECTRA comes back)

ELECTRA

Stop this, Mother, stop it!
You are frightening the child.
My father has done a great thing;
I saw it, and I know
It is pleasing to the gods.

(CHORUS)

What has happened? Tell us.

ELECTRA

First you must all stop weeping:
Give me the child.

(CHORUS)   Tell us.

ELECTRA (*Takes Orestes*) Listen, baby brother,
                    I will tell you such a tale.
                    When we came to the altar
                    All the army was waiting.
                    Then Calchas called for silence
                    And cried out to Artemis,
                    'Receive this clean sacrifice
                    And grant us a swift passage
                    To the army from the West.'
                    Then my father took the knife
                    And cut the dress from her shoulder
                    And so it fell on the sand
                    According to the custom.
                    Everyone but I
                    Lowered their eyes to the earth
                    But I watched my father's face;
                    His eyes were open also.
                    Then...then, Orestes,
                    Something wonderful, unwordable:
                    A flame, a flash of god-light,
                    A thud and a thrill of wind
                    And Iphigenia had gone;
                    And a deer lay on the altar
                    Gasping out its life-breath.
                    Then a whoosh of sea-birds
                    Soared up from the rigging
                    And the ship-sails leaped to the mast-heads
                    As if tugged by a thousand gods.
                    Then my father cried out
                    'Since Artemis has spoken
                    May her shrine never more
                    Be polluted by humans
                    And may the blood of innocents
                    No more stain holy altars
                    Lest the gods again be angry.'

CLYTEMNESTRA   I do not believe you:
                    It is not how things happen.
                    You have made it up to please me.

(Hugs the dead stag)

This is what is real,
This, the stench of stag-rot.

(CHORUS)

You must not be angry:
It is unwise to try
To understand gods' ways.
It is simpler and safer
Just to offer them libations.

(They do so)

CLYTEMNESTRA

Why should I be angry?
I pity my Agamemnon;
Such things are always paid for
In one way or another.
I weep for the man.

(She goes. ELECTRA calls after her)

ELECTRA

No tears for your daughter?
You do not love your children,
Not even this little one;
You only love your first one
Who died long ago.

(The wind has faded away)

Come with me, Orestes,
And I will show you how
A true mother should be.
When I have taught you language
You shall know all the high things
That a brave boy must know.
I will protect you
And hold you tight for ever
And I'll laugh and weep when you do
And Father will be so proud of us
When his ships bring him home.
Now the bright gods be praised!   (*)

(She goes with ORESTES. The sea sounds. The POET returns)

POET

All gone; the ships have gone.

(*He sits and drinks*)

(CHORUS)   Who is to blame?

POET   All, but all are innocent.

(CHORUS)   Could it have been otherwise?
    – Is that how it truly happened?
    – Why did it have to happen?

POET   Because that is the story.

(*Some dust falls from above. One of the ropes tying the rock frays and falls a little*)

PART II
The War

Play 4
NEOPTOLEMUS

THE WAR-CAMP AT TROY

CAST

First Woman   (–)

Second Woman   HELENUS/ THETIS

Third Woman   (–)

Fourth Woman   (–)

First Man   POET/ PELEUS

Second Man   AGAMEMNON

Third Man   ODYSSEUS/ CALCHAS *

Fourth Man   NEOPTOLEMUS

CHORUS

(*CALCHAS is not seen in this play, only his voice is heard)

*(Ten years later the POET is telling the
CHORUS and the SECOND WOMAN the
history of the war. It is evening and everyone
is at ease, eating and drinking. One or two
are playing instruments, including a drum)*

POET ... And so they buried Hector,
Tamer of Horses.
But many of the black ships
Had been burned and broken by him
So Priam called up fresh allies,
Penthesilea and her Amazons,
And they burned many more ships
Until Achilles killed her.
Then Memnon the Ethiopian
Came and burned more on the beaches
Till Peleus' son killed him also.
Then Apollo the City's Defender
Was angry with Achilles,
So he guided the bow of Paris
And Achilles leaves our story.
And so the tenth year came
And the towers and walls of Troy
Stood as high and brave as ever.

(Music ends)

(CHORUS) Tell us no more tales
Of the death of heroes, Poet.
– Go on to how the War-kings
Got into the city
– Go on to the Wooden Horse.

POET But first there is something tricky
Which we must try to make sense of.
Achilles' son Pyrrhus
Was only a boy at the time,
Yet it's said that he sacked the city
And slaughtered Priam himself.

(CHORUS) But if Pyrrhus killed him
How can he have been a boy
– No poet is to be trusted
On questions involving chronology.

POET   Then I will tell you a story
No other poet has told.

(CHORUS)   Then you've made it up? – Confess it.

POET   Not at all, I have made it cohere.

(CHORUS)   Then let us go into it.

POET   I will, but you can't.

(CHORUS)   Why not?

POET   No girls allowed in the war-camp;
There's not enough food now to feed them.
The army is so hungry
That they've had to eat their horses;
If they see you, you may be next.

(CHORUS)   Then we'd better not hear your story.

POET   If you just sit back and keep silent
If you're lucky you won't be noticed.
Watch, and see how old Peleus
Showed the West how to win the war.

       (*CALCHAS' voice is heard speaking to SINON*)

(CHORUS)   What is that?

POET   It is Calchas
Rehearsing the war-plan with Sinon.

(CHORUS)   What war-plan? – Who is Sinon?

POET   Don't rush me. Listen to Calchas:
He is telling all the army
How a traitor son of Priam
Has prophesied that Troy
Will not fall till three conditions
Are fulfilled by the West.
First, the image of Athene
Which fell into Troy from the sky
Must be stolen from the citadel.

(CHORUS)   What is an Image?

POET   You will see when Odysseus brings it.
Next, the shoulder-bone of Pelops

| | The first son of Tantalus |
| | Must be brought from Mycenae. |

(CHORUS) Presumably the replacement
          The gods made him when Tantalus
          Served him up at a banquet
          And one of them ate his son?

POET   Very good; go further off.
          This camp is no sight for young girls.

(CHORUS) But what is the third condition?

POET   That is the tricky bit,
          Achilles' son Pyrrhus
          Must be brought to Troy: here he is.
          Now sit back and be silent.   (*)

(CHORUS withdraw and watch, taking plenty of drink with them as NEOPTOLEMUS and AGAMEMNON appear. The ambience changes. It is now hot, dusty and dirty. The CHORUS react silently to what they see and hear)

NEOPTOLEMUS   Agamemnon, I am ready:
              You must give me my father's armour.

AGAMEMNON   Can you lift his spear yet and throw it?

NEOPTOLEMUS   Almost.

AGAMEMNON   Then keep practising.

NEOPTOLEMUS   I'm as old as my father was
              When he conquered the Mysians.

AGAMEMNON   But can you outrun a chariot?

(CALCHAS' voice is heard again)

              What is the hurry, boy?

NEOPTOLEMUS   Don't call me boy.

AGAMEMNON   Why not?
              It is what I call Orestes;
              He's the same age as you are.

NEOPTOLEMUS   He is at home with his mother;
              I am here and already a warrior.

AGAMEMNON	Not yet, but maybe you will be In some other war in the future.
NEOPTOLEMUS	I'll become a great one tonight When Odysseus brings back the image.
AGAMEMNON	Long before he's back Peleus your grandfather Will have brought Hesione home.
NEOPTOLEMUS	Hesione?
AGAMEMNON	She is Priam's sister. She was seized fifty years ago By Peleus' brother, Telamon. That's how the war began: Troy seized Helen in revenge. But Telamon is dead now So we've no just grounds to keep her. When Peleus brings her the war will end With a simple exchange of hostages Between myself and Priam.
NEOPTOLEMUS	You are going to speak with Priam?
AGAMEMNON	I am meeting him tonight At the ruined shrine of Apollo And there we will make peace.
NEOPTOLEMUS	But it's where they murdered my father.
AGAMEMNON	He too went there to make peace.
NEOPTOLEMUS	He would never have done that.
AGAMEMNON	Haven't they told you what happened?
NEOPTOLEMUS	No one speaks to me about it.
AGAMEMNON	It is time to tell you why.
NEOPTOLEMUS	Yes, I want to know the truth of it.
AGAMEMNON	He went to meet with Polyxena A Trojan royal princess.
NEOPTOLEMUS	How could they meet in a war-zone?
AGAMEMNON	Both sides agreed to treat it As a sanctuary where foes Could meet and drink together

And no weapons were allowed there.
When men are trying to solve
Something which seems insoluble
It is always best to meet
In pleasant surroundings if possible.
The grass was untrodden and green,
The streams ran pure and fresh
And the very air was holy.
But the trees and grass have withered
Since the god has departed.

NEOPTOLEMUS   But why did my father go there?

AGAMEMNON   To marry a girl he loved
And to seal a treaty of peace
Made by Priam and myself.

NEOPTOLEMUS   My father would never have agreed
To be part of any peace plan.

AGAMEMNON   Oh yes, he knew as we all did
We could never take the city
So he wished to have the honour
Of being the only peace-maker.
So he went to the shrine in secret
Without telling me or Priam;
But the Trojans knew of the meeting
And Paris' arrow killed him,
And that was the end of our peace-plan.

NEOPTOLEMUS   He loved this Polyxena
And she betrayed him to Paris?

AGAMEMNON   It did Troy little good.
When Odysseus and Ajax
Rescued your father's body
The shrine was defiled with blood
And Apollo was so angry
That he has deserted the city.

NEOPTOLEMUS   You hated my father, didn't you?

AGAMEMNON   No;
There were times that he made me angry
And times too when I loved him.

NEOPTOLEMUS	Then why did you quarrel so often?
AGAMEMNON	Men do when the pressures are great, And when each are both right and wrong It always leads to quarrels. But the blame for the wraths of Achilles Belongs most of all to his mother Who made some foolish prophecy Which made him fear death.
NEOPTOLEMUS	He feared nothing.
AGAMEMNON	All men fear something: What do you fear?
NEOPTOLEMUS	To lie. And you?
AGAMEMNON	The death of the city.
NEOPTOLEMUS	Then no wonder it has taken Ten years to destroy it.
AGAMEMNON	Do you know who really hated him? The army.
NEOPTOLEMUS	How can you say that?
AGAMEMNON	He would only fight when it suited him; Whenever his pride was hurt He would threaten to go home.
NEOPTOLEMUS	That's a lie; over and over He saved you all from destruction.
AGAMEMNON	True, but the man whom we honour Is not him whom our poets sing of: The victor of the plains And sacker of defenceless cities All rich in treasure and prizes And women to take for his pleasure, But the man whom we gave the title 'Defender of the Ships'.
NEOPTOLEMUS	Small men sneer at great ones; Do you know how the army despises you?
AGAMEMNON	It's the privilege of all armies To despise their commanders.

I rather despise myself, boy,
Because I have not been able
To end this pointless war.

NEOPTOLEMUS It will end when we take the city.

AGAMEMNON Why should you want to take it?

NEOPTOLEMUS Why? To avenge my father.

AGAMEMNON No, you want fame as he did.

NEOPTOLEMUS What do you want, Agamemnon?

AGAMEMNON Have you ever seen
Or been inside a city?

NEOPTOLEMUS No, Scyros is small.

AGAMEMNON Troy's towers are so high
One can see them from the war-camp.
I have always had a longing
To see inside the walls;
They say it is full of wonders,
Trees, gardens and fountains;
Priam told me he has planted
A fruit-tree rich with apples
In Ilion itself.
Sometimes in the evening
When the fighting is done
I've heard singing inside the walls
And dancing too and laughter
And music it seems I once knew.
Last night I dreamed, Neoptolemus,
That the daughters of Memory
Had made it their home.
I have come to love that city
Better than my own Mycenae;
So I mean when the war is over
To make that a fair place too.

NEOPTOLEMUS Is Mycenae a city too?

AGAMEMNON No, it is a citadel.

NEOPTOLEMUS While you sit here and dream
I'm going to look at the Horse.

(*As he goes, AGAMEMNON calls after him*)

184

AGAMEMNON	There will be no need of it now; Troy's walls will stand for ever! (*)

(CALCHAS is heard again. Enter PELEUS with a bundle)

PELEUS	What have you done to the war-camp? Shocking, disgusting, shameful: This camp is a stinking chaos, The dead unburied, the living Are like wraiths out of Tartarus, Starving, sick and despairing.
AGAMEMNON	Peleus, you are welcome! Your coming will put an end To the need for a war-camp at all. Tonight I will set my mark To a treaty of peace with Priam.
PELEUS	If this is the state of your army It looks as if you will have to.
AGAMEMNON	Where is Hesione, Peleus?
PELEUS	On the sea-bed, she died at sea.
AGAMEMNON	She is dead?
PELEUS	It was hot, So we threw her overboard.
AGAMEMNON	Why did you do that, Peleus?
PELEUS	Because I know better than you do How to deal with rotting bodies.
AGAMEMNON	Then how can I persuade Priam That I have fulfilled my promise To exchange Hesione for Helen?
PELEUS	That plan died ten years ago. I have brought her remains And a message she sent to her brother.
AGAMEMNON	What remains? What message?
PELEUS	She asked me to bring you the garments She wore when we took her from Troy: Some jewels and an old yellow dress.

AGAMEMNON	A yellow dress?
PELEUS	Of sacrifice; She wore it till her death's day.
AGAMEMNON	Where is it?
PELEUS	In this bundle Packed with Pelops' shoulder-bone.
AGAMEMNON	We won't need it now.
PELEUS	Then why did you ask me to bring it?
AGAMEMNON	You said that Hesione Sent some message to Priam…?
PELEUS	Yes, before she died, she said, 'Tell this to Priam, my brother: Since it was not the gods' will I should ever come home to Troy, I send you what is left Of the girl you knew long ago When my father dressed and bound me On the sea-shore as a sacrifice And they took me away to the West. I swore I would not change my dress Till I came home again, So take these remnants of me That Helen may also go home And all the world have peace.'
AGAMEMNON	I will take them to Priam tonight.
PELEUS	You're a fool, and I am thirsty. How has my grandson borne himself Since he came to Troy?
AGAMEMNON	Well enough. Odysseus took him to Lemnos To fetch Philoctetes.
PELEUS	Ha! He's brought the great bow of Heracles, The bow that never misses!
AGAMEMNON	Yes, it put paid to Paris.
PELEUS	My grandson has killed Paris?

AGAMEMNON   No, he is not yet strong enough
             To draw a great bow.

PELEUS   Give him time;
             Little shrimps must practise.
             Look, there he is, young Pyrrhus!

AGAMEMNON   The army do not call him
             Pyrrhus but 'Neoptolemus'.

PELEUS   'New Soldier', very good:
             Why do they call him that?

AGAMEMNON   He cannot lift his father's shield,
             So they say if he is to fight
             It must be a new sort of fighting.

PELEUS   He'll show them soon enough.

             (*NEOPTOLEMUS re-enters*)

NEOPTOLEMUS Agamemnon, it's almost ready;
             I have been inside it.

AGAMEMNON   Greet your grandfather, boy.

PELEUS   I salute you, Neo...
             What did you say they call him?

NEOPTOLEMUS Do not salute me yet.

PELEUS   Why not? You've avenged your father
             By bringing the bow of Heracles.

NEOPTOLEMUS Don't praise me; Odysseus forced me
             To get it by lying and a trick.

PELEUS   Odysseus knows how to win
             Which is more than the General does.

AGAMEMNON   By now Odysseus is dead.

NEOPTOLEMUS No, he has gone into Troy disguised.

PELEUS   Why should he want to do that?

AGAMEMNON   Because he is a fool
             And is acting like a traitor.

NEOPTOLEMUS Odysseus is fetching it now.

PELEUS   What is he fetching?

NEOPTOLEMUS The image of Athene
Which fell on Troy from the sky
As soon as it's brought to the war-camp
We shall all go into the Horse.
I've been inside it already.

PELEUS You've been inside a horse?
It's true that Zeus swallowed Metis
But there's no record of a boy
Ever getting inside a horse.

NEOPTOLEMUS It's an engine of war, grandfather.

AGAMEMNON Made out of broken ships;
Neoptolemus calls it a horse.

PELEUS Why?

NEOPTOLEMUS Because Odysseus
Has dedicated it to Poseidon.

PELEUS Why?

NEOPTOLEMUS Because Poseidon
Is both sea-god and god of horses.

PELEUS You mean that the son of Laertes
Is planning to go to sea
On a wooden horse?

NEOPTOLEMUS No, he means
To take the city with it.

AGAMEMNON To go to sea on a horse
Would be about as sensible
As the way he plans to use it.

(CALCHAS is heard rehearsing SINON again)

PELEUS What is this horse and that voice?

NEOPTOLEMUS It is Calchas rehearsing with Sinon
The story he means to tell Priam
To persuade him to take in the horse.

AGAMEMNON A story made up by Odysseus.   (*)

(A ragged BEGGAR enters and drinks and
washes at the pool. PELEUS kicks him)

PELEUS   Get out of here!

AGAMEMNON   Let him be.

PELEUS   But he's slobbering and washing
                In the only decent drinking water
                In the whole of your stinking camp.

AGAMEMNON   Yes, you stink like Philoctetes
                When you brought him from Lemnos.

ODYSSEUS   That is not surprising,
                These are Philoctetes' rags.

PELEUS   Odysseus!

NEOPTOLEMUS   Do you have it?

ODYSSEUS   How could you doubt it
                Since Athene was with me?
                The oracles are fulfilled.

                (*He unwraps the sacred image of Athene*)

NEOPTOLEMUS   It is lovely.

ODYSSEUS   Yes, as she is.

PELEUS   So you got through the guards?

ODYSSEUS   That was easy.

AGAMEMNON   No one saw you?

ODYSSEUS   Yes, Helen recognised me;
                She took me to her chamber
                In Ilion and bathed me.

PELEUS   Helen bathed you?

ODYSSEUS   She told me
                How she longs to go home.

AGAMEMNON   Because of Paris' death?

ODYSSEUS   Because the Trojans hate her;
                But just as she was telling me
                Hecuba came in.

PELEUS   Not an easy moment.

AGAMEMNON   Did she call for the guards?

ODYSSEUS	No, I negotiated:
	I swore that if she spared my life
	I would persuade the army
	To raise the siege for ever.
PELEUS	You swore that?
AGAMEMNON	You did well.
PELEUS	And Hecuba believed you?
ODYSSEUS	Everyone believes what they want to.
NEOPTOLEMUS	You should not have sworn it
	Unless you meant what you said.
ODYSSEUS	I did mean what I said
	But I doubt if she listened
	As closely as she should have
	To the actual words I used.
	I swore to persuade you
	To break camp and embark all the army
	And set sail for the West.
PELEUS	You swore to end the war?
ODYSSEUS	But I did not swear our ships
	Would not come back again.
PELEUS	Ha! Tell us more, Odysseus.
ODYSSEUS	My mind was on the plan
	All the Council had agreed on
	Before I went into Troy.
	When we climb into the Horse
	The General is to take
	The army out to Tenedos
	And wait behind the island;
	Hecuba will believe
	I have fulfilled my promise
	And Priam will be certain
	We have given up and gone.
PELEUS	This is a wondrous man!
	He should have been an Argonaut.
NEOPTOLEMUS	You lied again, Odysseus.

AGAMEMNON He had cause. You did well
But exceeded your authority.
Will anyone believe
Priam will swallow the tale
You have invented for Sinon?

ODYSSEUS Yes.

AGAMEMNON Leave us, Peleus,
And take your grandson with you;
I must speak alone with Odysseus.

(*CALCHAS' words to SINON are heard again*)

PELEUS Then I'll have a word with Sinon.

(*He sets down the bundle. ODYSSEUS takes
off his rags and starts eating*)

ODYSSEUS What's this?

PELEUS A nothing. Come, boy. (*)

(*He goes with NEOPTOLEMUS*)

AGAMEMNON Once before a beggar
Came to my hearth;
He brought no good to me.

ODYSSEUS Look at Athene's image;
It is lovely, as she is.

AGAMEMNON I salute you, Odysseus,
But you've overlooked one thing:
Priam and I have reached
Full agreement on peace terms.

ODYSSEUS Not again, Agamemnon?

AGAMEMNON This time they will hold;
Telamon is dead
So I've sent for Hesione.

ODYSSEUS So I've heard, but since she's dead
Your peace-terms are void.

AGAMEMNON I can fulfil them in spirit.
Before she died she asked us
To send her remains to her brother.

ODYSSEUS What remains?

AGAMEMNON   All that she wore
                    When they took her away to the West.

ODYSSEUS   So you think a ten years' war
                    Can be ended by sending Priam
                    Some faded rags and trinkets?

AGAMEMNON   Yes. Have you forgotten
                    Priam only seized Helen
                    To win back his sister?

ODYSSEUS   I have not forgotten.

AGAMEMNON   Then why should he want to keep Helen
                    When Hesione and Paris are dead?

ODYSSEUS   Why should he send her back
                    When he knows we are close to defeat?

AGAMEMNON   I know his mind; he'll do it.

ODYSSEUS   Your continual negotiations
                    Have driven our men to despair
                    But my plan has given them heart again.

AGAMEMNON   Your plan is a wild gamble
                    With the lives of all those men
                    For whom I am responsible.
                    Every time a Trojan fire-ball
                    Burns another precious ship
                    Each man knows that his chance
                    Of seeing his wife and children
                    Grows less and he no longer
                    Remembers or cares why he's here.

ODYSSEUS   We will never rescue Helen
                    Unless we take the city.

                    (*CALCHAS' words to SINON are heard again*)

AGAMEMNON   Priam will not be deceived
                    By the lies which you and Calchas
                    Have been teaching your cousin Sinon.

ODYSSEUS   When Hecuba sees our ships gone
                    She will know I've fulfilled my promise.

AGAMEMNON   But how can we take them to sea?
                    If we cram those hulks with warriors

	They will be destroyed as surely As you will be in the Horse.
ODYSSEUS	Then we must burn all the baggage And kill what's left of the horses.
AGAMEMNON	Our ships are too few and too rotten To carry the whole of the army.
ODYSSEUS	Then we must get rid of all those Who are unfit to fight or bear arms.
AGAMEMNON	The wounded?
ODYSSEUS	Our prisoners and slaves.
AGAMEMNON	And women prizes too?
ODYSSEUS	It has already been done.
AGAMEMNON	I gave no such orders.
ODYSSEUS	You are always slow in such matters.
AGAMEMNON	Did you give them, Odysseus?
ODYSSEUS	Yes, in the Council's name.

(*AGAMEMNON controls his anger before he goes on*)

AGAMEMNON	Let us suppose that the Trojans Did take the Horse into the city And you did light your signal in Ilion How could we be sure of seeing it? Sea-mists at night here are common.
ODYSSEUS	Calchas has taken auguries: The sky tonight will be clear.
AGAMEMNON	I trust Priam better Than the auguries of Calchas.
ODYSSEUS	What happens does not depend On you or me or the army But on the will of the gods.
AGAMEMNON	Yes, 'Trust in the will of the gods!' Since there are many gods All at odds with one other Such words have no meaning.

ODYSSEUS   When a man is lucky as I am
           And one of them speaks inside him
           If he's wise he will obey.

AGAMEMNON If all of us were to act
           As we thought a god had advised us,
           The world would soon be a chaos.

ODYSSEUS   It's your mind that is a chaos
           But Athene's head is clear.

AGAMEMNON How can you tell it's Athene
           Who speaks to you at all?
           The madness of men who assume
           They're obeying some god's command
           Will destroy the world one day.
           But in one thing you are right,
           We must each of us make choices.
           I have made mine, Odysseus:
           We will not use the Horse.

ODYSSEUS   You only think you have chosen.
           Do you really prefer to wait
           For some divine intervention?
           Perhaps for Poseidon to smash
           The walls that he built with an earth-quake
           Or to send in the sea to swallow them?
           Or perhaps for bright Apollo
           To drive the Trojans mad?
           Maybe you hope Zeus himself
           Will thump their gates with thunder-bolts?

AGAMEMNON Maybe, maybe not,
           But I know how your plan will be told of
           In the times that are to come:
           'Once upon a time
           Thirty fools climbed into a horse
           Made out of broken ships
           Labelled "Please handle with care";
           But the Trojans, being less foolish
           Burned the horse and the fools in it:'
           It will make a fine story.

ODYSSEUS   When some reality
           Seems to us insoluble

A story can turn it
Into a new reality.

AGAMEMNON You pretended to be mad
Before you came to Aulis;
Now you are truly mad;
Poor Ajax was saner
When he slew the sheep.
We are not on some wild venture
Mistold by old Peleus
Of things that never were
Because they never could have been,
But at the end of a war
Which both sides are sick of.

ODYSSEUS Is your mind too small to conceive
That mixture of cunning and courage
Which at times can change the world?

AGAMEMNON You're a clever man, Odysseus,
But you're caught in the delusion
That to win in some contest
Is the greatest thing of all.
I suppose you learned the habit
When you won the golden laurel wreath
For boxing at Olympus.

ODYSSEUS It was living leaf, not gold.

AGAMEMNON That boy is right, Odysseus;
He sees what I've always seen,
That you live by lies and trickery
Debasing all we have fought for.
You do not care about Helen;
You want to destroy a city
That is noble and beautiful
And full of innocent people.
There's no need now to destroy it:
To try is the act of a traitor.

ODYSSEUS Do not say that, Agamemnon.

AGAMEMNON It is treachery and treason
Against your own commander,
And it won't be for the first time.

ODYSSEUS   I have never been treacherous.

AGAMEMNON   What words would you prefer?

ODYSSEUS   Palamedes' death still troubling you?

AGAMEMNON   Yes, Odysseus, it troubles me.

ODYSSEUS   He was tried and convicted
Of attempting to betray the camp
To Priam. As his friend
Your position was a hard one
But that is no justification
For insulting me now.

AGAMEMNON   Yes, it is time to say it:
(*To audience*)   It was Odysseus
Who betrayed Palamedes
And I know why he did so.
When Paris died his father
Wanted to end the war
And with Palamedes' support
I could have made peace with Priam.
But Odysseus loathed him because
He was wiser and abler than he is,
So he planted a bag of gold
And a letter forged by some Trojan
In Palamedes' tent
As if they came from Priam
As a reward for betraying the camp.

ODYSSEUS   Palamedes lied when we questioned him
And it suited you to believe him.
Yet he never dared to say so
Either to me or the Council.

AGAMEMNON   Because I had no proof of it.

ODYSSEUS   And you have no proof now.
You kept quiet because you feared
The Council would replace you.

AGAMEMNON   I knew that it was true
Because I knew both of you.

ODYSSEUS   And I know why you have never
Even tried to take the city.

Tell truth, Agamemnon:
Long ago you made some promise
To your wife to protect it;
That is the real treason.

AGAMEMNON   I promised, as we all did,
To rescue my wife's sister.
The taking of the city
Has never been our war-aim.

ODYSSEUS   You talk like a woman.
Either we take it quickly
And your brother gets his wife back
Or we die here on the beaches.

AGAMEMNON   Enough of this, Odysseus.
I shall go and tell the Council
What I have agreed with Priam;
I shall then go into Troy
With the tokens of Hesione
And return to the camp with Helen
And we can all go home.

ODYSSEUS   Don't do it, Agamemnon,
You will be humiliated.
I do not want that.

AGAMEMNON   If you try to prevent me
I will have you stoned
As you stoned Palamedes.   (*)

(*Trumpets sound. Re-enter PELEUS and*
SOLDIERS with armour)

PELEUS   To your posts, it's begun!
They are climbing into the Horse.

AGAMEMNON   Who gave the order?

PELEUS   Your brother and the Kings.
When you brought back Athene's image
They knew what must be done;
Menelaus led them himself
And our bravest men climbed after him;
Even my grandson tried to
But his father's shield was too heavy.

O it is glorious!
All the camp is swarming
As my Myrmidons used to do
In the days when they were ants.
Tired fires are doused
And our ships are crammed with ash-spears
Like a fleet of porcupines.

AGAMEMNON   I shall stop them.

PELEUS   No, they know
Who really leads the army.

AGAMEMNON   Odysseus, come with me.

PELEUS   I've seen it all before:
An army's like a woman,
Moody, perverse and changeable;
It can happen in a moment.
There is only one problem;
Your cousin Sinon's drunk.

ODYSSEUS   That's serious.

AGAMEMNON   That is serious;
We must call off your plan.

PELEUS   No, it's only excitement.
We've thrown him in the sea;
He'll be fine by tomorrow morning.

ODYSSEUS   Fetch the boy, I have a use for him.

PELEUS   I'll fetch him. Now I feel
The old tingle in my veins:
There is no greater joy
Than to live through each moment
The night before a battle!

ODYSSEUS   The boy will be needed
Much more than I thought.
There's no more to be said;
You know that, Agamemnon.   (*)

(*PELEUS goes with the SOLDIERS.*
ODYSSEUS and AGAMEMNON arm
themselves)

(*To Agamemnon*)   But in one thing I agree with you;
                    The moods of Poseidon
                    Are at best uncertain.

AGAMEMNON   Is that why your engine
                    Is dedicated to him?

ODYSSEUS   It was, but I've changed it.

AGAMEMNON   The inscription?

ODYSSEUS   It now bears
                    The name of Athene.

AGAMEMNON   'To her who brings victory'?

ODYSSEUS   '...We dedicate this offering
                    To Athene in the hope
                    Of a safe return home.'

AGAMEMNON   If you change it you will anger
                    Poseidon and he will punish us
                    If we ever set sail for home.
                    I will take no part in this.

ODYSSEUS   Yes you will, because you are...decent.
                    You love your foolish brother
                    And you know that not only my plan
                    But the lives of all your comrades
                    Depend now most on you.
                    As usual it will be
                    A question of careful timing:
                    When the beacon's lit on Ilion
                    You must bring in the army quickly;
                    We cannot hold the citadel
                    For more than half an hour.

AGAMEMNON   Swear to me, Odysseus,
                    By your wife and your son whom you love
                    That if we take the city
                    You will not break your oath
                    To rescue Helen only.

ODYSSEUS   I've no wish to sack the city
                    Any more than you have.
                    If you bring in the army quickly
                    Once we have seized the citadel

What happens afterwards
Is for you to decide as General.
There can be no question
Of any needless bloodshed;
My plan depends most on you.   (*)

(PELEUS returns with NEOPTOLEMUS)

NEOPTOLEMUS   Agamemnon, you must hear me.
They have tried to stop me
From going into the Horse.
You must tell them –

AGAMEMNON   Be quiet,
I am speaking with Odysseus.

NEOPTOLEMUS   Have you forgotten the prophecy?
Troy cannot fall without me.

ODYSSEUS   We have not forgotten.

AGAMEMNON   Swear to me, Odysseus,
No violence will be used
Against any Trojan woman
Or any of their children.

ODYSSEUS   I swear it.

NEOPTOLEMUS   I also.

PELEUS   Such words are meaningless;
Always were, always will be.

NEOPTOLEMUS   The General is right.

PELEUS   Woman-talk, wife-talk.

ODYSSEUS   Do not mock him, Peleus.
The minds of all of us
Will be on our wives tonight.
Launch the ships, Agamemnon.

AGAMEMNON   Keep the old one out of the way
And the boy out of mischief.
Remember, Odysseus,
That the gods are apt to punish
Those who become too proud
Or too pleased with their own cunning.
Farewell.

ODYSSEUS	Farewell, Agamemnon. (*)

(AGAMEMNON goes)

NEOPTOLEMUS	Give me my father's arms.
ODYSSEUS	When you've fulfilled the prophecy.
NEOPTOLEMUS	How can I without arms?
ODYSSEUS	By an action which no one But you can undertake
NEOPTOLEMUS	Tell me what it is.
ODYSSEUS	Neoptolemus, 'New Soldier': The name suggests that you Must become one in some new way.
PELEUS	Excellent, but how?
NEOPTOLEMUS	Show me how!
PELEUS	Don't interrupt. What's in your mind, Odysseus?
ODYSSEUS	I fear that on one point The General may be right: If Sinon's drunk, old Priam May see through our whole plan Your task will be to persuade them: To take the great Horse in.
NEOPTOLEMUS	You want me to lie again.
ODYSSEUS	I want you to tell a story To uphold another story.
PELEUS	Good.
NEOPTOLEMUS	I will not do As you made me do on Lemnos.
ODYSSEUS	It got us what you wanted, The great bow of Heracles
PELEUS	And all the army honoured you. Now the prize is Troy itself.
NEOPTOLEMUS	How can I speak to Priam? He will know who I am.
ODYSSEUS	You must use another name.

NEOPTOLEMUS	If I did it would be a lie.
ODYSSEUS	Do you call it a lie When you tell someone a story?
NEOPTOLEMUS	Not if it's a true one.
PELEUS	But can one ever tell?
NEOPTOLEMUS	Sometimes but not always.
ODYSSEUS	Suppose that you told something Which you had already heard, You would be telling truly The thing that you'd heard told.
NEOPTOLEMUS	Don't play with words.
ODYSSEUS	When Sinon tells Priam What Calchas has prophesied Will his words be a lie Or simply a quotation?
PELEUS	If Calchas has said it It's no lie to repeat it.
NEOPTOLEMUS	Where are you leading me?
ODYSSEUS	Often when Calchas prophesies He does not speak his own words But those of the god inside him.
PELEUS	True.
ODYSSEUS	And can we deny That a god's words are true words?
PELEUS	We'd be rash, though we might.
NEOPTOLEMUS	What is all this to me?
ODYSSEUS	You too shall be bound To a stake on the sea-shore. When Priam has questioned Sinon He will come and question you also. Calchas shall tell you a story And you shall merely quote him.
NEOPTOLEMUS	I will not do that.
PELEUS	Odysseus, your plan Is ingenious and daring

	As your plans always are,
	But I spy a fatal flaw.
ODYSSEUS	No plan is flawless.
PELEUS	The Trojans know our customs;
	When we make a sacrifice
	It is always of a female.
ODYSSEUS	He shall say that since there were
	No women in our camp
	The blood of two males
	Was required by Athene
	As fitting compensation.
PELEUS	That would be helpful;
	I will have a word with Calchas.
NEOPTOLEMUS	You are both madmen.
ODYSSEUS	If you want to be a soldier
	You'll obey your commanders.
PELEUS	There is no alternative.
	Ha, wait, there is!
	One that will work on Priam
	Better than botched words
	From Sinon or a boy.
NEOPTOLEMUS	I am not a boy.
PELEUS	Precisely.
ODYSSEUS	Take us with you, old one.

(*PELEUS unties the bundle he has brought to AGAMEMNON*)

PELEUS	He shall go in Hesione's garments:
	It will be an exploit
	Worthy of Heracles.
NEOPTOLEMUS	I am going into the Horse.
PELEUS	Wait! You have just said
	You are not a boy. It's true;
	You're in between man and boy,
	So why not be a girl?
NEOPTOLEMUS	Stop him, he is senile.

ODYSSEUS   Let us consider this
Without speaking personally.
The crux is the mind of Priam.
He is subtle and skilful
In searching the minds of men
But it's said he is soft
When he looks in the eyes of women.
He would trust a girl's words
More easily than a boy's.

NEOPTOLEMUS   I am neither boy nor girl;
I am the son of Achilles.
I will take no part in a plot
Built on lies and pretences.

PELEUS   Don't talk like that
To senior commanders.

NEOPTOLEMUS   I won't because I cannot.

PELEUS   What's so hard about it?
Many boys at times pretend
To be girls just as a game.
If they're pretty, as you are,
They don't have to pretend;
People take them as they are.
I was confused myself once;
I was about to have her
When I found that she wasn't.

ODYSSEUS   Peleus –

PELEUS   He's being childish.

If you want to be a man
You must first be a girl:
Clear, simple, logical.

ODYSSEUS   It is not required of you
That you should become one,
Merely that you should act one.

NEOPTOLEMUS   What is acting?

PELEUS   That is a question
Your father asked me once.
It means...

NEOPTOLEMUS	Lying.
ODYSSEUS	It means skill,
	Skill in separating
	The truth of your acting
	From what you are or think you are.
PELEUS	Look at Calchas, when he's masked
	And the god speaks within him:
	He is still himself yet not himself.
NEOPTOLEMUS	Give me my father's armour!
PELEUS	Stop whining.
ODYSSEUS	Here are your orders:
	You shall say you're Achilles' child
	And that you have been treated
	Vilely by Odysseus
	Whom you hate and despise.
	Is that lying?
NEOPTOLEMUS	No.
PELEUS	If you're lost for words
	Go on quoting Calchas.
NEOPTOLEMUS	I cannot change my shape
	Or be other than I am.
ODYSSEUS	What is this? All who are human
	Change their shape every hour.
PELEUS	Your grandmother did it
	Every other second.
NEOPTOLEMUS	No, Odysseus, no!
	You can twist words but not me.
	I have heard how your lies
	Made them kill Palamedes.
	To me you are despicable.
ODYSSEUS	Good, your anger's good.
PELEUS	He is just like his father.
ODYSSEUS	Now channel it and use it.
NEOPTOLEMUS	I will be no part of this.

PELEUS

It is natural to be frightened
Before one's first battle.

ODYSSEUS

I don't think he is frightened.
When I went into Troy
I did not fear to die
But the shame of being dressed as a beggar.

PELEUS

It is much less shameful
To go as a King's daughter
Than a beggar, Neoptolemus.
Take this, you have your orders.

(*Presents the bundle*)

NEOPTOLEMUS

You are not our General;
I am going to Agamemnon.

ODYSSEUS

If you refuse to do this
Out of pride and stubbornness
You will fall into the same evil
As your father did before you.

PELEUS

What will they say of you
Far off in the future
If the Wooden Horse is burned
And all your father fought for
Was wasted by his son?

ODYSSEUS

If you do it, Neoptolemus,
You shall have your father's armour.

NEOPTOLEMUS

If I am to do it
You shall give me more than that.

ODYSSEUS

Time to bargain.

PELEUS

That is fair.

NEOPTOLEMUS

Both of you shall swear
Never to reveal to the army
Nor your friends nor to the poets
What my part was in taking the city.

PELEUS

That's fair too.

ODYSSEUS

We swear it.
Let us go.

NEOPTOLEMUS	Not so fast.
	You had yourself whipped, Odysseus,
	Before you played the beggar-man.
	If I am to say truly
	That I was to be sacrificed
	Calchas himself shall give me
	A wound in the shoulder
	With the sacrificial knife.
PELEUS	Very good.
ODYSSEUS	Agreed.
PELEUS	You have taught him much, Odysseus.
NEOPTOLEMUS	One thing more; when the Trojan women
	Are shared among our Kings
	I shall have the choice
	Of two from the Royal House.
ODYSSEUS	Two?
NEOPTOLEMUS	One for my myself
	And one for my father.
ODYSSEUS	You shall have them when you've earned them.
NEOPTOLEMUS	Swear it.
ODYSSEUS	So I do.
NEOPTOLEMUS	You shall hold him to it, Peleus,
	Or he will twist his words
	Just as he did with Hecuba.
ODYSSEUS	I'll not twist them, little warrior.
	When the fleet has set sail
	And no one can see you
	Sinon will come and bind you.

(*He starts to go*)

PELEUS	Wait. One thing which troubles me.
ODYSSEUS	What now?
PELEUS	Your dedication
	Of the Horse to Athene
	Is all wrong, it won't work

On Priam for one moment:
It is unsound divinity.

ODYSSEUS   It is done, and it will.

PELEUS   One should never make an offering
To the wrong god. Since it asks
For a safe journey home
It clearly should be made
To Hermes, God of Travellers.

ODYSSEUS   Prepare the boy, Peleus,
One word must rule us now:
Necessity. Embrace it.   (*)

(*ODYSSEUS goes. PELEUS places the bundle*
in front of NEOPTOLEMUS and undoes it)

NEOPTOLEMUS   I cannot do it, Grandfather.

PELEUS   You agreed, get on with it.

NEOPTOLEMUS   If I do it will destroy me.

(*NEOPTOLEMUS begins to weep*)

PELEUS   You are thinking perhaps of Pentheus?
He was stupid and arrogant
But you are much more intelligent
And prettier than he was.
It is good that you should weep;
Priam will find it touching.

NEOPTOLEMUS   I do not fear to die
But the shame I should have to live with
For the rest of my mortal life.

PELEUS   Did your father make this fuss
When his mother hid him on Scyros?
Have you forgotten the tales
You have heard of the old heroes?
Did Leucippus or Hymen
Or Heracles himself
Hesitate for one moment
When they did as you must do?
It is told how Zeus himself
Once turned into a girl
To win some woman he wanted.

Once the Horse is inside Troy
You can take any girl you fancy.

NEOPTOLEMUS That is not what I want.

PELEUS Then you should be ashamed:
Have you never had a girl?

(*NEOPTOLEMUS shakes his head*)

You shock me; you must start at once:
This dress might have been made for you.

NEOPTOLEMUS I do not want a dress!

PELEUS Put it on.

NEOPTOLEMUS I want my armour.

PELEUS This is now your armour:
It looks frail but it will give you
More strength and power than a spear.

NEOPTOLEMUS You're not sane.

PELEUS When a beautiful girl
Is lightly dressed and painted
And sparkling with rich jewels
It is true that she is vulnerable
And yet she is stronger
Than the warrior who woos her
For she makes that warrior soft
And so does as she will with him;
I speak from experience.

NEOPTOLEMUS I cannot lie.

PELEUS Let me remind you
Of a greater truth than yours.
It is told that in the beginning
The Wind wooed the Darkness
And she laid a silver egg
And out of it stepped Eros
And set all things in motion.
Eros is a perfect creature
For he is both male and female.
Sometimes he roars like a lion,
Sometimes he bellows and snorts

Just as I once heard the Minotaur;
Sometimes he hisses and sometimes
He bleats like a lamb; in all this
He is very much as you are;
That is why the tale is so useful.
It reminds all men and women
That they each have a bit of the other
Inside them. Accept it
And you'll find that ever after
You will be much more of a man.

NEOPTOLEMUS You can always twist old tales
Into any shape that suits you.

PELEUS It is time to change your shape
And endure the needfull ordeal
That the gods set all young warriors.

(*The two streams have begun to trickle*)

Look, do you see the streams?
They were dried up and dead this morning;
Now they've come to life again.

(*He drinks from them*)

O it tastes so fresh and sweet.
Drink, and it will free you
Of all your confusion and fears.

NEOPTOLEMUS What's the point? Whatever I do,
Priam will see through me.

(*He tastes the stream*)

PELEUS No, you'll go into that cave
And then you will surrender
To what is within you,
And your mind and your heart
Will grow as soft as a girl's.

NEOPTOLEMUS I am not going to do it.

PELEUS What we need most is some woman
To help with the dress and the paint.

NEOPTOLEMUS There are no women left in the camp;
It can't be done, Grandfather.

PELEUS

My wife could do it, of course;
She is skilled in the changing of shapes
But she never comes out of the sea now
So I'd better help you myself.

NEOPTOLEMUS

All that you are good at
Is pulling girls' clothes off.
Go away, you disgust me.

PELEUS

Go into that cave and think;
Think of your hopes of fame,
Of your father and of the army;
Think deep and wait in the darkness;
You may find that a prayer to the gods
May soothe you and even be helpful.

NEOPTOLEMUS

Truth, I love truth
More than my own life!
I know that if I lie
I shall lose my way:
Lies destroy, I know it.

PELEUS

Much truth may be found in caves.
I love them, it was in one
By the sea-shore in Thessaly
That I first encountered my wife.
Maybe she'll come and help you
So that when you come out in the day-light
You will find that you are in
Another world, the old one,
Where the heroes did such things
As men now think impossible.
Bellerophon, my friend,
Dared to tread the sky on an air-horse.
If you too have the courage
You also may become
A member of that world.

NEOPTOLEMUS

What was the name of that world?

PELEUS

We who were in it
Had no need to name it.
Time to go in, New Soldier.

(NEOPTOLEMUS drinks and goes towards the cave)

NEOPTOLEMUS When they ask me who I am
What name can I tell them truly?

PELEUS Use the name your father took
When his mother hid him on Scyros,
'Pyrrha', the same name as yours,
So you won't be lying when you say it.

NEOPTOLEMUS It means 'rage'.

PELEUS So it's a true name. (*)

(NEOPTOLEMUS cries out and goes in. PELEUS puts the bundle in after him and turns)

Ha! She is here! I sense it:
I can always tell when my love
Comes up out of the sea-deeps;
But I wonder what shape she will take:
A crab, a rock, a fish?
Where are you now, my darling?

(Enter AGAMEMNON)

AGAMEMNON What are you doing, Peleus?
Odysseus has told me your plan.
Where is the boy?

PELEUS In the cave.

AGAMEMNON Go now and join the ships.
If the Trojans find you here
They'll remember what you did
With Heracles to their city.

PELEUS But the boy —

AGAMEMNON I will bind him
As soon as he is ready,
And then we'll set sail for Tenedos.

PELEUS Why are you weeping, man?

AGAMEMNON Because I have just taken
My last farewell of my brother.

Go to the ships; I must offer
A prayer to the gods.

PELEUS   I am going.
If Heracles was still living
All this would not have been necessary.

(He goes)

AGAMEMNON   Boy, you can come out now:
Odysseus has told me
What the old man has planned.
It is not going to happen;
Neither you nor my brother
Nor the rest are going to die.
I love truth as you do,
So I shall go to Priam
And give him what you are wearing
And set my mark to true peace.
It is not going to happen!   (*)

(A WOMAN comes out of the cave)

WOMAN   Don't shout, Agamemnon,
It will happen as Zeus wills.

(AGAMEMNON is bewildered)

AGAMEMNON   You are fair.

WOMAN   Of course I am.

AGAMEMNON   I think that as you are
You might work on Priam.

WOMAN   Of course I could if I wished to.
Do I please you, Agamemnon?

AGAMEMNON   There's no need for that dress now.
Take it off, and go in again.

WOMAN   Take it off? You speak like Peleus;
I wear what I please.

AGAMEMNON   You speak like a woman
But you must not become one.

WOMAN   I am not a woman.

AGAMEMNON   That is what I'm saying.

WOMAN	I am a demi-goddess.
AGAMEMNON	You must stop this, you're a boy.
WOMAN	That is one shape
	Which I have never taken.
	You are foolish, Agamemnon,
	If you cannot distinguish
	A boy from a sea-nymph.
AGAMEMNON	Thetis...
	Thetis the foolish one:
	Why have you come back?
	No one has seen you
	Since your son Achilles died.
THETIS	I have come to help his son.
AGAMEMNON	Your help will destroy him
	As it destroyed Achilles.
THETIS	It is true he will be destroyed
	But it will not be tomorrow.
AGAMEMNON	I remember, you're a prophetess;
	Help me now by telling me –
THETIS	Help you? Their General?
	Till you came the sea was sweet to me
	And the sands here were golden
	And glorious to dance on.
	Now your war-hordes have made them
	As stinking foul as Tartarus.
	You have filled my lovely Ocean
	With garbage and dead soldiers.
	My grottoes are polluted,
	My dolphins are dying
	And can dance with me no longer;
	Even the greedy lobsters
	Are tired of eating seamen
	And old Oceanus
	Himself cannot sleep
	For fear of being crushed
	By broken ships and chariots.
	We that were denizens

Beneath the purple waves
Long before you earthlings
Or the coming of the gods
Live now in your war-horde's cess-pit.
In the time of Deucalion
When humans once before
Marred poor Mother Earth,
Zeus and Poseidon
Had to flood the world to cleanse her
And rest her for a while.
You forget that, don't you?
You will be punished:
The gods may be cruel
But humans bring more sorrow.

AGAMEMNON   You have cause for grief
But if all that is prophesied
Were true, human life
Would be unendurable.

THETIS   It is so; prophets merely
Remind human-kind
Of how it really is.
That is why I tried
To prevent Achilles living;
I knew he would be wretched.
Better not to have life
Than think you can be happy.

AGAMEMNON   I think it and I strive for it
With all my blood and bone.

THETIS   That costs, Agamemnon.

AGAMEMNON   I know.

THETIS   But it buys little.

AGAMEMNON   Whatever the cost
I will go on striving.

THETIS   That is why you will give
The gods so much pleasure
I too tried to make
My son Achilles happy.

AGAMEMNON   Your prophecy destroyed him.
             While I have life I mean
             To fight the lies of prophets.
             Troy must not fall.

THETIS   Why not?
             Why is it important?
             Why do humans think
             When some rock falls from the mountains
             Or the ground quakes and opens
             And crushes some crowded city
             That Gaia's the worse for it?

AGAMEMNON   You are not human, sea-nymph.

THETIS   No, I am thankful for it.

AGAMEMNON   Will my brother die tomorrow?

THETIS   He will die when it's his time.
             The Fates have measured out
             The life-thread of all of you
             And cut your cloth already.

AGAMEMNON   How can you be so indifferent
             To human creatures, sea-nymph?
             Help me to save your grandson
             As you tried to save your son.

THETIS   Do not remind me;
             You will make me weep.

AGAMEMNON   But it's said that you often
             Persuaded Zeus to spare him.

THETIS   So I did, Zeus loved me;
             I knew how to change his mind.

AGAMEMNON   Then make him change it now.

THETIS   I can do that no longer.

AGAMEMNON   Why not? Tell me why.

THETIS   Zeus has two great jars
             Where he loves to store his nectar.
             In one there are evils
             And in the other, blessings;
             For some there is singing,

For others there is pain.
The night before Achilles died
I went up to him on Olympus.
Zeus was sitting between the urns
And Apollo sat and watched him.
When I saw his mind was fixed
I asked him as he loved me
To give my son Achilles
Everlasting fame.
He did not look at me
But answered very coldly
That the fame of Achilles
Did not lie in his gift
Nor any of the gods
Nor any living humans
But rather that the smoke
Of the funeral pyres of heroes
Only lingers in the nostrils
Of singers yet to come
Who breathe it in and out again
As they turn it into tales.

AGAMEMNON   But will they tell truly?

THETIS   'True': that is a word
Humans have invented
To give them a sense of meaning;
Immortals do not use it
Nor do sea-nymphs understand it.

AGAMEMNON   There must be truth if there's to be
Any certainty or meaning.

THETIS   The only thing that's certain
Is the shift and turn of the tides.
But can you map or fix
That verge you call the sea-shore?
What is the truth of that?
Is it sea or land?
Tide out: time for children
To build citadels of sand

Or men to carve wise words on.
Tide in: all gone, no words,
No sandy citadels
And the verge is mine and Poseidon's.
Tide out: time again
For more golden sand to play on
And for poets to scratch tales on.
For those of us who have seen
All the tides that ever were
Since the birth of the Ocean
Our sense of truth and time
Is not the same as humans'.

(*PELEUS is heard calling*)

That is the voice
Of the man most hateful to me:
Time to change my shape again.

AGAMEMNON   Wait, sea-nymph!

THETIS   Why should I?
In five thousand years
Or five hundred thousand
What will it matter?   (*)

(*She disappears. Re-enter PELEUS*)

PELEUS   Son of Atreus, come!
All the army is waiting.
Ha! She's here, I smell her:
Where are you, my darling?
What shape have you taken now?

AGAMEMNON   Be quiet and come with me;
I am cancelling the order.

PELEUS   What order?

AGAMEMNON   The war-fleet
Will not leave the beaches.

PELEUS   It has, half our ships
Are already out at sea
And their brave prows are dancing
On the choppy road to Tenedos.

AGAMEMNON   I shall stop them.

PELEUS   You're too late;
             Kings shouldn't pray or talk too much
             When their troops are in action.

AGAMEMNON   Who gave the order?

PELEUS   I did, in your name.

AGAMEMNON   Stupid, evil old man...

PELEUS   You must go now and lead the army.
             Mass landings are tricky
             But everyone is happy
             Because at last it's happening.
             It is time to get your sea-legs:
             Put that fire out and hurry.

             (*He goes*)

AGAMEMNON   O my Iphigenia,
             O my darling in the darkness,
             Is this what you died for?
             Listen to me, Priam!
             I am calling to you
             High up there in Ilion!
             You have said our minds are as one;
             Listen and you'll hear me!

             (*He calls out. His cry is echoed in the distance*)

             Hesione is dead;
             Search the Horse and save your city;
             Burn it but spare my brother
             That he may take Helen home.
             For the rest, do your will,
             But first destroy Odysseus!   (*)

             (*He goes. The POET re-enters and the CHORUS come forward*)

POET   And that is how it was
             And how Peleus played his part in it
             And how they sailed to Tenedos.

(CHORUS)	We don't believe a word of it!
POET	Then tell me a better story To cover the facts as we know them.
(CHORUS)	Priam would see through Pyrrhus Even quicker than Sinon.
POET	It's easy to criticise When you're not taking part.
(CHORUS)	You said that we couldn't.
POET	You could if you went into it.
(CHORUS)	Do you mean into Troy?
POET	If you felt inclined.
(CHORUS)	If we went in We would soon learn the truth of it... — We could change the whole story Just as you have.
POET	Very good: Then just drink of the streams.
(CHORUS)	Yes, if we didn't drink That would be cheating.
POET	Drink and go in then. You will find that Trojan dresses Will make you look even finer Than the ones you wore in Scyros.

(*They drink of the streams*)

Of course there'll be complications.
If there weren't, human life
Would be quite unendurable,
Especially for poets.

(CHORUS)	We are going in! — We shall make our own story!

(*Music*)

POET	When you go in You will all look so pretty;

If you tell the truth to Priam
You may yet save the city.

(*CHORUS go into the cave for the first time*)

I had better go and help them...
Of truth I have great pity.

(*He follows the CHORUS in*)

Play 5
PRIAM

APPOLLO'S SHRINE AT THYMBRIA

CAST

First Woman	HECUBA
Second Woman	CASSANDRA
Third Woman	ANDROMACHE
Fourth Woman	POLYXENA
First Man	PRIAM
Second Man	(–)
Third Man	(–)
Fourth Man	NEOPTOLEMUS

CHORUS

(Outside the shrine of Thymbrian Apollo. Singing in the distance. The fire is out but still smoking)

CASSANDRA

Do you remember me?
Cassandra, Priam's daughter.
All is happening now
As it happened long ago
In my mind: is it possible
That because I foresaw it
I have somehow made it happen?

I can speak to you now because
Though you are yet to come
We share the same knowledge,
Though only a part of it.
This is where my parents brought me
And my brother when we were babies.
They feasted here all day
In honour of Apollo;
By nightfall both were drunk,
So they reeled back to bed
And forgot to take us with them.
In the morning they found us asleep
And the two sacred serpents
Were licking our genitals.
That is how we became prophets:
Because they forgot us,
Because they left us out.

When I saw what was to come
I tried to forget it,
So I went to the stream of Lethe
But by mistake I drank
Of the cold stream of Memory.
Ever since I have remembered
All that is going to happen,
But no-one believes me.

See how the sacred serpents
Twist and twine together.
Listen to what they're whispering
And mark the words they say:

'...The First Things and the then things
And the things that must follow...'
It is time for the Horse:
I curse you, Apollo.

(*Three or four TROJAN WOMEN run on,
some dancing. These are marked CHORUS A,
as some of the CHORUS (marked B) only
appear later*)

(CHORUS A)　　Ai... Ai... Ai!
– Gone – They've gone for ever!
– The black ships have gone
– Nothing's left but this stench
 And broken ships on the beaches
– Ten years of siege are over
 And their war-fires are all out!
– When the beaches have been cleared
 Of filth and dead horses
 We shall dance on our golden sands!

– Look, here's a flower!
– Not possible – Yes I found it
 By the entrance of this shrine
– Soon the grass will be green
 And the burned trees will bud again
 In the grove of Apollo
– Look there, in the cave-mouth
 The sacred serpents are back
– Apollo is our friend again!

– I hear bird-song – I hear music
– It is coming from the Horse.　　　　　(*)

(*Enter the rest of the CHORUS*)

(CHORUS B)　　What are you doing here?
　　　　　　　Why are you not at the Horse?

(CHORUS A)　　We came here to offer
　　　　　　　A libation to Apollo.

(CHORUS B)　　You must come with us quickly;
　　　　　　　They are questioning some man
　　　　　　　Who was left behind to be sacrificed
– Sinon's told us all their plans!

225

	—	They knew that we'd beaten them So Calchas told them to make A monstrous human sacrifice And leave the Horse as an offering Hoping they'd get home safely.
(CHORUS A)		They are beasts, not men.
(CHORUS B)		Cassandra's tried to spoil it.
(CHORUS A)		Of course — What has she done?
(CHORUS B)		She said there are armed men inside.
(CHORUS A)		That is not possible.

(CHORUS B)

No, but Laocoon,
Chief Priest of Poseidon
And of Apollo too,
Hurled a spear in its side to test it
— Then Cassandra screamed
That she heard the clang of armour
And cried out that we must burn it
— We all shouted her down
But we saw that it worried Laocoon
— He has gone to the sea-shore
To offer a bull to Poseidon
— While everyone is waiting
They are decking it with flowers.
— Let's go and join them
— It is over! It is over!   (*)

*(Music grows in the distance. They see
CASSANDRA)*

(CHORUS A)

— No, it's not, look who's there
— I wish they'd taken her with them
— No more prophesies, Cassandra.

CASSANDRA

What is the use of words?
Apollo, I hate you:
Leave me alone today.

(CHORUS)

You would have been happier
If you'd slept with the god when he wanted
you

Like any decent girl

	– We have suffered more from you Than the whole host of the War-Kings – You deserve to be punished.
CASSANDRA	All my life the god has punished me.
(CHORUS)	You were wrong and now you know it – Because you are unhappy You want everyone else to be – We have pitied her too long – Let's tear her prophet's robes off And throw her into the sea: The salt will wash the paint off And put an end to her screaming!

– We have suffered more from you
Than the whole host of the War-Kings
– You deserve to be punished.

CASSANDRA   All my life the god has punished me.

(CHORUS)   You were wrong and now you know it
– Because you are unhappy
You want everyone else to be
– We have pitied her too long
– Let's tear her prophet's robes off
And throw her into the sea:
The salt will wash the paint off
And put an end to her screaming!   (*)

*(They attack her. PRIAM enters from the
sea-shore, angry)*

PRIAM   Stop. This is the shrine
Of our city's chief defender.
I came here to offer
A libation to Apollo
And I find you showing violence
To his priestess the very day
That it seems the war is over.
Is this what we have fought for,
That our women should beat our women?
When they were here the Amazons
Were gentler than you are.

(CHORUS)   My lord, we are sorry
– She spoke ill of Apollo.

PRIAM   But what if she is right?

(CHORUS)   She never is nor has been
– The black ships have gone.

PRIAM   How can you be so sure
They aren't hiding behind Tenedos?
You should ask yourselves some questions:
Did you know that Sinon
Is the cousin of Odysseus
Who stole Athene's image?
Can you tell me why
The Horse is so huge?

	Could it be because It is bigger than our gates? Above all, why have they gone When their General and I Have agreed upon peace terms?
(CHORUS)	My lord, we have been hasty.
PRIAM	Nothing in this world Is as simple as it seems. Listen to what I've done And what I mean to do: I have set guards round the Horse And ordered sacred wood To be fetched from the mountains And laid underneath it; If the offering is peaceful We must not offend Athene.
(CHORUS)	Do you mean to burn it?
PRIAM	If need be, but first I will smoke it: If there are warriors inside They will not stay there long. Go back into the city And wait quietly in your homes Till Laocoon has sacrificed And searched a bull's entrails. When that's done I will decide What to do. Away with you. (*)

(CHORUS A and B go out separately. PRIAM looks out to sea)

CASSANDRA	You know the truth: burn it.
PRIAM	I will know when I have smoked it.
CASSANDRA	The smoke may blind your eyes.
PRIAM	The truth is behind Tenedos.
CASSANDRA	Since you know the truth, burn it.
PRIAM	I guess but am not yet certain.
CASSANDRA	Search deep and you'll lose your way.
PRIAM	To burn it at once would be rash.

CASSANDRA	No, you're afraid of Hecuba.
PRIAM	No, I fear Athene.
	We've offended her already
	By losing her sacred image;
	Much care is needed here.
CASSANDRA	I fear you, Priam; you have told
	The truth to those women already.
	Do not do as you've always done
	And put off great decisions
	Till you think you see more clearly;
	That always leads to sorrow.
PRIAM	I am only waiting
	For a little wood-smoke.
CASSANDRA	You waited fifty years before
	You tried to rescue Hesione.
PRIAM	I dreamed of her last night.
CASSANDRA	And the night before Achilles died
	He dreamed that he lay with Helen.
	Burn it, old man. Now.
PRIAM	I have made mistakes before;
	I will not make one now.
CASSANDRA	Troy will die tonight.
PRIAM	Only if I let it.
	Though you have often angered me
	You and I agree in much
	And are dearest to me of the children
	Who are still among the living.
	We dread the same horrors
	But we voice our dread differently.
	I speak to the people quietly;
	You must try to do so too
	And not let them call you
	Screamer or Doom-girl.
CASSANDRA	I cannot be as you are,
	However much I long to be;
	When the god speaks inside me

	You know I cannot silence him Unless you gag and bind me.
PRIAM	I do not wish to do that, Not today, Cassandra.
CASSANDRA	Priam, I am speaking now Gently and quietly, Not with the voice of Apollo But of what you heard yourself: The clang of arms and armour.
PRIAM	Yes, that sound in the Horse's belly... What it was is not yet certain.
CASSANDRA	Burn it, then it will be.
PRIAM	But suppose it was some god's voice?
CASSANDRA	Yes, Hades.
PRIAM	Do not name him.
CASSANDRA	Death is here, I smell it, And out at sea...

(*A sound far off*)

	Look, Father, Do you see?
PRIAM	I see nothing.
CASSANDRA	It is there, plain and palpable. Don't you see what is coming towards us?
PRIAM	It must be the ship Which is carrying Hesione Just as Agamemnon promised.
CASSANDRA	No, it is like the monster Which came here long ago To devour your sister.
PRIAM	Impossible.
CASSANDRA	Look again, you must see it.
PRIAM	I see the water thrashing With a shape coming towards us. Go and inform Laocoon; He will know what it means.

CASSANDRA   I know what it means:
             It means it's going to happen.

             (*She goes*)

PRIAM   Has Hesione has come back?
             Is it so? Is it possible?
             In the treadmill of time
             One law is certain:
             Good turns to evil
             And evil turns to good;
             But which comes first and when
             Is a harder thing to fathom.   (*)

             (*POLYXENA and CHORUS B enter from the
             horse*)

POLYXENA   Father, Sinon has told us
             Something else.

(CHORUS)   Something strange.

PRIAM   What is it, Polyxena?

(CHORUS)   He is not the only one
             That the War-kings left behind.

POLYXENA   She is here in Apollo's cave.

PRIAM   She? – Who is she?

POLYXENA   Sinon has explained to us
             Why they spared his life.
             Calchas said he was unclean
             For a sacrifice, and Athene
             Demanded a purer offering.

(CHORUS)   A virgin.

PRIAM   A virgin?

(CHORUS)   For Virgin Athene.

PRIAM   Some woman from the war-camp?

POLYXENA   Only one was still left there,
             Some child of Achilles,
             So they whipped Sinon and freed him
             And bound this girl in his place.

231

(CHORUS)	To a stake on the sea-shore
—	The very one your sister
	Was tied to long ago.
PRIAM	The same? On the sea-shore?
POLYXENA	Odysseus bound her
	And Calchas took the knife
	But just as he struck at her
	Zeus hurled a thunder-bolt,
	Poseidon stirred up the sea
	And the black ships tugged at their moorings
	As if they were in terror.
	All the army panicked
	And cried out, 'Let us go!
	It is clear that our offering
	Is unpleasing to the gods';
	So they all rushed into the ships
	And the War-Kings could not stop them.
(CHORUS)	And so they set sail for the West!
PRIAM	And the girl?
POLYXENA	When they'd gone
	Sinon untied her
	And she ran into this shrine.
(CHORUS)	We want to see her, Priam!
POLYXENA	I said she should be left there
	Till we had spoken to you.
PRIAM	You did well; it is clearly
	Another trick of Odysseus.
	Go in and fetch her.
(CHORUS)	We are not going in there.
PRIAM	What are you afraid of?
(CHORUS)	It is said that Achilles' ghost
	Still haunts the empty shrine. (*)

(*Enter ANDROMACHE*)

ANDROMACHE	You must come at once, Priam:
	You must come back to the Horse.

PRIAM

What is it, Andromache?

ANDROMACHE

Your soldiers have gone mad:
They are beating all the women
Who are dancing round it.

PRIAM

Why?
When I left them they were singing.

ANDROMACHE

When we tried to deck it with flowers
They flung us on the ground
And said that you had ordered
Fires to be lit beneath it.

PRIAM

Yes, to make smoke
To learn what's inside it.

ANDROMACHE

Nobody explained that!
When the women tried to stop them
Your brutes began to beat them
And one of them bound herself
To the legs of the Horse:
They whipped and kicked her, Priam.
When I told them to be more gentle
Your soldiers beat me too;
Is this what my Hector died for?
For our women to be treated
By Trojans as they would have been
If the West had won the war?

PRIAM

Fetch the girl, Polyxena.

*(POLYXENA and some of the CHORUS go
into the cave)*

Everyone has been foolish.
Didn't they hear that sound
When the spear struck the side of the Horse?

ANDROMACHE

Of course not, they were singing.

(CHORUS)

What was Laocoon,
A priest, doing with a spear?

PRIAM

He heard weapons in the Horse.

ANDROMACHE

Only the two priests heard them.

(CHORUS)

And one of them was Cassandra.

PRIAM	I have told everyone already That I will use smoke to test it.
ANDROMACHE	You didn't explain it clearly.
PRIAM	In confused situations There are always misunderstandings.
ANDROMACHE	You should not have mumbled When half of them were drunk.
PRIAM	Go and tell them to obey me.
ANDROMACHE	Tell them yourself.
PRIAM	I must first question a prisoner.
ANDROMACHE	Will you torture him as well?
PRIAM	Sinon has not been tortured.
ANDROMACHE	Everybody says so.
PRIAM	'Everybody says so': You should check the truth of rumours As I mean to do now. (*)

(*POLYXENA and CHORUS B bring in
NEOPTOLEMUS from the cave-shrine.
Underneath a cloak he is dressed and painted
for sacrifice, c.f. IPHIGENIA in Play 4*)

POLYXENA	Here she is, be gentle to her.
ANDROMACHE	Who is this?
POLYXENA	Achilles' daughter.
PRIAM	Why are her arms not tied?
POLYXENA	She is wounded, Father; We must try to stop the bleeding.
ANDROMACHE	Did Achilles have a daughter?
PRIAM	Andromache, be silent: You shall see that Priam Knows how to honour women. Girl, come closer to me And let me see your face.
POLYXENA	Don't be frightened of him.

PRIAM	I have heard Sinon's story; Now you shall tell me yours But first you must swear to answer Truly to all that I ask you.
NEOPTOLEMUS	I swear it.
POLYXENA	You must speak louder.
PRIAM	I hear her clearly.
NEOPTOLEMUS	I swear Only to speak truth to you.
PRIAM	If you lie I will know it. Are you Achilles' child?
NEOPTOLEMUS	Yes, and a suppliant.
PRIAM	Who was your mother?
NEOPTOLEMUS	Deidamia of Scyros.
PRIAM	And her father?
NEOPTOLEMUS	Lycomedes.
PRIAM	It is told that Achilles Has a son.
NEOPTOLEMUS	That is true.
ANDROMACHE	But a daughter?
NEOPTOLEMUS	I was born The same hour as he was.
POLYXENA	Then you must be his twin.
NEOPTOLEMUS	Call me what you will.
PRIAM	Why were you here in the war-camp And not at home with your mother?
NEOPTOLEMUS	A prophecy.
PRIAM	What prophecy?
NEOPTOLEMUS	That your city would not fall Unless I came to Troy.
ANDROMACHE	That is a strange prophecy.
PRIAM	What was the name of the prophet?

NEOPTOLEMUS	You should know your own son's name.
PRIAM	Was it Helenus the traitor?
NEOPTOLEMUS	Yes.
ANDROMACHE	This is unlikely.
PRIAM	And what is your name?
NEOPTOLEMUS	Pyrrha.
PRIAM	That means 'rage'.
NEOPTOLEMUS	You are wise.
ANDROMACHE	And with whom are you angry?
NEOPTOLEMUS	With Odysseus and Calchas; I hate them more than Trojans.
ANDROMACHE	Be careful what you say.
NEOPTOLEMUS	I have sworn to speak truly.
PRIAM	Why hate your own people?
NEOPTOLEMUS	For what they have done to me.
ANDROMACHE	Then why did you come here?
NEOPTOLEMUS	When my father lay dying He asked that I be sent for.
PRIAM (*To Polyxena*)	You were there, is this true?
POLYXENA	I remember him asking That his child or maybe his children Should come to his funeral.
PRIAM	Why did you stay in the war-camp When the funeral was over?
NEOPTOLEMUS	To see your city die.
PRIAM	It would seem that your hope Has not been fulfilled.
NEOPTOLEMUS	It would seem so.
ANDROMACHE	Speak more gently.
PRIAM	Sinon has told us The meaning of the Horse

And why you both were left here;
Tell us what happened next.

NEOPTOLEMUS I have lost much blood
And I need food and rest;
Take me into your house
And I'll give you the truth you ask for.

PRIAM You must answer my questions
And not make demands.

POLYXENA This is no way to treat suppliants.

ANDROMACHE It is, she is insolent.

POLYXENA That is because she's in pain.

ANDROMACHE Send her into the city;
You must go now to the Horse.

NEOPTOLEMUS If you do not trust me
Kill me now, old man;
After what has been done to me
I shall be glad to die.

PRIAM We do not kill suppliants,
Even those who speak rudely.
I've a debt to pay to your father.

ANDROMACHE What debt can you owe
To the man who killed my husband?

PRIAM When I went to Achilles' tent
The night that Hector died
Hoping to ransom his body
I was a suppliant too;
I wept and crawled and kissed his feet
And he was gentle to me.

NEOPTOLEMUS Then if you have any honour
You must pay that debt.

PRIAM I mean to.

ANDROMACHE (*To Chorus*) He will pay in his own way;
She is just how he likes them.

PRIAM Why do you speak so boldly?

NEOPTOLEMUS   How else should I speak?
               I am Achilles' child.

POLYXENA   Send her in, she is faint.

ANDROMACHE   Leave us to question her;
               She will speak more freely to women.

PRIAM   Very well, but one more question:
               What is Agamemnon doing?

NEOPTOLEMUS   I have told you as much as I can.

PRIAM   Has he sent for my sister?

NEOPTOLEMUS   Yes, she was sent for.

PRIAM   But has she come yet? Answer me.   (*)

               (*NEOPTOLEMUS pauses. CASSANDRA
               re-enters*)

               What is it, Cassandra?

CASSANDRA   Laocoon is dead on the sea-shore;
               He was preparing an offering
               To Poseidon when the sea-beast
               Came out of the waves and devoured him.

(CHORUS B)   What is she saying now?

ANDROMACHE   Why must you spoil this day?

PRIAM   Where is this creature now?

CASSANDRA   In the citadel itself.

POLYXENA   What does it mean, Father?

ANDROMACHE   Clearly Athene sent it
               When Laocoon struck the Horse
               He insulted her offering.

(CHORUS B)   Yes, it must be so.

PRIAM   That is unlikely.

               (*Re-enter CHORUS A from the city*)

(CHORUS A)   My lord!

CASSANDRA   Let these women tell you.

PRIAM   Control yourselves: what's happened?

238

(CHORUS A)	When the monster killed Laocoon We were glad that he was punished — But when it broke into the city We were frightened.
PRIAM	Where is it now?
(CHORUS A)	Curled up in Athene's temple — Hissing, snarling and roaring — It has three heads, my lord — One face makes the sounds — But one of them is smiling.
ANDROMACHE	It has come to honour Athene And to protect her temple.
(CHORUS B)	Then we too must honour it.
PRIAM	We must first know why it has come.
(CHORUS A)	Remember how when you were a boy A monster came from the sea And devoured many women — We know that it was sent By Poseidon or Apollo.
PRIAM	Yes, it was killed by Heracles.
ANDROMACHE	The world is full of monsters And every country has them; Some of them are terrible But others can be kind. Why assume that one is evil Because its shape is monstrous? We should treat beasts with reverence Until we know their nature.
(CHORUS A)	Three monsters have come to us — The first fifty years ago In the time of King Laomedon — The second was black with many heads But it sailed away last night — So this third one must be friendly.
PRIAM	That does not follow; How can you be so certain?

(CHORUS A)	Because it is curled up quietly Round the statue of the goddess Who has always been our enemy.
ANDROMACHE	It has come to protect us. Give the order, Priam, And take the Great Horse in.

(N.B. From here CHORUS A and CHORUS B become as one again)

CASSANDRA	Laocoon is dead for another reason: When he went to make a sacrifice To learn what was in the Horse He went to the wrong god.
(CHORUS)	What do you mean? – The wrong god?
CASSANDRA	Laocoon was Chief Priest Both of Poseidon and Apollo.
(CHORUS)	Why must she bring Apollo Into everything?
PRIAM	Why should Apollo Send a monster against Laocoon?
CASSANDRA	Because he broke his vow That as High Priest of this shrine He would never lie with a woman, But he lay with his wife here in secret Before the god's own image.
(CHORUS)	Unlikely.
CASSANDRA	I saw it.
(CHORUS)	She was spying on them to learn Something she needs to know about.
ANDROMACHE	Is it likely that Apollo Would kill his own priest?
CASSANDRA	Yes, it is likely.
(CHORUS)	Gag her and lock her up again.
PRIAM	No, her words may be important.
CASSANDRA	The Horse is what's important.

PRIAM	There is no need of haste; It will take nine days to fetch Sacred wood from the mountains As we did for Hector's pyre.
CASSANDRA	They have torn sacred wood From our temples already.
PRIAM	Why did my men not stop them?
CASSANDRA	Those that were sober helped them.
ANDROMACHE	Let them get on with it, Priam, And take the Horse into the city.
(CHORUS)	Yes, take the Great Horse in!
PRIAM	Do you want to throw away All that Troy has fought for And most of your husbands died for? Go back into the city And take the prisoner with you. Andromache, Polyxena, You are right when you say she will speak More freely to you than me; But be careful, girls are not always As innocent as they seem. I must go now to the Horse. (*)

(PRIAM goes)

(CHORUS)	You are among friends here: Tell us your story.
ANDROMACHE	First fetch some flax and oil So that we can dress her wound.

(One of the CHORUS offers a piece of cloth)

NEOPTOLEMUS	It is no longer bleeding; Let the King himself dress it When he takes me in.
POLYXENA	Be careful.
NEOPTOLEMUS	Does he not honour women?
POLYXENA	O yes, but it would be wiser To come with us rather than him.

241

ANDROMACHE	Drink this, you are shivering.
POLYXENA	And let me wipe your face; You look terrible, your tears Have smeared the paint all over it.

(*NEOPTOLEMUS snatches the cloth*)

NEOPTOLEMUS	I can bind my own wound.
ANDROMACHE	Drink first, and tell us more.

(*He drinks*)

(CHORUS)	Is it true that your grandmother Could really change her shape?
NEOPTOLEMUS	Yes, and that of others.
(CHORUS)	Are you married?
NEOPTOLEMUS	No.
(CHORUS)	That's not good – Does it mean That you are still a virgin?
NEOPTOLEMUS	It means what it should mean; I have sworn that I will never Lie with a man.
(CHORUS)	That's a shame.
ANDROMACHE	Cassandra swore that too But it has not made her happy.
NEOPTOLEMUS	I am as Athene is, Virgin but warrior, And as Artemis, Patroness Of virgins and hunters.
(CHORUS)	Warrior and hunter? She is delirious – It's the drink, she needs food.
POLYXENA	In Troy we honour virgins.
ANDROMACHE	Yes, while they're virgins.
POLYXENA	You shouldn't have asked my father To take you in himself.
(CHORUS)	She knew what she was doing – Once she's been bathed and scented

242

	And given a new dress All will go easy between them.
NEOPTOLEMUS	I will never be Other than I am.
(CHORUS)	What is that supposed to mean?
ANDROMACHE	Girls like to say such things But they all know as you do They were born to please a man.
NEOPTOLEMUS	I will never lie with Priam.
(CHORUS)	Come, your lips and does' eyes Were made to give men pleasure — And to get it – It is natural.
POLYXENA	Leave this, you have frightened her.
NEOPTOLEMUS	No, they make me angry.
ANDROMACHE	You said that you love truth So that is what we're giving you.
(CHORUS)	What you want is irrelevant — When Priam likes a girl He takes her – Or he tries to.
ANDROMACHE	He tried it with me the night Before I married Hector.
POLYXENA	Don't say such things.
ANDROMACHE	Why not? This girl's father Took any girl he wanted Whenever he sacked some city.
NEOPTOLEMUS	That's a lie.
(CHORUS)	No, it's true: He took hundreds.
ANDROMACHE	So why grudge us Some payment in kind?
POLYXENA	Andromache –
ANDROMACHE	He even made love to Penthesilea After he'd killed her.
POLYXENA	Stop this.

NEOPTOLEMUS   That is a vile story
    Made up by Thersites;
    My father killed him for it.

ANDROMACHE   Then drink some more and forget it.

    (*NEOPTOLEMUS drinks*)

POLYXENA   What you said to her was cheap.

ANDROMACHE   Forgive me, and tell us
    Did you ever know your father?

NEOPTOLEMUS   I know of all his deeds
    And his nobleness and courage.

ANDROMACHE   Has no one ever told you
    How he really was?

(CHORUS)   It is time she should know it.

POLYXENA   Not now, Andromache.

NEOPTOLEMUS   I know what has been said of him
    By men like Agamemnon.

(CHORUS)   Did they tell how he chased Hector
    Seven times around our walls
    To make his death more shameful?

ANDROMACHE   He was evil, Pyrrha.

(CHORUS)   Brutal – Cruel – Vicious.

POLYXENA   Only in a part of him;
    When he did bad things he wept for it.

ANDROMACHE   And when he'd wept and eaten
    He slept, rose fresh in the morning
    And did them all again.

POLYXENA   Just like our own warriors.

ANDROMACHE   Ours did not laugh when they looked
    In the eyes of those they slaughtered.

POLYXENA   You must not go on thinking
    Only of your Hector.

ANDROMACHE   She loves truth, let her have it.

NEOPTOLEMUS   If you go on, I shall kill you.

POLYXENA   Leave it.

ANDROMACHE   You are right,
               She has courage; I am sorry.

               (*Pause*)

POLYXENA   You are so like your father.

NEOPTOLEMUS   How can you tell?

(CHORUS)   She knew him:
               She was with him the night he died
               Here at the shrine of Apollo.

NEOPTOLEMUS   Here?

(CHORUS)   Yes, she was with him
               When this shrine was destroyed.

POLYXENA   You should not have told her.

NEOPTOLEMUS (*To Polyxena*) You are his murderer.

POLYXENA   You could say so.

ANDROMACHE   She was not,
               She was quite innocent;
               Paris killed him.

POLYXENA   Leave this.

(CHORUS)   But she wants to know the story!

NEOPTOLEMUS   Tell me.

ANDROMACHE   When Priam told her
               That she must marry your father
               To put an end to the war
               She asked me what to do
               Because she was frightened and hated him
               For what he'd done to Hector.

NEOPTOLEMUS   And how did you advise her?

ANDROMACHE   I told her she must come here
               And do as her father asked.
               When she said all she wanted
               Was to tell him how vile he was
               I knew she was in love with him.

(CHORUS)   You wanted revenge for Hector.

245

ANDROMACHE No, I wanted peace
And to put an end to the madness.

(CHORUS) So you went and told Paris
About their secret meeting.

ANDROMACHE No, I spoke to no one
But Hecuba overheard us.
She hated Priam's peace-plan
And wanted her darling Paris
To win honour in the field
Because all the city hated him.
She dragged him out of Helen's bed
And made him follow Polyxena.

POLYXENA Why didn't you come and warn me?

ANDROMACHE All the world knew
Achilles was invulnerable;
I never thought Paris could harm him.
Not Apollo himself
Who guided Paris' bow
Could have killed him if she hadn't –

POLYXENA If I hadn't made him tell me
The place where he was vulnerable.

NEOPTOLEMUS You made him tell it?

POLYXENA   Yes.

ANDROMACHE She didn't know Paris was listening.

POLYXENA I wanted to find out
What kind of man he was
Underneath the brutality;
I wanted to find out
If I could marry him,
And whether he was vulnerable,
Not in his body
But in his mind and heart.

NEOPTOLEMUS You destroyed him.

POLYXENA   Yes,
But I did not mean to;
He was not as I'd thought he was.
O yes, he was a monster

But kind and gentle too;
He feared death like all warriors,
Just as Hector did.

ANDROMACHE   Don't say that.

POLYXENA   Both did vile things in battle
As all warriors will and must,
But when he died I wept for him.

NEOPTOLEMUS   You killed him.

POLYXENA   I think so.

(CHORUS)   No, Paris killed him
—   She is quite innocent.

POLYXENA   None of us are innocent,
Not any longer.
I know I will be punished.

ANDROMACHE   Why should you be punished?

POLYXENA   The gods are not kind
But sometimes they are just.

ANDROMACHE   Where are you going?

POLYXENA   I want no part of this;
I shall go and sit alone
And weep awhile on the sea-shore
But I do not want my tears
To spoil this day for others.   (*)

(*She goes*)

NEOPTOLEMUS   She will be punished: all
Who are to blame will be punished.

ANDROMACHE   If you must blame someone
Blame Apollo who guided the bow.

NEOPTOLEMUS   So I do.

(CHORUS)   Be careful,

He may hear you.

NEOPTOLEMUS   I would say it
To his face if he was here
And demand compensation.

ANDROMACHE   You are a strange creature.

NEOPTOLEMUS   Yes, I am a creature.

ANDROMACHE   You want revenge of course.

NEOPTOLEMUS   It is natural.

ANDROMACHE
                    Yes, to want it
          But to take it is stupid.
          If I wanted revenge for Hector
          I could take it now on you
          And part of me would like to
          But what would that solve?
          Revenge wins nothing back:
          It is only the beginning
          Of a pointless, endless cycle
          That goes on and on for ever
          Till nobody remembers
          How or why it began.

          Everybody knows it
          Yet everyone forgets it;
          So the womb of revenge
          Never withers but goes on teeming
          To the very end of time,
          Breeding fools who believe
          That what they do is noble;
          When they suffer for it
          They think they are heroes
          And their friends call them martyrs.

          What you feel now is natural;
          I felt it too when Hector died
          But I did not exult
          When Paris killed your father;
          I knew someone else would kill him,
          And so it will go on.

NEOPTOLEMUS   I fetched the bow that killed him.

ANDROMACHE   Then you're revenged already.
          Forget it now and you'll find
          Your life will be much happier.   (*)

          (*Re-enter PRIAM*)

248

PRIAM	Have you questioned her?
ANDROMACHE	Yes, She is quite innocent; She has not yet learned how to lie. Have you punished your soldiers And explained your plan to the people?
PRIAM	I have not been to the Horse.
ANDROMACHE	Why not?
PRIAM	I could not find it.
(CHORUS)	Not find it? – What is this?
PRIAM	There's a mist, a sea-mist Between the shrine and the Horse.
ANDROMACHE	A sea-mist on the plain?
PRIAM	It has drifted in from the sea And is covering all Dardania.
CASSANDRA	It is coming in from Tenedos.
ANDROMACHE	But how could you lose your way?
PRIAM	For a while it was as if I was nowhere and a nothing.
ANDROMACHE	You couldn't find the place Where the women were singing?
PRIAM	Yes, I did hear singing But it was only one girl's voice.
(CHORUS)	That is strange – It must have been Some nymph or some goddess.
PRIAM	We must think clearly and separate What belongs here and what doesn't.
(CHORUS)	The Horse belongs to us.
PRIAM	But why is a sea-monster Curled round Athene's statue? To protect us or to warn us? And why if they are defeated Should the war-men dedicate Their offering to Athene Whom they honour as Goddess of Victory?

249

If they wanted a safe voyage home
Why did they not offer it
To Poseidon who hates them?
Above all, what is in the mind
Of their General? What is happening?

(*He calls out*)   Agamemnon, answer me!

(*Sound of sea-birds*)

One thing alone is clear to me:
We must wait till the mist
Clears here and round Tenedos.   (*)

(*Enter HECUBA*)

HECUBA   There is no mist here, Priam,
Except in your own mind.
By the Horse and over the city
The friendly sun is shining:
As I looked down from Ilion
I could see the crags of Tenedos;
There is nothing there but sea-birds
And though the sea between
Is thick and foul with flotsam
The dolphins have come back
And are leaping in the sunlight;
They have quicker wits than you have.
All your life I have seen
How the weight of great decisions
Has clouded your subtle mind
But a woman sees more clearly;
So when your mind has been troubled
You have often been glad
To let me choose for you
And so my truth in the night
Has given you strength in the morning.
We have won the war
And the War-Kings have gone,
Not by years of bargaining
With your friend Agamemnon
But by myself with Odysseus
Who is their real General.

PRIAM
: You let him steal the image
Of Athene from the city,
The image which preserved us;
Do you call that a bargain?

HECUBA
: How should I know that he'd hidden it
Underneath his beggar's rags?
When I found him with Helen
He grovelled and screamed for life
And so I let him have it
As a bargain, not through pity.
He swore that he would make
The War-lords go home
And he has; I remember
The exact words he said to me:
'I give my solemn oath
That our General Agamemnon
Will break up the war-camp
Launch our black ships in the water,
Embark the whole army
And set sail for the West.'

PRIAM
: Were those his exact words?

HECUBA
: They were, I remember.

PRIAM
: They may have been his words
But I can read his mind
Better than you can.
Why should the General do that
When he and I had reached
A different agreement?
What I need to read now
Is the mind of Agamemnon.

HECUBA
: He has done as Odysseus promised.

PRIAM
: But Agamemnon has sworn
To send back our Hesione;
Till I see her, all this makes no sense.

HECUBA
: You will never see her.

PRIAM
: Yes, I saw her last night...

HECUBA
: Another dream, Priam?

PRIAM   She had come back to us
                And she was wearing the same dress.

HECUBA   Your dreams have always muddled you.

PRIAM   Hesione will come back
                Just as the General promised.

HECUBA   Promises lead nowhere,
                Least of all between kings.

PRIAM   Agamemnon thinks as I do.

HECUBA   That is why the war
                Has gone on for so long.

PRIAM   None of this is his doing;
                I must know his mind.

HECUBA   He is standing on his ship's prow
                Looking towards Mycenae.

ANDROMACHE   He is thinking as we are
                Of his home and his children.

CASSANDRA   He is standing on Tenedos
                And watching us.

PRIAM   I know him:
                He keeps his word as I do.

HECUBA   He may be like you, Priam,
                But that doesn't mean you know him.

PRIAM   There are too many signs!

HECUBA   The horse will rot on the sea-shore
                If you start trying to unravel them.

PRIAM   The monster is a sign.

HECUBA   The monster is asleep now.

PRIAM   The thunder is a sign.

HECUBA   Yes, of rain; it's a sign
                You'll catch cold if you stay here.

PRIAM   The girl is a sign.

HECUBA   I have been told of her;
                We shall treat her with honour.

PRIAM	I have not yet questioned her To confirm Sinon's story.
HECUBA	You can question her in Ilion; Take her in and rest.
PRIAM	I will not go in Till I know more about her.
HECUBA	You used to be wise; Why are you now so stubborn?
PRIAM	Yes, I am stubborn, Stubborn for the truth.
NEOPTOLEMUS	Take me in and I'll give you All the truth you search for.
(CHORUS) (*Aside*) –	The sacred serpents are coupling That sign is a happy one
PRIAM	But what's in the mind of the gods? Do they bless us or warn us?
CASSANDRA (*To Priam*)	Careful, old hound, You were on the track this morning; Now you lose the scent.
ANDROMACHE	No, he's right to remind us Of the gods.
(CHORUS)	But of which god? Apollo or Poseidon? Or even Zeus himself?
ANDROMACHE	None of these, but of her To whom the Horse is dedicated.
(CHORUS) –	Why should we speak of Athene? She has never been good to us.
PRIAM	That has been a great sorrow to me.
ANDROMACHE	Yet we have always honoured her; Although she fought against us She was surely only testing us. When Odysseus stole her image She turned against the War-Kings.
HECUBA	That is why they've tried To appease her with this offering.

	Will it please her if you light
	Fires underneath its belly?
ANDROMACHE	Have you forgotten her nature,
	Her true nature, old man?
PRIAM	No, she is Goddess of Victory.
ANDROMACHE	Then you have forgotten;
	Women, remind him.

(CHORUS)   She invented flutes
            As well as the blare of trumpets
        —   Pottery and ploughs
            Elegant and useful
        —   She invented ships
            Long before men misused them
        —   It was she who first taught us
            How to count with numbers
        —   And she gave us the arts
            All women are skilled in
        —   Cooking – Spinning – Weaving.

ANDROMACHE   Not just skill: wisdom.

PRIAM   Yes, but what is wisdom?

(CHORUS)   Knowledge? – Understanding?
        —   Searching and questioning?

CASSANDRA   Suffering and accepting.

(CHORUS)   And perhaps a kind of healing?

CASSANDRA   Dreaming.

PRIAM   It is possible.

HECUBA   Leave this, you'll confuse him.

ANDROMACHE   One thing is certain:
             It was the West, not we,
             Who distorted her true name.
             We know she much prefers
             Peaceful persuasion:
             It is that which gives true victory.

HECUBA   That's why the Goddess of Victory
             Is a female.

PRIAM
>   Victory
> Is not how a war ends
> But how true peace begins.
> That is a labyrinth
> More fearful and perilous
> Than the hurtle and crush of chariots.
> War in its way is simple
> But peace requires more cunning
> And it takes much more time.
> If we act hastily
> In honour of her only
> We may anger the other gods
> Who for ten years have fought for us:
> Apollo and Poseidon
> Are quick to take offence.

(CHORUS)
> They are great but Zeus is greater.

HECUBA
> What does it matter
> Which god we honour
> When no one can be certain
> Of their nature or their minds?
> It's our brothers, sons and husbands
> Whom we should honour now
> Who died for our city
> So as to give us life;
> This day should be theirs,
> Not ours for speculation.
> Take the Horse in for their sake
> And let gods do the debating.

(CHORUS)
> She is right – She is right, Priam.   (*)

PRIAM
> But how can we be sure of it?

CASSANDRA
> Ask Pyrrha one question:
> What is in the Horse?

ANDROMACHE
> Yes, that is sensible.

PRIAM
> You are right, that is the first thing:
> Answer us.

NEOPTOLEMUS
>   The first thing
> Is her who began it.

(CHORUS)	Who does she speak of?
—	Is she talking of Helen?
PRIAM	What are you saying, girl?
NEOPTOLEMUS	Look...

(NEOPTOLEMUS takes off and throws down rings, necklaces, and jewels in front of PRIAM)

(CHORUS)	What is she doing?
NEOPTOLEMUS	Look at them, Priam.
PRIAM	I cannot stoop to see.
NEOPTOLEMUS	Give them to him, women.

(CHORUS pick them up and show them to PRIAM)

PRIAM

Agamemnon, I thank you:
You have sent our Hesione home!
But where is she, girl?
In the cave or on the sea-shore?

NEOPTOLEMUS

She is dead, she died at sea.
These remnants were brought here
On Agamemnon's orders
By Peleus my grandfather.

ANDROMACHE

This girl must have stolen them.

NEOPTOLEMUS

No, before she died she asked
That everything she had worn
When Heracles took her from Troy
Should be sent back to her brother:
Take them and remember her.

(PRIAM weeps)

HECUBA	This is your dream's meaning.

CASSANDRA

It was a true dream, Father,
True and false mixed together.

ANDROMACHE

Why did Agamemenon
Not bring them himself to Priam?

NEOPTOLEMUS

Odysseus put her remnants
On me so as to mock you;

256

	But before she died she sent him A message.
ANDROMACHE	Do you know it?
NEOPTOLEMUS	I heard it.
(CHORUS)	Tell us.
PRIAM	Tell us.
NEOPTOLEMUS	I will tell you as Peleus told them: 'Since it was not the gods' will I should ever come home to Troy I send you what is left When my father dressed and bound me For sacrifice on the sea-shore And they took me away to the West. I swore I would not change my dress Until I came home again, So take these remnants of me That Helen may go home also And all the world have peace.' (*)
ANDROMACHE	Speak to us, Priam.
PRIAM	I cannot, I'm afraid.
HECUBA	What are you afraid of?
ANDROMACHE	She is the sign you've searched for.
HECUBA	Why must you always Mistrust a good meaning And look for some bad one?
PRIAM	Because I fear what lies Beneath what we call meaning.
HECUBA	Leave that to our philosophers, It is no fit talk for kings.
ANDROMACHE	Why can you not Let yourself be happy?
CASSANDRA	He is right, that is why The gods send us dreams, Not to help us but remind us Of the way the world really is:

                            Nothing's solved, nothing fits;
                            We only pretend it does.

HECUBA   Be quiet, girl, it does fit.
                            We have won the war
                            And all our dreams of empire
                            Will now become reality.
                            As the gods sometimes bring
                            A dead child to life again,
                            So old defeat in time
                            May be reborn as victory.
                            We shall mount an expedition
                            To win back Athene's image
                            Take the Great Horse in!

(CHORUS)   We have won the war!
        –   Troy is itself again!
        –   Our walls will stand for ever!
        –   Take the Great Horse in!

ANDROMACHE   It does fit, my darling.

                            (*Pause*)

PRIAM   Yes it all fits...
                            That is why I suspect it:
                            Cassandra speaks the truth.
                            You must try to understand
                            That when we think we have solved things
                            We may only have imposed
                            Some meaning that we long for,
                            Some pattern in our mind
                            That we groped for long ago.
                            Great signs are not solutions,
                            They are more often warnings.
                            When we humans cry 'It fits'
                            All the gods start laughing.

HECUBA   They'll laugh if you reject their gifts
                            And speak like a clever idiot.

ANDROMACHE   You are weary as Zeus himself is
                            When his own thoughts weigh him down.
                            Take this girl in and rest:

	And then she will tell you all You think you need to know.
(CHORUS)	The gods themselves have sent her To renew you and refresh you.
PRIAM	That is not what I need now.
ANDROMACHE	It is just what you need, old man.
HECUBA	I was watching you, Priam, As they talked of Athene; Your thoughts were not of her But rather of Aphrodite.
(CHORUS)	That is how it should be And as ours will be tonight!
HECUBA	Question her in the morning When she will have restored Your natural zest and vigour.
NEOPTOLEMUS	You speak of me as if I was one of your city's whores. Show me more honour, Trojan.
HECUBA	You need not remind Trojans Of what is and is not honourable.
ANDROMACHE	She is right to remind us; She's the daughter of a King.
(CHORUS)	She must speak as she does In front of all of us; Once she is in Ilion She will speak and act more freely.
NEOPTOLEMUS	Kill me now and have done.
ANDROMACHE	Pyrrha, I laugh at you. The day I first shared Hector's bed I was just as frightened. It is natural, it will pass.
(CHORUS)	It is natural – We are friends here – We pity you for all The war-men have done to you.
NEOPTOLEMUS	I am friend to no Trojan; If I could I would kill

	All my father's enemies.
	Those who dressed me for sacrifice
	Showed me more respect than you do.
	Kill me now in honour
	Of any god you wish
	And I will end the war
	As Iphigenia began it.
(CHORUS)	This puppy has spirit
—	She is just how Priam likes them.
HECUBA	Quiet, girl. This war began
	When your grandfather Peleus
	And Telamon seized Hesione.
NEOPTOLEMUS	No, it began when you
	Made your vile son seize Helen.
HECUBA	Hesione was raped
	But Helen was a hostage;
	That she fell in love with Paris
	Should not blur that distinction.
PRIAM	Hecuba, both of you, leave this!
HECUBA	This girl has been neither
	Raped nor taken hostage;
	What passes between you tonight
	Is up to you and her.
(CHORUS)	Let them work it out together.
ANDROMACHE	That is usually the best way.
ALL	Take the Great Horse in!
PRIAM	Too many voices
	Are banging in my head!
	All of you, be silent!
	I put my faith in wood-smoke,
	Not in words. Smoke the Horse. (*)

(Re-enter POLYXENA)

POLYXENA	O my father, a wonder!
PRIAM	What is it, Polyxena?
ANDROMACHE	Why are you weeping?

POLYXENA   The women are taking
     The Horse into the city.

PRIAM   They will not get very far;
     They do not have the strength.

POLYXENA   Yes, the gods have given them strength!
     How else could they be moving it
     Over the stony ground?
     It is gliding along as easily
     As if it sailed on a sea-road.

(CHORUS)   Let us go and help them!

PRIAM   Even if they drag it
     Right up across the plains
     It's too high for our gates.

POLYXENA   It will not be too high;
     Your soldiers have already
     Begun to break the walls.

ANDROMACHE   Do you still not see
     That Athene is behind this?

HECUBA   The gods have chosen for you.

(CHORUS)   Take the Great Horse in!

NEOPTOLEMUS   Take it in and take me with you.

PRIAM   Wood-smoke, must try wood-smoke;
     We must stop this, and I will!

HECUBA   Gently, Priam, gently.
     We know what has disturbed you;
     This girl from the West
     Reminds you of your sister
     Whom you always loved too much.
     But this is not Hesione,
     She's a gift the gods have sent you.
     Do what you always do:
     Take her in as your wife.
     You yourself have said
     That after a war is over
     It is good to make friends of enemies;
     It is why you wished Polyxena

	To marry this girl's father.
	What better way can there be
	Of showing your magnanimity?
(*To Neoptolemus*)	And if you go on refusing him
	Your father's ghost will curse you.

Take her into Ilion:
And when she is bathed and scented
You shall share a meal together
And do as the wine inclines you
Either for sleep or pleasure.
If the gods bless your bed
You shall have such loving
As Zeus had with Hera
The night before our Hector died
And they lay among the flowers.

(CHORUS)   –   Time to dance the wedding-dance!
           –   And we will dance with you!

ANDROMACHE   She cannot dance the wedding-dance
             Dressed like this.

POLYXENA   Then I'll fetch her one.

HECUBA   Yes, all must be done
         According to the custom.   (*)

(*POLYXENA goes*)

HECUBA   Why are you silent, girl?

NEOPTOLEMUS   Do you think I will dance with him
              In the place where my father died?

(CHORUS)   Then let it be done here
           And then you shall go in together
           When the Great Horse enters the city.

CASSANDRA   Yes, do it, do it now!
            But before she puts on the wedding-dress
            She must take off the old one!
            That Trojan cloak dishonours
            This Princess of the West.

NEOPTOLEMUS   No, only Priam
              Shall see me as I am.

(CHORUS)	Let her be, she is shy now
–	That is natural – Only natural
–	But we want to see her face
–	Let us wipe the paint off
	We want to see the bride
–	Come, we will help you.

(CHORUS pull off NEOPTOLEMUS' cloak. PRIAM cries out when he sees the yellow dress)

CASSANDRA	Here is your dream, Priam.

(NEOPTOLEMUS slowly circles PRIAM)

(CHORUS)	She is fair – But she is shivering
–	When she is in Ilion
	He will soon warm her
–	I think she will warm him
–	Her hips are like a boy's
–	Her legs are strong and long enough
	To outrun a mountain-deer
–	Just like her father
–	That is how Priam likes them.

ANDROMACHE *(To Priam)* Why don't you look at her?

(CHORUS)	Something in him fears to
	As if it was forbidden
–	Yes he is afraid
	That he's too old to please her
–	He is never easy
	Before he takes a girl
–	That is how it should be
–	That is how it was with me
	When he took me in his orchard
–	You are fools to doubt a man
	Who has had fifty children.

ANDROMACHE	How can you say these things?
	None of you know anything. (*)

(CASSANDRA pokes the fire)

CASSANDRA	That is well said:
	This war-fire is not out.
	Look on the light of Apollo!

(She takes a brand from the fire. Flames appear from it)

(CHORUS)	It's the flame of Apollo!
–	The god has not left us!
–	Praised be our Apollo!
CASSANDRA	Apollo... Apollo...!
PRIAM *(To Cassandra)*	Priestess of Apollo,
	Take the brand to the Horse!
	When you have smoked it
	I will make my decision.
NEOPTOLEMUS	No, let it be our wedding torch:
CASSANDRA	No need to smoke horses, Priam!
	Pyrrha spoke truth when she said
	That the first thing is here.

(She runs at NEOPTOLEMUS to set fire to the yellow dress. He seizes the brand and throws her to the ground)

(CHORUS)	See how she threw her!
–	She is surely Achilles' child!
–	Yes, it's told how her father
	Could wrestle with a bear.
CASSANDRA	Apollo! Apollo!
	This is not a girl;
	I felt a man's strength in him.
(CHORUS)	Because some god is in her!
CASSANDRA	Apollo! Apollo!
	Pull off the dress and tear him.
PRIAM	Is this your promise, Cassandra?
CASSANDRA	Here is the truth, Father!
NEOPTOLEMUS	Is this the mad girl
	All the world has heard of?
HECUBA	Take her back to her cell.
CASSANDRA	Do you want the truth?
	Give me the brand again.
(CHORUS)	We know your truth!

(They knock down CASSANDRA and kick her)

NEOPTOLEMUS	Let her be:
	Let us have no more blood
	At the shrine of Apollo.
	Look on this torch, Trojans;
	Wedding-fire is sacred.
CASSANDRA	It is death-fire to us all.
	Go on, bring back the monster
	With a thousand heads of death!
	It will destroy you, Father;
	Apollo... Apollo...! (*)

(She begins to speak in Greek, c.f. Euripides' 'Trojan Women' lines 308-313, as NEOPTOLEMUS speaks the same words in English)

HECUBA	Shut Cassandra's mouth and bind her.
(CHORUS)	She mocks the god of Marriage.
NEOPTOLEMUS	Burn, light, high!
	Burn bright and strong!
	Lord of Marriage, hear me;
	Here's my prayer, my flame.
	Bless me and bless him
	When I lie by his side;
	A bride at a wedding
	Always has light.
PRIAM	Is this your will, Apollo?
(CHORUS)	Yes, raise the wedding-torch!
—	And sing the wedding-song!

(The CHORUS gag and bind CASSANDRA)

NEOPTOLEMUS	Priam, Lord of Troy,
	Take me into Ilion
	Show me where you looked
	Down onto the war-camp;
	Show me the battle-plains
	And winding Scamander
	That still runs thick with blood
	Down to the empty sea-shore.

This torch shall be a beacon
That shall flame the victory
Throughout the West and Asia
And all the world shall see
How Priam has at last
Made peace with his enemies
And your long war is done!

HECUBA   That is how it should be.

NEOPTOLEMUS   Take me in, Priam,
And I'll burn more bright than torches;
Do I not please you?
Does not my body
Set a tingling in your veins
And make your old blood fiery?
I am fiery too.
Yes, let there be dancing!

(He begins to dance as his father did before he went to war, c.f. Play 2. N.B. The following speech also is a parody of CASSANDRA in 'The Trojan Women' c.f. same passage)

Dance with me, women,
Dance like birds flying,
Dance for all your dead men,
Dance for my father's sake,
Dance in your pretty dresses;
My fate is your fate
And all of you are mine!

(All begin to dance. POLYXENA comes back with a red dress)

POLYXENA   Pyrrha, this is the dress I wore
When I came to marry your father:
Put it on for his sake
And he will bless your marriage.

ANDROMACHE   See how she honours you!
Come into the cave
And we will help to dress you.

NEOPTOLEMUS   No, I must go in alone
And offer a libation

	In the place where my father died That I may do all things fairly.
POLYXENA	Let us help you.
NEOPTOLEMUS	No: In the West brides are dressed By their mother or their grandmother; Thetis, come to me! Help to change me now.

(He goes into the cave)

POLYXENA	Why are you silent, Father?
PRIAM	I have heard it said That what we believe will happen Never does happen, Yet what cannot happen Sometimes does happen. Whether by the hands Of the bright gods or by humans All happens as it must.
HECUBA	Then let us give thanks to all To whom we have built temples.
PRIAM	Help me to kneel, Hecuba, And then I will decide it. (*)

(ALL kneel. As they do, half-chanting and half-speaking, CASSANDRA prophesies apart: her words are from the Pyrrhus speech in 'Hamlet'. The CHORUS prayer can overlap)

(CHORUS)	First, as is fitting, Sky-lord, we honour you: Your plan is now fulfilled.
ALL	Zeus, we Trojans honour you.
HECUBA	Apollo, we honour you, Our defender and our champion, Lord of Light, the beautiful, Our victory is yours.
(CHORUS)	Poseidon, we honour you, God of the sea and horses;

May the waves, your sea-horses
Smash the black ships for ever.

Ares, war-god, we honour you:
You fought for us and we thank you.
Now go back to your home in Thrace
And live there in quietness.

Hephaestus, we honour you,
Fire-god and Smith-god,
Turn your forge to peace again
And make us jewels, not armour.

Artemis, we honour you:
If Poseidon spares the ships,
Stop the wind and let them rot
In a dead sea-calm for ever.

Demeter, we honour you:
Refresh and bless our fields
That our corn may turn to gold again
And grow as high as the Horse.

Aphrodite, we honour you
Who here bore our Aeneas;
Be with us in Troy tonight
And teach us how to laugh again.

POLYXENA   Athene, we honour you,
Although you fought against us;
May the Horse take the place of your image,
We are sorry that we lost it.

ANDROMACHE   Hestia of the Hearth,
Sweetest to us and dearest,
Quench all the world's war-fires:
May our hearth-fires burn for ever.

*(Music lifts. NEOPTOLEMUS re-enters in the
red-dress, dressed and painted by THETIS
within)*

HECUBA   Hera, Queen of Marriage,
Bless their bed of love tonight
And may this girl, a stranger,
Live in quiet in our city.

NEOPTOLEMUS	You have left one god out Who today deserves most honour: He whom we do not name Who lords it under the earth.

(*Music ceases*)

(CHORUS)	Why should we honour him?
NEOPTOLEMUS	Because all the dead are with him And because each one of us Shall sooner of later meet him.
PRIAM	Well said, we must honour him: You whom we do not name We honour for their sake.

(*A silence*)

NEOPTOLEMUS	What do you wait for, Priam? Achilles' child is waiting.
HECUBA	On your feet, Priam; Say what you must.

(*PRIAM rises*)

PRIAM	Take the great Horse in.

(*Music and dancing: a serene celebration of peace. NEOPTOLEMUS leads the wedding dance. All go, some dust falls from above. The sea sounds.*)

Play 6
ODYSSEUS

THE WAR-CAMP AT TROY

CAST

First Woman	HECUBA
Second Woman	HELEN
Third Woman	ANDROMACHE
Fourth Woman	POLYXENA
First Man	(–)
Second Man	MENELAUS
Third Man	ODYSSEUS
Fourth Man	NEOPTOLEMUS

CHORUS and SOLDIERS

(As many SOLDIERS as possible, including the
CHORUS at the end. At every entrance they are like
stage attendants, visored and impersonal)

(*Thymbria again. Smoke and fires in the
distance. HECUBA and ANDROMACHE and
all the TROJAN WOMEN are sitting or lying
round the fire. All are wearing red dresses*)

HECUBA

You! You up there,
Zeus, what are you doing?
Watching us? Or sleeping
After last night's feasting?
When they tumbled Ilion
Did you laugh or weep?
That story's over, Zeus:
Now watch me make a new one.

Women, stop this weeping;
We shall never meet again
So we must all prepare ourselves
For what must now be done.
You know the kind of men
That we shall have to deal with;
Butchers of our husbands,
Destroyers of our homes,
Each of whom will choose
One of us as prizes.
But whatever they do to us
We must not show our suffering;
If we weep and show our weakness
We'll encourage them to treat us
With the contempt we deserve;
If we rage we will anger them
And they'll make us suffer more;
But if we all endure it
With dignity and courage
They will learn to respect us
And we will learn as quickly
How to handle barbarians.
I am now your General
And command you, no tears:
Stand up and stop snivelling.

CHORUS

Why have you made us
Put on our wedding-dresses?

HECUBA	To show them who we are.
	I have received a message
	From the General himself
	That all wives of high-born Trojans
	Will be treated honourably.
CHORUS	My husband was a common man.
HECUBA	Then keep quiet and you'll be safe.
	Agamemnon will come to me
	As soon as he has restored
	Order in the city.
POLYXENA	There is no city now.
HECUBA	Then we'll have to build a new one.
	It is time to remind him
	Of the rights of a royal house.
	All of you stand up
	And show me what you're made of.
ANDROMACHE	I put this on to remind myself
	Not them, of who I am.
	When the citadel was taken
	I bathed and washed my hair,
	Put on my rings, my girdle
	And the perfume which Hector
	Brought me from Lydia
	To remind me of my wedding-day;
	Then I knelt and kissed our marriage-bed
	And looked in my mirror
	And smiled at what I saw.
	When they came and brought me here
	Their soldiers knelt as I passed them;
	They know how to behave
	Before a Trojan Princess.
HECUBA	That is how it should be.
CHORUS	You were lucky.
HECUBA	If you cringe
	You will suffer and deserve to.
CHORUS	Whose wedding-dress is that
	Which Polyxena is wearing?

HECUBA	It belongs to some dead woman;
	I made her put it on.
ANDROMACHE	Why? She's Achilles' wife,
	So she's safer than all of us.
	Where is Cassandra?
CHORUS	Probably she screamed so much
	That they cut off her tongue.
HECUBA	Then they were sensible;
	She would shame us
	If she were with us now.
	When they take us into their ships
	We must go in proudly
	And then they will honour us
	For the sake of our dead husbands.
POLYXENA	Don't say these things, Mother.
HECUBA	I say what I must
	Though it will not be easy.
	When they take you to their beds
	Some of you will weep,
	That is allowable;
	Some of you may vomit,
	That would be understandable;
	One or two may like it,
	That would be despicable;
	But if any of you weep
	Or scream or beg for pity
	You will not be true Trojans.
	You are women of a city
	That is greater and more famous
	Than any in the world.
POLYXENA	We were. It was. It isn't.
HECUBA	Troy was destroyed before
	And we built it up again;
	We shall do the same thing now.
POLYXENA	We are going to be punished.
ANDROMACHE	Why? We have done no wrong.

POLYXENA | Yes, we have been stupid:
We took the Great Horse in.

HECUBA | We were right, Polyxena.
When we broke the city walls
And danced into the city
What we felt then in our hearts
Was our truth and our glory. (*)

(*Enter ODYSSEUS with SOLDIERS*)

ODYSSEUS | I have brought you some food;
You must sit if you want to eat it.

(*SOLDIERS lay down food*)

HECUBA | Odysseus, you swore to me
When I saved your life in Ilion
That you would prevent this.

ODYSSEUS | I said so and I tried to
But sometimes the gods
Confound our oaths; I'm sorry.

HECUBA | What have the gods to do with it?
When men do something vile
They always blame the gods,
But whom do they hope to deceive?

ODYSSEUS | I do not deceive myself;
I'm ashamed at what has happened.
The General and our Council
Are full of grief and sadness.

HECUBA | So they send you to say sorry:
Why has the General
Not come to me himself?

ODYSSEUS | He is trying to restore order.

HECUBA | But why did he give the order
That led to all this?

ODYSSEUS | He didn't.

HECUBA | Then why is the city burning?

ODYSSEUS | We gave our men strict orders,
No killing and no looting;

275

	But I fear that in war There is always a risk of mistakes.
HECUBA	You call this a mistake?
ODYSSEUS	Confusion, doubt and chaos, Those are the three Furies That confound the plans of men. It began when Achilles' son Pyrrhus killed your husband; Young warriors are eager.
HECUBA	A boy cannot have done What was done to Priam.
ODYSSEUS	No, one would not have thought so. The task that we gave him Was to slip through the trap-door And open the Horse's belly. So he did and we seized the gates While he went up into Ilion To light the signal-beacon To the General on Tenedos. But there seems to have been Some delay or misunderstanding Between us and Agamemnon Or perhaps by the boy himself. Maybe there was a sea-mist: But for whatever reason The army came in too slowly And with no clear instructions.
HECUBA	What is all this to me? It is what they did when they got here, The brutality, the destruction -
ODYSSEUS	That was not what we planned. But the boy found his sister With your husband unlawfully And so he killed both of them.
ANDROMACHE	He killed his own sister?
ODYSSEUS	It seems some madness seized him. He ran naked into the street

And stabbed whoever he found
Unarmed or drunk or sleeping.
I have seen all too often
How one single death
Can lead to a general massacre.

HECUBA   Do you want me to believe
A boy did it all alone?

ODYSSEUS   No, but he began it;
It was as if the dark spirit
Of his father was in him.
When the army heard
The war-cry of Achilles
They thought it was his ghost
And it turned them into beasts.
By the time the General arrived
The whole city was on fire.

HECUBA   Do you expect me to believe this?

ODYSSEUS   No, but it is so.

HECUBA   You talk of your plan
As if it was to be bloodless.

ODYSSEUS   That is what Agamemnon hoped.

HECUBA   Send him to me.

ODYSSEUS   I mean to.

HECUBA   You are lying, Odysseus;
You are trying to hide your own guilt
By putting it on others.

ODYSSEUS   When a boy needs to prove his manhood
It may lead to some extravagance
No man would ever think of;
It was the same with his father
When we landed in Mysia.
I regret it deeply, Hecuba,
But he's earned his father's armour.
In all human dealings
Good and ill go together.

HECUBA   In all human dealings
The guilty blame the innocent;

	It was you who betrayed me, Not the boy or Agamemnon.
ODYSSEUS	I may not be a good man But I am not treacherous.
HECUBA	Do you hear that, women? Remember what he did? He came here disguised, but I found him And took him in and fed him: I pitied him.
ODYSSEUS	It is true.
HECUBA	Yes, it's true, and do you remember What happened next, Odysseus; Helen came in and told me Who you were?
ODYSSEUS	A bad moment: I remember it very clearly.
HECUBA	So you grovelled and clutched my dress And begged me for your life; Your hand was cold as you groped me.
ODYSSEUS	I was acting a part; I find it Helpful in such situations.
HECUBA	But out of kindness and pity I said I'd let you go If you swore you'd end the war And send the army home.
ODYSSEUS	That is not quite what I swore.
HECUBA	How can you deny it?
ODYSSEUS	May I repeat the exact words I spoke to you when I swore them?
HECUBA	Yes, admit what you promised; Repeat them word for word.
ODYSSEUS	'I give my solemn oath That our General Agamemnon Will break up the war-camp, Launch our black ships in the water, Embark the whole army

And set sail for the West.
When you see the ships' keel-marks
Scraped across the sand
You will know that Odysseus
Has done what he has sworn to.'
I have fulfilled
Every word of my oath.

HECUBA   Word-twist, Odysseus:
When I pitied you and spared you
You lied and betrayed me.

ODYSSEUS   You did not pity me;
You used the situation
Just as I'd have expected
Of a Queen with your intelligence.   (*)

ANDROMACHE   Leave this, both of you.
Tell us what you've come for:
Which of us is to be
The prize of which War-King?

HECUBA   No need to tell, I know it:
I shall go with the General.

ODYSSEUS   Agamemnon did not choose you.

HECUBA   Then he insults me.

ODYSSEUS   He did as he is apt to do:
He waived the right of choosing.

HECUBA   Then who had the first choice?

ODYSSEUS   I did;
The Council thought it fitting.

HECUBA   Whom did you choose, Odysseus?

ODYSSEUS   Naturally I chose the person
To whom I owed my life.

HECUBA   You chose me? You?

ODYSSEUS   To cherish and protect you.

HECUBA   Cherish? In your bed?
I am old, it's disgusting.

ODYSSEUS   That is not what I want.

HECUBA	Then what do you want? Perhaps You prefer boys or animals?
ODYSSEUS	Seizing women for one's bed Is to me contemptible; I love my wife Penelope And want no other woman.
HECUBA	Yet it's said you love Athene.
ODYSSEUS	Yes, she is pure.
HECUBA	It would seem she has had Little influence on you.
ANDROMACHE	Did the General choose no one?
ODYSSEUS	When the rest of the kings had chosen, He took the one nobody wanted.
HECUBA	Cassandra? He'll regret it.
ANDROMACHE	Where is she? We were told That she was violated In the temple of Athene.
ODYSSEUS	Yes, an attempt was made But Agamemnon rescued her.
HECUBA	He wanted her in his bed?
ODYSSEUS	I think he wished to save Some of the sacred relics In the temple. Her attacker Has of course been punished.
HECUBA	Does he want her as a prophetess?
ODYSSEUS	No, I do not think so.
ANDROMACHE	What does it matter? Who had the next choice?
ODYSSEUS	All agreed that Neoptolemus Should be given two choices.
HECUBA	Two?
ODYSSEUS	One for himself And one for his father Achilles; All the Council agreed

	Some prize must be given To the greatest of our warriors.
HECUBA	How can you give a dead man A living, breathing woman?
POLYXENA	I understand him, mother.
ODYSSEUS	I am glad of it, Polyxena.
HECUBA	Explain.
ODYSSEUS	Your daughter will fulfil A ceremonial function By his tomb at Sigaeum.
HECUBA	What does he mean, Polyxena?
POLYXENA	He means I shall be punished For my part in Achilles' death.
HECUBA	But you were quite innocent.
ANDROMACHE	What function, Odysseus?
ODYSSEUS	Calchas says that Achilles' ghost Will keep our fleet wind-bound Unless she is sacrificed At his tomb.
HECUBA	I forbid it!
ODYSSEUS	So would I if I could; Both the General and I Told the Council that dead men Have no rights over living women.
HECUBA	You were right.
ODYSSEUS	We were outvoted.
ANDROMACHE	Does Achilles want revenge?
ODYSSEUS	Calchas did not tell us.
HECUBA	Apollo's sister Artemis Hates all impurity; My daughter cannot be sacrificed: It is her time of the moon.
POLYXENA	She is lying to try to save me.

HECUBA

But she has done no wrong!
Send Agamemnon to me.

POLYXENA

You must stop this, mother;
Be quiet and listen to me.
After Achilles died
Cassandra told me what would happen
But I shut it out of my mind
As you are trying to do now.
Quiet, Mother. You have spoken
Fine words about the future
Because it's against the rules
For those who govern kingdoms
To dare to speak the truth.
You left out the one word that matters:
We are slaves. Each one of you
Will scrub floors and be whipped
If you do not please your masters;
You will sweat all day in the fields
And at night share some brute's bed
And his snores will mock your memories.
I would rather die than be chosen
For the bed of the butcher-boy
Who killed my dear father.

Take me to my husband
And let Calchas cut my throat;
I want that, yes, I want it:
It is said that all dead men
Love to drink the blood of the living
Because it gives them the sense
Of being alive again.
Achilles does not call for me
Because he wants revenge
But because he loves his wife.
If there had been time
For us to be together
As a man and wife should be
We would have made peace
Between Troy and the West
And I would have learned to love him.

If my blood now can give him
A little sense of life
I shall be a true wife to him.

ANDROMACHE   How can you speak like this?

HECUBA   You say dreadful things.

ODYSSEUS   No dead man has ever drunk
The blood of his own wife;
He wants revenge, it's simple.

POLYXENA   Yes, to minds like yours.

HECUBA   Why do you want to die?

POLYXENA   Because I shall see my father
Underneath the earth
And meet all my brothers
And Hector will hug me
As he did when I was little.
Why should I fear Asphodel
When at last I will be able
To tell Paris what I think of him?

ODYSSEUS   Because I am ashamed
Of what must be done now.

HECUBA   You should be ashamed
Of what has been done already.

ODYSSEUS   Maybe I am.

POLYXENA   Cover my he̎ad, Odysseus,
And take me into the darkness.

ANDROMACHE   Honour this girl, Trojans,
And bear yourselves as she does.   (*)

*(Enter NEOPTOLEMUS in his father's armour.
His face is bloody. The CHORUS see
NEOPTOLEMUS and begin to scream)*

CHORUS   Achilles! Achilles!
  —   It's the ghost of Achilles
  —   He has come to take her.

ODYSSEUS   This is Pyrrhus: by his courage
He has won his father's armour.

283

HECUBA	Is this the boy who did it?

(SOLDIERS carrying slave-dresses follow NEOPTOLEMUS)

NEOPTOLEMUS	Do what must be done.

(SOLDIERS bind POLYXENA and the rest)

HECUBA	Let me see his face. Wipe my husband's blood off; Show your face, butcher-boy: He's ashamed to let me see it.
NEOPTOLEMUS	I will wipe it off When I've done what I came for. Why should I be ashamed? And why is the girl not yet Prepared for sacrifice?
ANDROMACHE	You can see she is ready.
NEOPTOLEMUS	Then why is her face not painted? You know what must be done: She must put on the dress of sacrifice According to the custom.
HECUBA	Send Agamemnon to me! This is not what he promised me.
ODYSSEUS	We must act with care, Neoptolemus; The gods may not grant us A fair wind to the West If our rites here anger them.

(NEOPTOLEMUS presents HESIONE's yellow dress)

NEOPTOLEMUS	Put this on.
POLYXENA	I will never wear The one that your sister wore.
NEOPTOLEMUS	On her it was not honourable; On you it will be.
ANDROMACHE	She loved your father, Pyrrhus.
NEOPTOLEMUS	She betrayed him to his death. Take off what you are wearing Or I will tear it from you.

ODYSSEUS	That would be unworthy Of you and of your father: Don't do it, Neoptolemus.

(NEOPTOLEMUS takes the sacrificial paint and smears it on POLYXENA's face)

Is this the way to treat
Your own father's wife?
I cannot prevent you
From shedding this girl's blood
Since Achilles' ghost commands it,
But if you also try
To humiliate Polyxena
It is you who will be humiliated
And held in contempt
For the rest of your mortal life.
Already in the army
Some speak of you with horror.
When you first came to Troy
You were clean and pure and noble;
Now you are soiled and polluted.
You must listen once again
To the spirit of truth inside you
Or the rest of your life be wretched.
Are you not ashamed
Somewhere inside you?

NEOPTOLEMUS   If I have changed
It is you who have changed me.
It is you who have made me contemptible.

ANDROMACHE   Moral now, both of them.

ODYSSEUS   Let me speak to you for a moment
As I once spoke to your father.
Let me remind you
How it was with the old heroes
When passion overtook them:
At times they also turned
Into monsters as you have,
But they overcame their wrath
As your father did and you must
If you wish to be thought a hero.

	Men like their heroes to be noble, Or at least to act nobly.
HECUBA	That is well said, Odysseus.
NEOPTOLEMUS	Act? I have heard you Use that word too often.
POLYXENA	No more words, either of you: Take me to my husband.
HECUBA	Speak to me, my darling; Let me hold you to my breasts.
POLYXENA	Tell me, Odysseus: The girl who was sacrificed So that you could sail from Aulis, What words did she use When they took her to the altar?
ODYSSEUS	She called upon Zeus To hold high the flame of dawn So that she could say farewell To the sunlight that she loved.
POLYXENA	That was well said; I should like to have known her.
NEOPTOLEMUS	Maybe you will.
POLYXENA	If we go quickly We shall reach Sigaeum by daylight. The loveliest thing on this earth Is the dawn that gives birth to the day And the sun up there, shining: Hail and farewell, Sun-light that I love! Put it on me, Odysseus.

(*ODYSSEUS hoods her*)

NEOPTOLEMUS	Take her to Sigaeum.	(*)

(*Some of the SOLDIERS take POLYXENA out.*
Others lay slave-brands on the fire.
ODYSSEUS goes)

HECUBA	Now you know what stuff Trojan girls are made of.

NEOPTOLEMUS	But the rest have yet to show it. Why are those dresses still on them?
HECUBA	You cannot touch any of them; They are all of the Royal House.
NEOPTOLEMUS	All these are your daughters?
HECUBA	All.
NEOPTOLEMUS	That is strange; It is known you have many daughters But they're married to your allies And they all live far off.
HECUBA	All are my daughters now And under my protection As I am under Odysseus'.
NEOPTOLEMUS (*To Soldiers*)	Do not lie to me, Hecuba. Tear off this mockery And put on what befits them.
ANDROMACHE	Slave-gear?
NEOPTOLEMUS	Never pretend To be what you are not. Do it.

(*SOLDIERS tear off the CHORUS' dresses and dress them as slaves*)

HECUBA	Stop this, I command you.
NEOPTOLEMUS	Do it.
ANDROMACHE	You are a nauseous Brutal little boy.
NEOPTOLEMUS	Is this the wife of Hector?
ANDROMACHE	I am.
HECUBA	She at least Is of the Royal House.
NEOPTOLEMUS	She must do as the rest; Take off your dress.
ANDROMACHE	Take off your master's armour; You have yet to earn it, boy.
NEOPTOLEMUS	I won it in battle.

ANDROMACHE You won it by murdering
An old man and your own sister.

NEOPTOLEMUS Yes, I killed her, she was tainted.

ANDROMACHE She was noble, not as you are.

NEOPTOLEMUS No, she was marred
As soon as she was made;
If I had let her live
I should have been sullied too.

ANDROMACHE How was she sullied?

NEOPTOLEMUS By a foul old man who tried
To force her to his bed.

ANDROMACHE And you killed her for that?
You are unnatural.

NEOPTOLEMUS She was, not I.

HECUBA I doubt if Priam touched her;
Why are you so squeamish?

NEOPTOLEMUS He soiled her.

ANDROMACHE How can you tell?

NEOPTOLEMUS What does it matter?
She is buried for ever
Under the rubble of Ilion.

(*To Soldiers*) Are the slave-brands ready?
Do what you have come for.

CHORUS Don't let him hurt us!

HECUBA Obey him, let them do it.
You will all find it easier
If you sing. Begin, I'll lead you.

(*HECUBA starts to sing and the women join in
as the SOLDIERS brand them. Each hide their
pain*)

Mark them well, Pyrrhus;
This is a kind of courage
That you will never know of;
It is you who will be branded

Forever, and not them.
Take your prize and leave us.   (*)

(NEOPTOLEMUS looks at ANDROMACHE)

NEOPTOLEMUS   This is the one I have chosen.

ANDROMACHE   Then you're mad as well as vicious.

HECUBA   Be careful, Andromache.

ANDROMACHE   Go back to the Council
Where it seems that they still honour you,
And when you have told them
Your shame, go back to Scyros
And brand the pigs in their sties:
That is all you are fit for.

NEOPTOLEMUS   I wish to do honour
To a great warrior's widow;
But I am a warrior too
And have done more than he did:
I have won the war.

ANDROMACHE   You are not a warrior
And you never will be;
You are a little boy.

(He strikes her)

NEOPTOLEMUS   I am a man now;
I shall teach you to treat me so.

ANDROMACHE   Do you think you can please a woman
Who has shared the bed of Hector?
Do you think if you take me
Into your brat-bed
You'll be able to look in my eyes?
I see yours now, New Soldier,
In that golden armour which is too big for you;
Don't you see, if you take me
That I'll always be comparing
A real man and a false one
For the rest of your life of shame?

NEOPTOLEMUS   No one knows the future;
We must both forget what's past;
Take off that dress and burn it.

ANDROMACHE   He is trying to humiliate me
             As his father did with Hector.

NEOPTOLEMUS You do not know my mind yet:
             Take it off. Re-heat the brand.

HECUBA   Agamemnon promised me
             No member of my family
             Should be touched: fetch Odysseus.

NEOPTOLEMUS The Council gives the orders now.

ANDROMACHE   Brand me and you'll brand
             Yourself inside for ever.

NEOPTOLEMUS This is foolish, Andromache,
             And will do you no good.

ANDROMACHE   Good? Where is goodness?
             How can any one that's human
             Do such things to humans?
             Where does such evil come from?
             Why must others suffer
             When one sick boy is angry?

NEOPTOLEMUS That is better, weeping
             Suits you better than scolding.

HECUBA   Take it off, Andromache,
             Or he will tear it off you.

ANDROMACHE   While I do, no one touch me.

NEOPTOLEMUS Do it quickly then as they have.

ANDROMACHE   Hector... Hector... Hector!

             (*As she begins to take off her dress,
             ODYSSEUS returns with two SOLDIERS*)

ODYSSEUS   You must leave this, Neoptolemus,
             There's a quarrel in the Council
             And much of it concerns you.

NEOPTOLEMUS I will go. (*To Soldiers*) Come with me.
             When my prize is ready
             Send her to me, Odysseus.   (*)

             (*He goes with his SOLDIERS*)

ODYSSEUS   I have brought some oil
             And some ointment for each of you.
             I must speak to the Queen.

             *(ODYSSEUS' SOLDIERS dress the burns on
             the womens' shoulders. ANDROMACHE
             stands apart, holding her dress to herself)*

HECUBA   What now, Odysseus?

ODYSSEUS   I am not a cruel man:
             I have compassion
             And sometimes too much;
             It is not the smoke of the city
             That works now on my eyes.
             I am sent to tell you
             What Calchas has prophesied.

HECUBA   I guess it; shall I make it
             More easy for you by telling you?

ODYSSEUS   If you know it, speak it.

HECUBA   You have not yet touched on
             A custom we are told
             Is common in the West.
             Did Calchas perhaps prophesy
             Some danger in the future
             Sometimes posed by royal children?

ODYSSEUS   You have a prophet's skill.

HECUBA   All our men are dead,
             Isn't that enough for you?

ODYSSEUS   Some boys are still living.

ANDROMACHE   Stop this.

HECUBA   Quietly now.
             I have no young children:
             At my years –

ODYSSEUS   Understood.
             But Andromache has a son;
             Some name him Scamander
             And others Astyanax;
             I find the first name sweeter.

ANDROMACHE   You cannot mean – you cannot –

HECUBA
Let me handle this, Andromache.
Everybody knows
That little boys are harmless.

ODYSSEUS
Everybody knows
That little boys grow up;
Many tales are told
Often involving shepherds,
But I need not remind you;
Sometimes it works out well
And sometimes not so well.

ANDROMACHE
Stop this, Odysseus!

ODYSSEUS
We've heard you have one son left
Who is young, though not a baby;
His name is Polydorus.

HECUBA
He is safe, you will never find him.

ODYSSEUS
Let us hope not for his sake
And for yours.

ANDROMACHE
         Scamander:
Nobody must touch him!

ODYSSEUS
That's what I'm charged to speak of.

HECUBA
You mean they plan to kill him?

ANDROMACHE
Don't try to frighten me.

ODYSSEUS
I regret it very deeply.

ANDROMACHE
I left him safe at home!

ODYSSEUS
Your home is no longer standing.

ANDROMACHE
Where is my boy, Odysseus?

ODYSSEUS
It is given out that he jumped
From the walls before they were broken.

HECUBA
That was noble.

ODYSSEUS
         But not true.

ANDROMACHE
Tell me what's happened to him!

ODYSSEUS
By order of the Council
He was thrown from the walls.
I voted against it.

ANDROMACHE	Why? Tell me why!
ODYSSEUS	Calchas prophesied He would avenge his city.
ANDROMACHE	I do not believe you; No man would dare to do that.
ODYSSEUS	You are right, when Calchas spoke None in the army were easy And some showed open disobedience; That is always a danger After a victory.
HECUBA	So?
ODYSSEUS	So I did it.
ANDROMACHE	You?
ODYSSEUS	I am sorry; there are times When it seems that such horrors Are somehow meant to happen.

(ANDROMACHE holds herself in till here. Now she breaks down)

HECUBA	Come here, Odysseus. You swore you would be good to me; Now is the time to prove it. You must make the Council cancel All that Calchas has commanded: They must if they are human.
ODYSSEUS	They are human, so they won't.
HECUBA	But you spoke for Polyxena?
ODYSSEUS	Yes, I am trying to save her.
HECUBA	You must also make them promise To kill no more children And bring us her son's body.
ODYSSEUS	I should be glad to do so; I also have a son, Young and very dear to me.
ANDROMACHE	Make him go away! Get him away from me!
ODYSSEUS	I will do what I can.

HECUBA	Then bring me Priam's body And send Agamemnon to me. (*)

(He goes. ANDROMACHE stands shivering. She has not put on the slave-dress and is naked, clutching the slave-sacking to protect herself)

Let it out now, my darling,
And when you go to Pyrrhus
You will be strong again.

CHORUS	How can she put her misery And grief into words?
HECUBA	You are right, true grief is wordless; We have all lost sons.
CHORUS	We have all lost everything.
HECUBA	When they bring Priam's body They will bring Scamander's too And we'll bury them together.

(HECUBA holds her. ANDROMACHE begins to sing quietly)

Put it on.

ANDROMACHE	Don't touch me.
HECUBA	Put it on, you're shivering.
ANDROMACHE	Don't touch me!
HECUBA	You must go on: Curses can give one strength.
ANDROMACHE	Don't say such things, Hecuba! I cannot bear this.
HECUBA	We may all have to bear More than we know of yet.
CHORUS	None of us can bear More than we're suffering now.
HECUBA	Careful; you'll tempt the gods.
CHORUS	But how can we bear it?

(ANDROMACHE laughs)

ANDROMACHE	I bear it, I bear it:
	You didn't know that, did you?
HECUBA	What are you saying?
ANDROMACHE	The night before Hector died
	He was frightened and could not sleep
	Because he knew Achilles
	Would kill him the next day,
	So I held him in my arms
	And sang until he smiled
	And then we had such loving…
HECUBA	And?
ANDROMACHE	And I conceived.
HECUBA	Are you certain?
ANDROMACHE	O yes.
HECUBA	It will be a boy, I know it;
	That is good.
ANDROMACHE	How can I bear
	To be soiled by Neoptolemus
	When I carry Hector's child?
HECUBA	This is very good.
CHORUS	How can you say that?
HECUBA	She must go into his brat-bed
	And let him take his pleasure.
ANDROMACHE	She is mad, keep her away from me.
HECUBA	You must make the boy
	Believe it is his own.
CHORUS	How could she do that?
HECUBA	It has been done before.
CHORUS	Only in stories, lady.
HECUBA	She must make her own story now
	And in time her son will become
	A great King in the West
	Who will destroy our enemies.
ANDROMACHE	You're not sane, you are dreaming.

HECUBA

Don't frighten your master
With your proud and fierce looks;
You must handle him gently.

ANDROMACHE

How can I pretend?
I have lost my child!

HECUBA

Stop this, no self-pity;
I have lost more children
Than your womb will ever yield.
It is true that to bear children
Is the greatest thing of all
And the sweetest to a woman
And yet it is nothing
Unless such children live
Brave lives and win such fame
That all the world remembers them.
That is why I did not grieve
When death took my sons;
They won honour for my country
And high words will be told of them.

CHORUS

Not of Paris, your darling.

HECUBA

Of him most of all.
By his courage and his beauty
He won Zeus' daughter
And fame for our city.
For ten years we held it
Against a great army
Which could only get in by trickery.
Troy won the war: that is how
After-ages will tell of it.

CHORUS

How can she say that?
— So that she can bear it.

ANDROMACHE

If I lie with Neoptolemus
I will have to bear his child.

HECUBA

Rather say, bear your own.
We can still turn ill to good.

ANDROMACHE

This is our doomsday:
Some may be lucky

And suffer with dignity
But I won't and I can't.
I will go now as I am
And tell them they are evil
And that will be the end
Of the story of Andromache.

HECUBA

Tears won't help your child;
Use your wits and you'll survive.

ANDROMACHE

I don't want to survive.

HECUBA

Your child is inside you
And he will give you strength.
I, your Queen, command you
As a War-Queen to her warrior.
Revenge often takes
Many years in the making
But the aim will sustain you
And you will grow strong again.
Wipe your eyes and get up;
The soldiers are coming back.
Do you want them to see
The wife of Hector snivelling?
Put this on, Andromache.

(HECUBA puts a blanket over
ANDROMACHE as Neoptolemus' SOLDIERS
enter. ANDROMACHE throws the slave-dress
on the fire)

ANDROMACHE

Hector! Hector! Hector!   (*)

(SOLDIERS take out ANDROMACHE. The
CHORUS break into weeping)

CHORUS

Apollo! Apollo! Apollo!
Why have you left us?
Why have you betrayed us?
Why? Tell us why?

HECUBA

Trojans, listen to me!
Apollo is still with us.
We must forget the past
And make a new beginning:
We must go on.

CHORUS	How can we?
HECUBA	By going where we must.
CHORUS	Where's that?
HECUBA	Sit, I'll tell you How we will heal our wounds.
CHORUS	What is she saying?
HECUBA	Before there can be healing There must be a wound But before there's a wound Blood must be spilt...
CHORUS	You speak strange words, lady.
HECUBA	Do you remember How our city began?
CHORUS	Yes, they tried many sites Before Troy was founded.
HECUBA	Good, tell me the story.
CHORUS	Ilus, Priam's grandfather Won a prize at some games From some king now forgotten Who told him he must follow it Wherever it might wander Till it lay down and rested.
HECUBA	And what was this prize?

CHORUS	It was a dappled cow
	   – Where it lay would be the place
	Where he must build our city
	   – So he followed it and pondered
	As it wandered and it browsed
	Till they came to the spot
	That the gods had appointed
	   – And there he reared up Ilion.

HECUBA	The tale is a good one But you tell it vilely. The cow was not dappled But splotched and smeared with blood

From the bulls in the slaughter-house.
Now a herd of cows
Bloody and branded
Must go across the sea-lanes
And when the herd is parted
Each must help to found
A new Ilion...a Troynovaunt:
Odysseus will help us.

CHORUS   Don't trust him.

HECUBA   No, I'll use him.
He will respect a woman
Who does not show weakness.

CHORUS   He is coming.

HECUBA   Then mark me.   (*)

(Enter ODYSSEUS and SOLDIERS. He is very weary)

ODYSSEUS   I have brought you some hot drink
With some herbs and honey in it.
Put it on the fire
And it will help to warm them
And keep up their strength.

(The SOLDIERS do so and ODYSSEUS dismisses them)

You must not catch cold now.

HECUBA   What kind of man are you?
Sometimes you show kindness,
Sometimes you twist words
And sometimes you kill babies;
It does not seem to trouble you.

ODYSSEUS   It troubles me deeply
But I did not kill him;
He was killed by Neoptolemus:
It did not seem the moment
To say so to Andromache.

HECUBA   You should have told her;
It will lead to greater grief
Between them later on.

ODYSSEUS   I think so; when it does
            He will have to handle it.

HECUBA   Have you done as I asked you?

ODYSSEUS   I have done what I could
            But the minds of the Council
            Were on other things.

HECUBA   Some quarrel?
            It is common after a victory.

ODYSSEUS   Drink that, while it's warm.
            It began when Menelaus
            Promised his daughter Hermione
            To Neoptolemus.

HECUBA   Pyrrhus?
            That boy has too many prizes.
            But why should it lead to a quarrel?

ODYSSEUS   Because long ago at Aulis
            Menelaus promised his brother
            That if he led the army
            Orestes should marry her.

HECUBA   Orestes?

ODYSSEUS   The General's son.

HECUBA   Then his first oath is binding.

ODYSSEUS   I think so, but the Council
            Upheld Pyrrhus' claim.

HECUBA   That boy is greedy.

ODYSSEUS   The boy is not to blame
            For what happened once he'd set
            The beacon-light on Ilion.

HECUBA   That was your plan, Odysseus.

ODYSSEUS   If you have to blame someone
            You should blame Agamemnon.

HECUBA   Agamemnon wanted peace.

ODYSSEUS   Yes, it's sad. When he saw
            The beacon-light from Tenedos
            It seems he did not give

The signal to the army
Who were waiting in the ships.
The plan was to come in quickly
Before Troy could arm
But they waited half an hour
Till they heard cries in the city.
Agamemnon himself
Did not come till it was over.

HECUBA   Is this true?

ODYSSEUS   It is possible:
Menelaus said so to his face
Which is why they started quarrelling.

HECUBA   Send Agamemnon to me.

ODYSSEUS   He has gone.

HECUBA   Gone?

ODYSSEUS   He's set sail
For the West with your daughter.

HECUBA   Then fetch Menelaus
Or has he gone too with his war-prize?

ODYSSEUS   No, he is weeping alone.

HECUBA   What has he to weep for?

ODYSSEUS   Calchas has foretold
That he and his brother
Will never meet again.

HECUBA   Then both of them are lucky.

ODYSSEUS   They are sorry that they quarrelled.
Menelaus knows that his brother
Has done most to rescue his wife.

HECUBA   But what will he do with her now?

ODYSSEUS   He means to put her on trial.

HECUBA   For what crime?

ODYSSEUS   He says
He wants to know that happened
When Paris came to Sparta.

HECUBA	All the world knows what happened.
ODYSSEUS	But perhaps not who began it.
HECUBA	If he hopes for cuckold-comfort He will never know the truth.
ODYSSEUS	He will try her at Delphi.
HECUBA	He's unwise to trust Apollo.
ODYSSEUS	I agree, I prefer Athene. (*)
	(*They drink*)
HECUBA	What do you want, Odysseus?
ODYSSEUS	I want us to help one another.
HECUBA	You mean it is time to bargain.
ODYSSEUS	There is a real danger Of mutiny in the army.
HECUBA	You wish me to speak to them?
ODYSSEUS	Go on drinking and listen.
HECUBA	I should be glad to speak to them.
ODYSSEUS	When your son seized Helen Menelaus told the army He had also seized much treasure, So if they rescued Helen His gold would be shared among them.
HECUBA	Paris seized no treasure Beyond the girl he loved.
ODYSSEUS	Maybe not, and yet –
HECUBA	One has to say such things.
ODYSSEUS	We understand each other.
HECUBA	But now the army hold Menelaus to his promise?
ODYSSEUS	Of course the Atreidae hoped To meet their commitments From the treasury of Priam.
HECUBA	Of course.

ODYSSEUS	But we cannot find it.
HECUBA	The last of our gold Was spent on Hector's ransom.
ODYSSEUS	Yet Priam raised fresh allies; How were they rewarded?
HECUBA	Naturally we promised payment After the war was over.
ODYSSEUS	Naturally, but all kings Keep some reserve in secret In case they are defeated And forced into retirement; It is natural.
HECUBA	It is natural. You had better dig Under Ilion till you find it.
ODYSSEUS	Is it there?
HECUBA	Old dogs forget Where their best bones are buried.
ODYSSEUS	You are playing games with me. Finish your drink, Hecuba, And tell me where it is hidden.
HECUBA	Then you must first promise me Three things.
ODYSSEUS	Three is too many.
HECUBA	First, Priam's body Must be brought to me for burial.
ODYSSEUS	That is already arranged.
HECUBA	Next, you must prevent The sacrifice of Polyxena.
ODYSSEUS	That is harder but I'll try. In his heart the boy is gentle, Just as his father was.
HECUBA	Lastly, you shall swear By the goddess you hold dearest That if ever you find my son,

	My last son still living, Polydorus, you will protect him.
ODYSSEUS	I swear that I will cherish him As I do my own Telemachus.
HECUBA	Will the Council agree to it?
ODYSSEUS	They will hold it a small price To appease an angry army. Where is the gold?
HECUBA	In Thrace.
ODYSSEUS	With King Polymestor? Good, In winter the northern route Is the quickest way home and the safest.
HECUBA	Then go back to the Council And do as you have sworn to. (*)

(*ODYSSEUS rises*)

ODYSSEUS	There is only one problem: In strict terms of law I fear I have no power To deal on your behalf.
HECUBA	What does that mean, Odysseus?
ODYSSEUS	Although I protect you You are not my slave.
HECUBA	What of that?
ODYSSEUS	It's unfortunate You do not bear my mark Which would ensure your safety: That troubles me.
HECUBA	But surely Even in the West They do not brand Queens?
ODYSSEUS	I fear there are precedents.
HECUBA	There are always precedents.
ODYSSEUS	You speak wisely as always.
HECUBA	I forbid it, Odysseus.

ODYSSEUS	There could be advantages.
HECUBA	Go away.
ODYSSEUS	A brand's purpose Is not to humiliate But to protect whoever bears it. Our soldiers are rough men But they are taught from childhood To treat brands with respect: It prevents them stealing cattle.
HECUBA	Go away, Odysseus.
ODYSSEUS	But perhaps you fear the pain? That is understandable.
HECUBA	I cannot suffer more Than I am suffering now.
ODYSSEUS	Maybe not, but suffering Is not the same as pain.
HECUBA	Do you think that I fear pain?
ODYSSEUS	Grief can be endured But pain is unendurable.
HECUBA	First a little kindness And then some half-promise And then something vile: I read you, Odysseus, The trick is an old one. Do you think you can frighten Hecuba?
ODYSSEUS	I have no wish to do so But these women are watching you; How will you answer me?
	(Pause)
HECUBA	If I'm branded no one can touch me?
ODYSSEUS	That is the law among us.
HECUBA	We are all Trojan women And we suffer together. But you yourself must do it; Take the brand from the fire

	Or perhaps you are frightened?
	Have you ever used a brand?
ODYSSEUS	Only on sheep and cattle.
HECUBA	Then you're rising in the world,
	Get on with it, Ithacan.

(She uncovers her shoulder as he takes the brand from the fire)

ODYSSEUS	There seems to be a brand-mark
	On your shoulder already.
HECUBA	Yes, it's an old one.
ODYSSEUS	Whose is it, Hecuba?
HECUBA	I had it as a child;
	He who made it is dead.
ODYSSEUS	What was the man's name?
HECUBA	Heracles.
ODYSSEUS	Heracles?
	That is not his mark.
HECUBA	The shapes left by great ones
	Are soon blurred by time.
	Are you afraid of the dead?
ODYSSEUS	I would be foolish not to be.
HECUBA	But Heracles is immortal.
ODYSSEUS	Your words are wise, as ever.
	Overbranding is held
	A grave crime in the West.
	You please me, Hecuba,
	You and I think alike;
	I will put all you ask to the Council.
	But I fear a storm is coming;
	When they've brought your husband's body
	You must do your rites quickly;
	As soon as you hear my trumpet
	You must come to the ships. (*)

(He goes. HECUBA laughs)

CHORUS	Why did you tell Odysseus That there is gold in Thrace?
HECUBA	To see my son Polydorus; He is hidden there in the light.
CHORUS	Lady, that is dangerous.
HECUBA	The King of Thrace is powerful And his wife is my daughter; They have sworn to protect my son.
CHORUS	Then there's no need to go there.
HECUBA	It is always wise to renew Oaths sworn between kingdoms.
CHORUS	But is there any gold there? – Don't tell us – Such knowledge Could be dangerous.
HECUBA	Yes it's dangerous But I must teach my boy The high things he must know When he rebuilds our country.
CHORUS	But he's a little boy.
HECUBA	Odysseus spoke rightly, Little boys become great kings.

(*ODYSSEUS' trumpet sounds*)

CHORUS	That is Odysseus' trumpet – We must go to the ships.
HECUBA	Not till they've brought Priam's body. (*)

(*Enter SECOND MAN as MENELAUS, holding a bundle. His head is partly bandaged and hidden. The women do not recognise him*)

MENELAUS	Which of you is Hecuba? I have brought her what is left Of the body of her husband. It is all that could be found Under the stones of Ilion.
HECUBA	This? Did Odysseus Send you to mock me?

MENELAUS   No, the Council of the West
             Wished you to have it.

HECUBA   Then it is a mockery;
             Do they think that I will weep
             For a bone-bag of some nobody?

MENELAUS   No Trojan bones are nobody.

CHORUS   Let us take them and honour them.

HECUBA   Tell the Council they must dig
             Till they send what was promised me.

MENELAUS   The Kings of the Council
             Have set sail for the West.

             (*ODYSSEUS' trumpet sounds again*)

CHORUS   We must go.

MENELAUS   First lay them gently
             On the fire and honour them.

HECUBA   Get on with it.

MENELAUS   Sometimes
             A warrior who is nameless
             Is remembered longer
             Than the city that he died for.

             (*CHORUS lay the bundle on the fire. HECUBA
             starts to go. Flames and smoke begin to rise*)

CHORUS   Look, lady, at the light
         —   What is this sweet smell?
         —   Maybe one of those we love.

MENELAUS   Where there is love
             Hearth-fires never die.

HECUBA   That is well said, stranger.

             (*A flame rises from the fire, thin and high*)

CHORUS   See how the flames
             Leap up to Olympus.

HECUBA   Up you go, old bones.
             Zeus, are you watching?
             If you exist

Greet this flame and honour it;
Sniff the smoke in your nostrils
Of all my city's children.
Do you remember
What Priam once said to us
When Heracles enslaved us
All those years ago?
When some doom crushes us
Or when some great rock falls
It is not our story's end
But a trial put upon us
By the everlasting gods
To see what stuff they made
When they first took clay and earth
And shaped a human woman.
Gods may begin things
Though that is not certain,
But humans go on
Questioning and challenging.
Laugh, Zeus, if you will
As you swill down your nectar
But watch us and wonder:
We are worth the watching.

(*The CHORUS chant and beat the ground*)

MENELAUS

Fine words may ease the heart
But they cannot give life again.

HECUBA

Words can change the world!
While I have language
And a true tongue to sound it
I am stronger than the spears
Of all the world's war-hordes:
My words are flames of fire!

(*ODYSSEUS enters with SOLDIERS as his
trumpet sounds a third time*)

ODYSSEUS

Must I fetch you myself?
On your feet, all of you:
The storm at sea grows closer.
You should leave too, Menelaus,
If you want to outwit Poseidon.

HECUBA	Is this the bull of Sparta?
MENELAUS	You must go now to the ships.
HECUBA	O my lord Menelaus! You threw away your nectar Ten years ago in Sparta. You are a foolish bull To try to hide your horns But you are a gentle one. This one man, Odysseus, Has treated me with honour; You have yet to prove to me What kind of man you are. Follow me, women, Follow the dappled cow.

(Trumpet sounds again. HECUBA leads the CHORUS out singing)

ODYSSEUS	Are you coming, Menelaus?
MENELAUS	Soon.
ODYSSEUS	You are waiting Till the army's gone, that's wise.
MENELAUS	Farewell.
ODYSSEUS	In my opinion Your brother was right to be angry With what you did and said to him; After all he has done for your sake You should not have given your daughter To Pyrrhus but to Orestes As you promised long ago.
MENELAUS	We have all acted wrongly.
ODYSSEUS	Of course, but we've won. May your voyage be swift and happy.
MENELAUS	I have waited long.
ODYSSEUS	We have all waited long. (*)

(He goes. MENELAUS looks at the fire. Music. Mist begins to appear slowly from the cave. The sea sounds)

HELEN (*Within*)   Apple day… Apple day…

(*A golden apple rolls out of the cave*)

It's for you, Menelaus.

MENELAUS   It was stolen by Eris.

HELEN   But now it is your turn…

MENELAUS   It is not yours or mine.

HELEN   Yes, she gave it to me
And I have kept it for you.

MENELAUS   Come out, we must go home now.

HELEN   Pick it up and I'll come to you.

(*HELEN appears in the mist. She is painted gold all over and is naked except for a mass of gold necklaces, bangles, rings, girdle etc, which partly cover her. MENELAUS does not look at her, but at the apple*)

Free, I am free again!

(*She begins to dance*)

What will you do with your apple-girl?
Choose, Menelaus; If you do not want me
Give Hera the apple
And you shall get back
All the treasure you have lost.
If you can't decide
Then give it to Athene.

MENELAUS   Yes, I'd like to be wiser.

HELEN   Wisdom is a mist.

MENELAUS   They say truth is wisdom.

HELEN   What nonsense are you speaking?
O yes, I have heard
You will try me at Delphi.

MENELAUS   It is said all truth is found there.

HELEN   Let us try the truth now.

(*She begins to dance*)

I am your war-prize:
Don't you want me, Menelaus?

(*Throws off some necklaces. She dances round him, he laughs*)

MENELAUS

You look ridiculous;
You are right to take it off.

HELEN

Wives are expendable
But gold lasts for ever.

(*Throws off more*)

MENELAUS
(*Calls*)

I do not want the gold.
Where are my soldiers?

HELEN

But you do wish to try me,
So you shall have your will.

(*She goes on dancing, enter MENELAUS' SOLDIERS*)

Ah, here are my loyal Spartans,
Brutal, brave and beautiful.
How you have all suffered
For my sake and my husband's,
Take this as your reward.

(*She throws jewels and rings at the SOLDIERS*)

MENELAUS
(*To Soldiers*)

Don't touch them, I have gold enough
To reward you when we're home.

HELEN

But I hear you and your brother
Promised gold to everyone;
If my husband will not pay it
A loyal wife knows her duty.
I am what is lost
And I am what men long for.

(*Throws off more jewels and a golden apple*)

Pick them up, don't be frightened.
Don't you remember
How when you all were little
They told you of a Golden Age
Which is lost but still to find?

If you search long and are lucky
Each one of you may find it;
This apple is a bit of it
And I am all the rest
And I will refresh you.
It wasn't Eris, no,
But Aphrodite herself
Who plucked it from the tree
Of gold in Hera's garden.
Have you all forgotten
The streams of Hesperides
Still bubble far off in the West?   (*)

(The streams run. MENELAUS picks up the apple)

MENELAUS I will take this to Cheiron
And try what it is made of.
Cover her with my sea-cloak
And take her to my ship.

HELEN Yes, try me on ship-board:
We will need a lot of blankets:
Rowing-benches are hard:
I know, I have experience.

MENELAUS If we do not leave before the storm
We may never reach Sparta.

HELEN O I am glad of it!
On my first night with Paris
There was such a noble storm
That we had to beach at Cranae;
The Four Winds clashed above us
And the waves frolicked over us
All wanting to be part of us;
The wings of sea-birds stroked us
And a dolphin leaped too far
And flopped and thrashed beside us;
It puffed and it eyed us
So it may have been my Father
Seeing us fulfil his plan;
All the oarsmen cheered us
And the steersmen got so drunk

That we ended up in Egypt.
Now it is your turn;
Here I stand, Menelaus,
Living, breathing, shining:
Take your golden girl and taste
Your golden world again.

MENELAUS   Very good, Helen.
These displays are of course
Familiar to all of you,
But we know that underneath
She is as she has always been,
Insecure and frightened.
Those who are vulnerable
Need to seem invulnerable.
I know, I have experience;
And those who don't know who they are
Need most to make images
Of what they would like to be.
It is good for her to try
To humiliate me now
But after ten years in the war-camp
Such things have ceased to trouble me.
She knows, as I do,
That a touch of self-mockery
Is very often helpful.

But don't you think, Helen,
You are punishing yourself
By appearing in the image
That the world has put upon you?
It is only a mask
And masks may be useful,
Which is why prophets use them
Since their faces are rarely
As noble as their words.
You had better put this cloak on
Or you really will catch cold.

(*He smiles and she laughs. He puts his cloak
on her. She makes a strange sound which is
echoed in the sky*)

HELEN   I am cold, hold me, husband.   (*)

(She snuggles by him. Music)

Once upon a time
There was a little girl
Who came out of an egg
So at first she felt special.
But one day they told her
That she was a rape-child
And she became uneasy;
Should she be proud of it
Or was it something shameful?
After that she never knew
Who she was nor why;
Nurse told her that this feeling
Is common among rape-children
But she grew shy and private
And terrified of men.

One day when she was picking
Flowers in a water-meadow
Close to the bull-rushes
By the bank of the Eurotas
She found she had gathered so many
That she had to pull her dress up
To make a basket for them.
Suddenly she saw
Cruel eyes in the bull-rushes
Peeping where they should not
When a girl lifts her dress.
Then a huge ancient man
Sprang out and flung her down
And raped her in the bull-rushes.
She ran home bruised and bleeding;
But when she told her father
What Theseus had done to her
Tyndareus beat her and said
She herself must have provoked him.
Soon she realised what was happening
And that another rape-child
Was coming into the world.

She wanted to get rid of it
But she didn't know how;
When it was born
They never let her see it
And so she never knew
If it was dead or living.

Then Tyndareus said,
'I wash my hands of you:
I must marry you at once
To some King who is worthy.'
She wept, since in her experience
Few kings were ever worthy
And she feared that her husband
Would be some brute like Theseus.
But he wasn't, he was gentle
And taught her the best ways
Of making love kindly.
Nurse used to say
He did it so well
Because he used to eat
The testicles of bulls
But she didn't believe that;
Bulls are sacred to him.
O, it is so good
That you are going to try me:
You will try me, won't you?

MENELAUS   There's a mark on your shoulder
Which wasn't there before;
Did Paris or some Trojan
Hurt you in some way?

HELEN   Father put it on me.

MENELAUS   Tyndareus?

HELEN   Zeus.

MENELAUS   Surely Zeus has no brand-mark?

HELEN   His brand is on all of us
Though it does not show so clearly;
Mine is on me for ever.

MENELAUS	Time to go home now; I want to see our daughter.
HELEN	Hermione?
MENELAUS	Of course.
HELEN	Must we really see Hermione? She is such an ugly child. You should not have promised Hermione to Pyrrhus.
MENELAUS	I had to.
HELEN	I know, but she won't be happy.
MENELAUS	Who will be? ...Shall we go?
HELEN	Yes, let us go.

(*She picks up and gives him the apple*)

Zeus, Father, I have done;
Your plan is fulfilled.
Some lost, some won;
It is as you willed.

(*All go. The sea sounds*)

Play 7
CASSANDRA

THRACE NEAR THE SEA-SHORE

CAST

First Woman	HECUBA
Second Woman	CASSANDRA
Third Woman	ILIONE
Fourth Woman	(–)
First Man	POLYMESTOR
Second Man	AGAMEMNON
Third Man	ODYSSEUS
Fourth Man	(–)

CHORUS and SOLDIERS

(Thrace. The sea-shore opposite Sigaeum near to the entrance of the Hellespont. Night. It is raining. It is cold and windy and there is a storm at sea. From time to time the tips of waves break over the edge of the ambience. The CHORUS are lying asleep and shivering. HECUBA is sleeping in her tent in front of the cave. CASSANDRA enters wearing AGAMEMNON's sea-cloak)

CASSANDRA

Now it is Thrace's turn
To make a mistake:
Thrace, where King Polymestor
Breeds the great Thracian horses.
The gods have raised a sea-storm;
They are angry with the victors
And have shattered their war-fleet.
Agamemnon's ship was blown here
Though he longs to go home.
I long to go with him
That my story may be over.

But it is not over.
When the war began
Both sides wooed the Thracians;
Their hearts were with Troy
Because Polymestor's wife
Was one of Priam's daughters;
But they feared to cross the War-Kings,
So they tried to keep a balance
By trading with both sides.
That was their first mistake.

The war made Thrace rich:
Troy needed food supplies
When the Troad was ravaged;
The West wanted timber
Because their ships were rotting
Or burned on the beaches.
So Odysseus came and demanded
Thracian wood as no trees
Were left standing in the battle-zone;
He spoke of building an engine

That would put an end to the war.
Polymestor did not trust him
So he sent Odysseus packing.
That was their second mistake.

Then the West sent Palamedes
Who told them Agamemnon
Would soon make peace with Priam;
But his army was starving
And without oil and fruit
Plague would break out in the war-camp.
So Thrace gave him all he asked for,
But Odysseus was humiliated
When he saw Palamedes thrive,
He tricked the desperate War-Kings
Into thinking he was a traitor
And so the army stoned him,
And Odysseus built the Horse.

But Troy was starving too;
And when Achilles killed Hector
Priam had to empty his treasury
To ransom my brother's body
And had no more gold to buy allies.
He knew then that Troy was doomed,
So he sent his youngest son
Polydorus to Thrace in secret
Who swore he would protect him.

Now Odysseus is back again
And his men are burning and looting
Searching for Thracian gold
Which Hecuba has told them
Will help the West pay for the war.

(ILIONE enters cautiously)

This is my sister Ilione;
She was born in Troy
But Polymestor persuaded
My father to make her his wife
To protect Troy's northern shores.
That was his third mistake.

She is trying to cope
But no one copes in a god-game.

(*She withdraws and watches*)

ILIONE (*To Chorus*) Where's Hecuba? Wake up.

CHORUS   Be quiet, we're trying to sleep.

ILIONE   I must speak to my mother
                          Before Odysseus comes.

CHORUS   It's Ilione – Speak softly
                        – She's in there, sleeping.

ILIONE   O how you all have suffered!
                          I have brought you a little bread.

CHORUS   Give it us – Why haven't you
                          Brought her son and your husband?

ILIONE   I must speak to my mother first.
                          Is it safe for them to come here?

CHORUS   Nobody is safe now.

ILIONE   No, Odysseus is threatening
                          To do dreadful things;
                          He has seized Thracian hostages
                          And swears he will kill them
                          If Polymestor does not tell him
                          Where Priam's gold is hidden.

CHORUS   Then you had better tell him.

ILIONE   We have told him we have no such gold
                          But Odysseus doesn't believe him.

CHORUS   Does he know Polydorus is here ?

ILIONE   No.

CHORUS   You should have brought him
                        – What is it ? You look frightened.

ILIONE   There is something I can't tell you.

CHORUS   Yet you look as if you need to
                        – You can trust us – Tell us.

ILIONE   My husband is a good man,
                          He didn't mean to do it...

CHORUS	What has Polymestor done?
ILIONE	He has drowned the boy…
CHORUS	How could he?
ILIONE	He feared that Odysseus Would find out we are hiding him. What shall I tell Hecuba?
CHORUS	Wisest to tell her the truth — No, that would break her.
ILIONE	But what am I to do ? I have honoured the gods, I have done no evil…
CHORUS	That is not always possible.
ILIONE	O why was I born a Trojan In the family of Priam? (*)

(*HECUBA* calls out from within)

HECUBA	Who is that? Is it Ilione?

(*HECUBA* drags herself out of the tent)

	My son, is he safe?
ILIONE	O Hecuba…
HECUBA	Why didn't you come sooner?
ILIONE	How you have suffered, Mother.
HECUBA	Is he safe?
CHORUS	Look what she's brought you.
ILIONE	Some cakes I baked myself.
HECUBA	Is he safe?
ILIONE	Yes, safe.
HECUBA	Polymestor will not give him To Odysseus?
ILIONE	No, never.

(*HECUBA* rises)

HECUBA	Why haven't you brought him with you?

ILIONE
Why did you tell Odysseus
Father's gold was hidden here?

HECUBA
So that none of our enemies
Shall know where it really is.

ILIONE
But we have no gold, you know that.

HECUBA
Of course I know.

ILIONE
You must tell him
The truth or he'll destroy us.

HECUBA
He has come with eight ships only;
What is your army doing?

ILIONE
You know we have no army;
Do you want Thrace to suffer
As you have?

HECUBA
If necessary.

ILIONE
Mother, listen to me:
You must face reality.

HECUBA
Only one thing is real now,
The lives of the children
Of the royal house of Troy,
The house which you belong to;
Polymestor must swear
To rear my son as his own.

ILIONE
What's the need? He has sworn already.

HECUBA
Because he's weak like you.

ILIONE
He's a good man, he loves Troy.

HECUBA
Then he should have fought beside us.

ILIONE
We sent help when you needed it.

HECUBA
And you sent it to our enemies.

ILIONE
We had to be careful.

HECUBA
Careful?
If you'd not supplied Palamedes
Troy would not have fallen.

ILIONE
Do you want our children
To be butchered as yours were?

HECUBA	Your son's blood is Trojan You alone are free to act now.
ILIONE	When a woman takes a husband She belongs to a different family.
HECUBA	You are bound by the blood you were born with To protect your own blood-brother.
ILIONE	I have done all I could.
HECUBA	Not yet. Why have you not Brought your husband with the boy?
ILIONE	He dare not leave his own son Unprotected in the citadel.
HECUBA	Who is he most afraid of? Odysseus or me?
ILIONE	Odysseus has threatened To put him to the torture.
HECUBA	Of course, but he has sworn To protect me and mine; I will protect both of you.
ILIONE	If you want to protect Any gold that is hidden Would it not be safer To tell me where it is?
HECUBA	Your husband made you ask that.
ILIONE	No, the thought was mine.
HECUBA	Bring him and we'll discuss it.
ILIONE	You must promise to persuade Odysseus That it is not in Thrace.
HECUBA	I promise; go quickly.
ILIONE	But Odysseus may see us.
HECUBA	Bring him to the back of my tent, And bring your own child too; If Odysseus sees my son He will think he is one of yours.

Why are you waiting, Ilione?
I could always read your face;
There is something you've not told me.
What is it?

ILIONE   It is fear.

HECUBA   What are you afraid of?

ILIONE   You. You frighten me.

HECUBA   Good, but I love you;
No more words, Trojan: fetch them.   (*)

(ILIONE goes)

I have slept, I am strong again
And there's work to be done.
Don't sit there, sullen and sulky;
You must make my tent ready
For our royal guests.

CHORUS   Lady,
You are in great danger.

HECUBA   No, Odysseus will protect me,
And I still have four children
With whom to remake our city,
Three daughters and a son.
Ilione is weak
But she fears me more than Odysseus;
She will do what I ask of her.

CHORUS   Ilione will not help you.

HECUBA   Maybe not, but Odysseus has promised
That Polyxena will be saved.

CHORUS   She is dead. While you were sleeping
We saw a great fire
Across the straits at Sigaeum
 — We saw Achilles' burial mound
Reared high up on the headland
So that all of Europe and Asia
May honour him for ever
 — She is dead; we are sorry.

HECUBA   There was always a risk
Neoptolemus would kill her

326

	Before Odysseus could stop him; There is no time now to weep.
CHORUS	Lady, don't trust Odysseus – You think that you are using him But he is playing with you – Ilione was trying to warn you.
HECUBA	I do not believe you.
CHORUS	Cassandra has confirmed it.
HECUBA	Cassandra's half-way to the West In the ship of the General.
CHORUS	No, they landed here last night; Agamemnon's ship was blown northward By the storm; it's on the beach And they're trying to repair it.
HECUBA	Good, I shall speak with him: Polydorus will be safe now.

(*CASSANDRA comes forward*)

CASSANDRA	Polydorus is dead.
HECUBA	Go away, Cassandra, Go back to your master.
CASSANDRA	Go down to the sea-shore And see for yourself.

(*Two of the CHORUS go*)

HECUBA	How can this be true? Who would have killed him?
CHORUS	Polymestor killed him.
HECUBA	Who said so?
CHORUS	Ilione told us – Her husband fears Odysseus As we do and you should.

HECUBA (*To Cassandra*) Fetch Agamemnon: fetch him!
                He will control Odysseus.

CASSANDRA	He won't.
HECUBA	What has he said to you?

CASSANDRA He has not yet spoken to me:
He sat on the ship-stern alone
Looking back towards Troy and weeping.

HECUBA Shame.

CASSANDRA His men said it was something
To do with his brother.
See, Mother, Poseidon
Has brought your last son to you.

(*The sea-sounds as the CHORUS return with POLYDORUS' body*)

HECUBA This...? How did he die?

CASSANDRA As you will, at sea.

CHORUS They drowned him – O Hecuba,
Polydorus and Polyxena...
– Lady, we weep for you.

(*HECUBA goes and looks at the body. She cries out. The cry turns into a howl and then to a kind of growl*)

– That is good; let it out
– She will feel the better for it
– But she is not weeping
– What is she doing?

(*HECUBA begins to scratch in the earth*)

HECUBA Work to do, work to do.

CHORUS Rest, your work is over.

HECUBA First we must bury the dead...

CASSANDRA Then she must go to sea
And climb Odysseus' ship-mast...

CHORUS Shut your mouth – Why should she try to?

CASSANDRA To look back on our country;
But she'll fall dead onto the deck
And all that will be left of her
Will be an old black bitch-dog.
Look at her, she's begun
To change her shape already.

HECUBA	Got to get it.
CHORUS	What?
HECUBA	That which must be got.
CHORUS	She is talking of the gold
	— She thinks it's in the earth.
HECUBA	Not gold now, something better:
	Revenge on Polymestor.
	We will kill him and his child.
CHORUS	How can we?
HECUBA	I will tell you.

(HECUBA takes a shell and breaks it)

HECUBA
When he comes to my tent
Use this on your fingers:
Thrust them into his eyes
And crack his skull with stones.
We will teach him that Trojan girls
Are braver and more dangerous
Than Achilles in his wrath.

CHORUS	But we would suffer for it.
HECUBA	No, Odysseus will protect us.
CASSANDRA	What is the point, Mother?
HECUBA	What is the point of Justice?

When will you understand?
The great gods are testing us
To see if we are strong enough
To turn what is done to us
Into something rare and noble.
Though all that we suffer
Is not of our own making
What we make of it is ours;
If you don't understand that
Our story has no meaning.
The gods may move strangely
But in the end it is certain
That they mean to do us honour.
For ten years our little city

Beat the War-Lords to the beaches;
Could we have done that
If the gods had not loved us?

CHORUS What is ten years or a hundred?
   – To the gods that is nothing
   – For fifty years we thrived
Till Heracles destroyed us
   – Then we won another fifty
And here we are now, broken
   – Our little age is over
And our everlasting city
Is dead children and dead stones.

(*They weep*)

HECUBA Our story is not yet over:
Many tales are told
Of a family or people
Suffering so long
That none of them remember
How their suffering began;
Yet at last they rose again
And grew greater than before.

CHORUS It would take a thousand years
For that miracle to happen.

HECUBA No, in some of you
It may have begun already.
Did no war-man take you
The night the city fell?
You will bear fresh sons in the West
And teach them to love our city.

CHORUS Do not say such things
   – Such sons would not be ours
   – How can we win back
What is gone for ever?

HECUBA I will tell you, puppies.
Listen to me, Cassandra:
You alone are safe
Because you belong to the General.
There are times when daughters

330

	Are more valuable than sons And if they have weak husbands They can have greater power.
CHORUS	— Agamemnon is married already When Cassandra speaks Nobody listens to her.
HECUBA	What she says doesn't matter; What is done in bed with bodies Is what makes kingdoms great.
CHORUS	But she's Apollo's priestess —
HECUBA	Perhaps it's begun already; Is his seed inside you?
CASSANDRA	The man has not touched me.
HECUBA	Then remember what I named you.
CASSANDRA	'Defence against Men'.
HECUBA	Not 'Defence' but 'Entangler', 'Entangler of Men'. Time to do it, puppy; Take off her prophet's robes, Wipe off the god-paint And show us if you know How to dance the wedding-dance.
CASSANDRA	Do not touch me, any of you.
CHORUS	Dance for us, Cassandra!
HECUBA (*To Chorus*)	When the General comes You shall teach him the truth Of how the world began.
CHORUS	Dance, dance, Cassandra!
	(*They pull off her cloak. She is wearing a yellow dress. She begins to dance, speaking Greek from 'The Trojan Women' again*)
CASSANDRA	This is my wedding-dress.
HECUBA	Take it off. Where did you find it?
CASSANDRA	In a chest in my master's ship.

331

CHORUS You found a dress of sacrifice?
— It must be precious to him.

HECUBA But you are not a sacrifice;
Take it off or you will anger him.

CASSANDRA I am a sacrifice.

HECUBA To whom?

CASSANDRA To Apollo,
To Apollo's mind within me.

HECUBA Take it off her! (*)

CHORUS Wait:
Polymestor is coming
With Ilione and their child.
— If they are, Odysseus
Will not be far behind
— What will you say to him
About the gold?

HECUBA Nothing,
Because I will have no words.

CASSANDRA You have too many, Mother.

(*HECUBA growls again*)

HECUBA When we've punished Polymestor
My work will be over
And I shall not need a tongue.
Come into my tent.

CHORUS What does she want of us?

HECUBA Before there is healing
There must be a wound
But before there's a wound
Blood must be spilt...
This sea-shell is sharp
So when our work is done
Silence my tongue for ever:
Swear you will do it.

CHORUS We dare not – If Odysseus
Asks us about the gold
How shall we answer him?

HECUBA   Tell him it's in Egypt,
                Libya, Tauris, Sicily:
                Make him grow old
                Searching in the sea-lanes,
                Looking for a treasure-hoard
                Which he will never find.
                Let us go in to our guests.

                (They start to go. HECUBA turns back)

                'There they stand yet...'
                The walls and the towers...
                If I should live again
                And knew my story's ending
                I would not change it.

CASSANDRA   She has learned nothing.

                *(CASSANDRA starts to chant quietly in Greek,
                using HECUBA's words in 'The Trojan Women'
                beginning at line 1240)*

HECUBA   It's she who has learned nothing.
                The joy we felt in our hearts
                When we danced the Horse through the gates,
                That is our Trojan truth.
                What else can humans do
                As they look towards the future
                But live in the moment?
                A moment does not last,
                It's a fragment of a second,
                Yet we're always in the moment
                Then, now and always:
                There is no other way.
                If we embrace that
                That is the high thing,
                That is the noble.
                Now and for ever
                Take the Great Horse in:
                For so it will be told...!

                *(As HECUBA and the CHORUS go into the
                tent singing, CASSANDRA repeats part of the
                speech she has been chanting from the 'Trojan
                Women')*

CASSANDRA 'If we had not suffered
Who would have remembered us?
When we are dead things
We shall be remembered
In stories and in songs'. (*)

(*ODYSSEUS enters from the sea-shore*)

ODYSSEUS Where is your mother?
In her tent?

(*Music within*)

She has guests?

CASSANDRA Of course.

ODYSSEUS Polymestor?

CASSANDRA And his wife.

ODYSSEUS I am glad,
They'll persuade her to be sensible.

(*He sits*)

Cassandra, I believe
Though others may not do so
That a god speaks inside you
Because very often
One does so to me;
But Athene's voice is quiet
And her counsel's clear and sensible,
So I speak her words in kind
And no one thinks me mad.

CASSANDRA You are fortunate.

ODYSSEUS But of course
You are not mad at all;
It's your god who is the madman.
To build a city twice
And twice to destroy it
Is at best inconsistent.

CASSANDRA No, he punishes those
Who do not honour him.

ODYSSEUS You are saying that he will punish us
Because we destroyed his temple?

334

CASSANDRA   You destroyed all our temples
So all the gods are angry;
Your Athene is friends again
With Apollo and Poseidon.
The storm that will destroy your ships
Will be the work of all of them.

ODYSSEUS   Yet Athene's temple stands;
I forbade our men to touch it.

CASSANDRA   Yet she's angry at what was done
To me in her sanctuary.

ODYSSEUS   The violence done to you
Was a serious offence
Against the rules of sanctuary.
Yet it is strange to me
That you fled for refuge
To Athene and not to Apollo.

CASSANDRA   His temple was on fire.

ODYSSEUS   She is a virgin as you are;
Is that why you went there?

CASSANDRA   It is usual when seeking sanctuary
To run to the nearest temple
That is still left standing.

ODYSSEUS   Yes, the practice is common.
But before he died I spoke
With the man who had tried to rape you:
He swore that he only wanted
To take away your mask.
He was drunk and mistook
The paint on your face
For something he could take home
As a trophy to please his children.
Many men are excited
By a woman masked or painted;
They long and they fear
To see the face behind it.
I too am curious;
I should have thought a mask
Would be more convenient.

CASSANDRA   Gods do not always
Require what is convenient.

ODYSSEUS   This tale that is told
Of Apollo having cursed you
Because you would not lie with him
Suggests you cannot give yourself
As a woman should to a man.

CASSANDRA   A god is not a man.

ODYSSEUS   For a girl to refuse a god
Is unusual, even these days.
I suppose it makes you feel special.

CASSANDRA   What do you want of me?
Even your Athene
Cannot help you find a nothing.

ODYSSEUS   A nothing? Ah, the gold-hoard;
That is not Athene's business.
But surely your Apollo
Can help to shed some light?

CASSANDRA   His light is not one to search with;
Sunlight blinds and scorches.

ODYSSEUS   So does war-fire and the flames
Of a great city burning.

CASSANDRA   You have not yet seen the light
Of the burning of the world.

ODYSSEUS   If his light is so terrible
Shed the paint and be free of him
And let me see your face:
My words seem to frighten you.
What is it that they say?
'The thing that we fear most
Is the thing that always happens.'

CASSANDRA   What is your thing, Odysseus?
Never to see your wife again
Or your home or your son?

ODYSSEUS   All warriors fear that
Till they hoist sail for home.

CASSANDRA	To set sail may not be The same thing as to get there.

(Screaming and shouting within)

ODYSSEUS	What's that noise?
CASSANDRA	Human Justice. (*)

(CHORUS run out, barking and howling. HECUBA crawls in dragging the dead body of ILIONE's son and snarling. Screams of pain within)

ODYSSEUS	Quiet, all of you! Tell me what has happened.
CHORUS	Justice has been done!
ODYSSEUS	By whom?
CHORUS	By all of us!

(HECUBA barks like a dog)

ODYSSEUS	Hecuba, what have they done?
CHORUS	She cannot speak, Odysseus – She has no tongue to tell you What you long to know.

(HECUBA howls as he goes to her)

ODYSSEUS	Who has done this?
CHORUS	She has: – She's beaten you, Odysseus! – We all have!
ODYSSEUS	What have you done?
CHORUS	We have given him Justice! – Hecuba's blinded the King! – And we have killed his children!

(HECUBA snarls by the body of their child)

ODYSSEUS	Why have you done this?
CHORUS	Because he killed her son – Look there – Polymestor drowned him.

ODYSSEUS *(To Hecuba)* Now I understand you:
This is where you hid the boy

And why you wished to come here;
I did not think you so foolish.
But to kill this Thracian child...
That was something else.

CHORUS   It was just!

ODYSSEUS   To kill me
Would have been more straightforward.

CHORUS   We would have if we could.

ODYSSEUS   But you couldn't, so you killed
This innocent child instead;
You killed the only creature
Weaker than you are.

CHORUS   – We didn't plan to do it
                – It just happened.

ODYSSEUS   Yes, it happened.

CHORUS   We went in to help her
To punish Polymestor
But it was dark inside
And we could not see clearly
                – It was as if the tent
Was full of a thousand people
                – All were screaming with rage
                – We only tried to defend ourselves
                – It just happened to us.

ODYSSEUS   That is generally how things happen.

CHORUS   Yet the old law is a good law:
Blood for blood, Odysseus.

ODYSSEUS   You have all been stupid.

CHORUS   Revenge isn't stupid
                – Not when it is just.

ODYSSEUS   You want justice? You shall have it.
You and your mistress
Have broken a law
Sacred to all peoples
And in all human homes.

CHORUS   We have no home now.

ODYSSEUS
If a tent has a hearth-fire
Then it is a home
And when strangers come there
You are bound to protect them.
But you took them in, Hecuba,
To maim and to kill;
That disgraces me, your master.
Why did you do it?

CHORUS
To show we are not slaves.

ODYSSEUS
You have shown that you are,
Slaves to your misery
And the part in you that's animal.

CHORUS
If you were human
You would understand.

ODYSSEUS
If being human means
Hurting those who have hurt you,
Yes, I understand.
You will go to the ships
And there my men will whip you
To teach you a little dignity.

CHORUS
If you want us to have dignity
Treat us with dignity
– Give us back our country
– Our children and our homes.

ODYSSEUS
It is true that you have suffered
And I am sorry for it.
If you learn to behave sensibly
You will find we can be kind.

(*HECUBA growls again*)

What is it, Hecuba?
I am sorrier for your son's death
Than I am for what your sufferings
Have led you to do here.
If you'd told me the truth
I would have protected him
As I swore to you in Troy.
Soon you and these women

Must go back into the ships;
But before we brave the storm
We shall all share a meal
As our warriors used to do
Before going into battle.
You too, Hecuba,
Must try to eat a little
To build up your strength.

(*He offers food*)

CASSANDRA   Without a tongue one cannot
Eat or drink: one dies.

ODYSSEUS   I have heard it said so
But I have as yet no proof of it.
Let me help to feed you
With some bread soaked in wine.

(*He offers some to HECUBA and she spits at it*)

Gently now, Hecuba;
Dogs that have been damaged
Often refuse to eat
From the hands of their master.
I have one such in Ithaca;
He too must be old now
But when his master's home again
He will eat from this hand,
Just as you will, Hecuba.
In a few days time
You shall help me to feed him.

(*He offers again to feed her*)

CHORUS   Whip her first and feed her afterwards.

ODYSSEUS   She has suffered most;
You should pity her.

CHORUS   She began it.

ODYSSEUS   Only gods begin things.

CHORUS   Once upon a time
She bore a little boy

340

And all our Trojan prophets
Told her he'd destroy us,
So she sent him to the mountains
And gave him to a shepherd;
— But when he was found again
She rejoiced. It was human.

— When she sent him to seize Helen
Priam said, 'Send her back'
— She said, 'My boy shall keep her;
What he wants is only human.'

— When Priam gave orders
To smoke the Wooden Horse
She made us take it in
— That too was human.

— When the city fell
She said, 'It is not over,
I must see my last son'.

ODYSSEUS   Yes, it was only human.

(While they have been speaking, HECUBA has started to crawl away. She holds the dead child in her mouth)

What are you doing, Hecuba?

CASSANDRA   She is taking him to your ship
To share the same sea-grave.

(HECUBA makes animal sounds as she goes)

ODYSSEUS   What is she trying to say?

CASSANDRA   She is singing her bitch-song
For herself, and for all
Who were and will be drowned
In the place where old Peleus
Pitched the corpse of Hesione:
'Cynossema', the Bitch's Grave',
So to be named by sailors.

(HECUBA has gone)

ODYSSEUS   There seem to be words
Which she wanted to say to me.

Perhaps they were about the gold;
You have tongues, can you help me?

CHORUS

My lord, we know nothing.

ODYSSEUS

But women love to share
Secrets with one another.

CHORUS

We know nothing.

ODYSSEUS

But you do,
You know about pain as she does.

(*He nods. The SOLDIERS put brands in the
fire*)

To be branded once is painful
But it's less so than a second brand
Stamped on the first one
As it begins to heal.

CHORUS

Don't hurt us any more!

ODYSSEUS

I've no wish to, I assure you.

CHORUS

Ask Cassandra, she knows everything
– Yes, I saw her mother
  Whisper to her this morning
– She can tell you where it is
– The God of Light himself
  Whispers truth inside her.

CASSANDRA

Take the brand, Odysseus;
Do you think I fear it
When I have already
Been burned inside by the sun?

CHORUS

Try her, Odysseus
– It would be just!   (*)

(*Enter ILIONE, with blood on her face and
dress*)

ILIONE

First give me justice.

ODYSSEUS

You shall have it, Ilione.
Have they wounded you also?

ILIONE

This blood is my husbands';
Their broach-pins in his eyes
Went into his brain-pan.

342

ODYSSEUS	I am sorry, Ilione. Sit down and compose yourself.
ILIONE	First give me justice On these women and my mother.
ODYSSEUS	I know the story; They have done you much harm.
ILIONE	Then you must help me heal What is left of our kingdom.
ODYSSEUS	I should be glad to help you: You have some plan perhaps?
ILIONE	I must rule here now in Thrace For the sake of our people.
ODYSSEUS	Yet you too are a daughter Of the royal house of Troy.
ILIONE	I rejected my house And my parents long ago.
ODYSSEUS	But how can one reject The blood that one is born with? If we could then perhaps It would be a better world.
ILIONE	I do not want philosophy, I want Justice.
ODYSSEUS	You shall have it: But Justice works two ways. You too have offended Against those human laws Which bind every one of us When guests come to our homes. You and your husband Killed a child, your own brother Whom you'd sworn to protect.
ILIONE	I did not kill Polydorus.
ODYSSEUS	Yet you condoned by silence.
ILIONE	I tried to prevent it.

ODYSSEUS   Your position was not easy,
            No one's ever is,
            But you'd help yourself better
            Not by talk of Justice
            But by helping me, Ilione,
            With a matter which is troubling me.

ILIONE   We have no gold, Odysseus.

ODYSSEUS   So I'm told, I am sorry.

ILIONE   I swear by all the gods,
            Both the little ones of Thrace
            That live beneath our earth
            And the Great Ones on Olympus
            That we have no gold nor know of none.

ODYSSEUS   That is possible, but first
            It is sensible to sift
            True gold from baser metal,
            And the surest means is fire.

            (*The SOLDIERS take up the brands*)

ILIONE   I am cursed to belong
            To the family of Priam!

ODYSSEUS   That statement is accurate:
            Do what must be done.

            (*The SOLDIERS seize her*)

ILIONE   Women, make them stop this!

CHORUS   Don't trust her, Odysseus
        —   Look, she's like an animal
        —   We kept our dignity
        —   It is right to give her justice.   (*)

            (*As the SOLDIERS seize her, AGAMEMNON
            enters*)

AGAMEMNON   Stop this, Odysseus.
            What are you doing here?

ODYSSEUS   As I have always done,
            Serving your best interests.

AGAMEMNON   I gave you no orders
            To come here to Thrace.

ODYSSEUS   No, the Council gave them
            After you sailed away:
            Priam's gold is hidden here.

AGAMEMNON   This woman is in pain.
            Untie her Odysseus
            And go home to your Penelope.

ODYSSEUS   Not till she's said where the gold is.

AGAMEMNON   What gold?

ODYSSEUS   Hecuba told me
            That Priam's gold is hidden here.

AGAMEMNON   If it is, which I do not believe,
            It is none of your business.
            You swore to rescue Helen
            And your oath is fulfilled.

ODYSSEUS   I shall be glad to obey you:
            I see there's no more to be done here.

AGAMEMNON   Is this the Queen of Thrace.

ODYSSEUS   She.

AGAMEMNON   Untie her.

            (*ODYSSEUS releases ILIONE*)

                    I am sorry
            For what this man has done here.
            Where is your husband?

ILIONE   Hecuba has killed him.

ODYSSEUS   Because he killed her son.

AGAMEMNON   I am sorry. And these women?

ODYSSEUS   Hecuba's, they helped her.

ILIONE   They killed my child, Agamemnon.

AGAMEMNON   Who began this?

CHORUS   Odysseus!
          — Punish him, Agamemnon.

AGAMEMNON   Blame is seldom single:
            We must all share some blame
            For the horrors of these years.

345

ODYSSEUS   Save such words for the victor's speech
                You will make back in the West.

AGAMEMNON   It is natural now that you hate us
                But if we are sensible
                I believe it is possible
                In time to reach some harmony
                And even reconciliation.

ILIONE   These men have many words
                But they do not know their meaning.

AGAMEMNON   Then perhaps all we can hope for
                Is to clear up the mess.

(*To Soldiers*) Untie each one of them.

                (*SOLDIERS untie the WOMEN*)

ILIONE   It is told, Odysseus,
                You so loved your son and wife
                That you tried not to join the war
                And yet it does not trouble you
                When other families suffer.
                And you, Agamemnon,
                How can you allow
                Such men to do such things to humans?

AGAMEMNON   I too have asked these questions;
                I do not know the answer.

ILIONE   Then keep quiet about healing:
                There can be no healing here.

AGAMEMNON   When you've buried your son and your
                                                husband
                You must rule here in Thrace
                As my wife rules in Mycenae;
                And since by blood you are Trojan
                You must forgive these women;
                They did as they did
                Because of what we have done to them.
                Take them with you now
                Not as slaves but free subjects.

ODYSSEUS   Fine words, Agamemnon.

CHORUS	Don't send us with her!
–	She will not forgive us
–	She will be revenged.
AGAMEMNON	You prefer to go to the West?
CHORUS	If we are treated kindly.
AGAMEMNON	Then you shall go with me
	To my home in Mycenae.
	May the High Ones grant you
	A safe and quiet journey.
(*To Soldiers*)	Take them to my ships:
	Gently now and kindly. (*)

(*The CHORUS go out singing, escorted by the SOLDIERS. The singing continues during ILIONE's next speech. ILIONE takes the dead child in her arms. She begins to leave and then turns back. Thunder*)

ILIONE	All you gods, hear me,
	And you trees and fields and beaches
	And you, Earth Mother, hear me!
	The wolves of the forest
	Have come out of the West
	And brought fear and fire
	To our fair eastern plains.
	Troy towers, broken, gone,
	Thrace the peaceful, going,
	All our good world going.
	Our olive-trees are stripped,
	Our granaries are ransacked,
	Our people slain like cattle
	And our cattle slain like men.
	Our brave Thracian horses
	Are crammed into your ships
	So that you may make war
	On each other in the West.
	Gods, don't let them get there:
	Smash the black ships, sea-god;
	Winds, blow their bloody hulks
	Over the edge of the Ocean.

	May you never see your homes; If you do, may your hearth-fires Leap up and devour you And the good earth you have fouled Open up and swallow All War-lords for ever.
ODYSSEUS	Rhetoric is useful When speaking to large crowds; When spoken by a criminal It is merely self-indulgence.

(*ILIONE goes with the dead child*)

| CASSANDRA | Each of them has taken
One anothers' child. (*) |

(*The storm at sea fades*)

AGAMEMNON	I curse you, Odysseus.
ODYSSEUS	Good, you'll feel the better for it.
AGAMEMNON	Gods, teach this man The moral laws that rule us.
ODYSSEUS	Maybe I know them Better than you do.
AGAMEMNON	You do not know their meaning, Only how to play on them.
ODYSSEUS	They mean one thing, Agamemnon; We shall all be punished, Not so much for our crimes As for our mistakes. I shall launch my ships at once; We will never find the gold now.
AGAMEMNON	You swore there would be no looting.
ODYSSEUS	But you'll need gold to fulfil Your promise to the army.
AGAMEMNON	They'll be paid from our coffers When we get back to the West.
ODYSSEUS	We agreed in full council A share of Priam's gold.

AGAMEMNON	I never heard of it.
ODYSSEUS	No, you were too busy Shouting at your brother.
AGAMEMNON	I'm ashamed that we quarrelled; I was wrong and I was stupid. But you have been stupid too; If there's gold here, which I doubt, Its weight would sink your ship In the storm which the gods Have rightly raised to punish us.
ODYSSEUS	I agree. Yet when the War-Kings Learn of my thorough search It may help them to moderate Their demands on you and your brother. I shall launch my ships at once.
AGAMEMNON	That could be your mistake: The storm will destroy each one of them.
ODYSSEUS	The sooner I set sail The sooner I'll get home again.
AGAMEMNON	While they repair my ships I shall try to make good The harm that has been done here.
ODYSSEUS	Whenever you say that I dread what will follow.
AGAMEMNON	What more can kings hope for? As a war-wound may heal So in time I believe That in all human dealings There can also be healing. It does not take long For burned fields and vineyards To grow green and bear fruit again And so with homes and cities.
ODYSSEUS	You are trying to impress This woman here who pleases you.
AGAMEMNON	She is not a war-prize.
ODYSSEUS	It is said that she is fair.

AGAMEMNON   I have not seen her face.

ODYSSEUS   It is strange of you but typical
Not to see what you have chosen.

AGAMEMNON   When no one else wanted her
I took her to protect her.

ODYSSEUS   You will love her, of course.

AGAMEMNON   Why?

ODYSSEUS   Because you've rescued her;
You are obsessed with rescues.

AGAMEMNON   I will not touch a woman
Who belongs to a god.

ODYSSEUS   Are you sure you are wise
Not to have branded her?
Your wife may not understand
Your motives as well as I do.

AGAMEMNON   I want to save one member
Of the house you have destroyed.

ODYSSEUS   Is that all the thanks I get
For ten years of faithful service?

AGAMEMNON   Go away, Odysseus:
But before you brave the storm
You would be wise to offer
Some libation to the gods
Of this land where we are guests.

ODYSSEUS   I will offer no libation
To a god I do not know.

(*AGAMEMNON kneels and lays his helmet on the earth*)

AGAMEMNON   You little ones that dwell
In this bruised earth in silence
Remember all travellers
And grant this country Peace
Which is dearest to all mortals.
Teach the High Ones of the Mountain
To take her in among them.

(CASSANDRA takes fire to the beacon)

ODYSSEUS

Grey-eyed one, lovely,
Be with me on my journey;
Give me strength in peril
And bring me safely home.

(CASSANDRA lights the beacon. Thunder and lightning)

CASSANDRA

Ai, ai, Apollo!

ODYSSEUS

What is the girl doing?

AGAMEMNON

I have already lit
Beacons from Mount Ida;
All the West knows we are coming.

CASSANDRA

Look on the beacon
For the journey of Odysseus.

(She begins to prophesy in Greek, c.f. lines 431-440 from 'The Odyssey'. They listen for a moment)

ODYSSEUS

I need no beacons;
I know all the sea-lanes.
Your war-prize speaks of places
Which do not exist.

AGAMEMNON

Maybe they will
Once you have discovered them.
Poseidon is angry.

ODYSSEUS

But Athene is more cunning.

CASSANDRA

Remember, Odysseus,
What you fear most
Is the thing that always happens.

ODYSSEUS

Time to go.

AGAMEMNON

       Time to go.   (*)

(As ODYSSEUS goes, POLYMESTOR comes out of the cave. He is blind and his face is bloody and mask-like)

POLYMESTOR *(Calls after him)* Greet your wife for me, Odysseus
She'll be happy when she sees you.

AGAMEMNON   Who is this?

POLYMESTOR   King Polymestor:

(*He has sudden pangs of pain, like TELEPHUS in Play 3*)

O the pain! I cannot bear it!

AGAMEMNON   I was told you were killed by Hecuba.

POLYMESTOR   She tried to: they blinded me
But I live.

AGAMEMNON   Then you are lucky:
You deserve to be dead.

POLYMESTOR   Oh, oh…

AGAMEMNON   Why is he dancing?

CASSANDRA   To be free of his pain.

AGAMEMNON   He deserves his punishment
For murdering a child.

POLYMESTOR   Did you never kill a child?
If you did, you'll be punished too.

AGAMEMNON   Not by you, dancing man.

POLYMESTOR   And did you not kill
Your best friend Palamedes?

AGAMEMNON   I was not one of those
Who voted for his death;
I tried to prevent it.

POLYMESTOR   But you dared not stand up to Odysseus;
You feared that the War-Kings
Would replace you as General
Because you and Palamedes
Were trying to end the War,
So you did not dare to defend him
And we were all destroyed.

(*The pain returns for a moment*)

AGAMEMNON   Yes, I am ashamed
That I did not save him.

POLYMESTOR	Just before he died, Remember what he said?
AGAMEMNON	Yes, I remember: 'Truth, I mourn for you: You have died before me...' I have not forgotten.
POLYMESTOR	And do you remember The meaning of his name?
AGAMEMNON	Yes, it means 'Ancient Wisdom'. (*)
POLYMESTOR	His father, old Nauplius Will make you pay for it.
AGAMEMNON	He's an old man, what can he do?
POLYMESTOR	He has used a device of his son's.
AGAMEMNON	Palamedes' inventions Are a blessing to men.
POLYMESTOR	But they are often not used In the way their inventor meant Do you remember, ship-lord, The meaning of Nauplius' name?
AGAMEMNON	Yes, 'Navigator': Sound navigation Is a blessing to men.
POLYMESTOR	Very good, that is why his son First invented lighthouses To guide ships into harbour.
AGAMEMNON	Yes, when we reach home We will all be glad of them.
POLYMESTOR	Blazes on the headlands...!
AGAMEMNON	Yes, we will see their beacons.
POLYMESTOR	But you will not see the promontories Of punishment beneath them Where old Nauplius has moved All the beacons and the bonfires: All the thousand ships of Aulis Will be crushed against the rocks!

AGAMEMNON   Then I'll steer by our watch-towers
             And bring in my ships by daylight.

POLYMESTOR   But you will not see the rocks
             That are hidden in the palaces.

AGAMEMNON   What is this, rocks in palaces?

POLYMESTOR   No rock is more dangerous
             Than the wrath of angry wives:
             Nauplius has told them
             That each War-King responsible
             For the death of his son
             Has broken his oath
             Sworn long ago at Aulis
             To lie with no Trojan girl
             Until the war was over
             Saying they'd be home by winter.
             Now each of their wives is troubled:
             Even the wife of Odysseus
             In Ithaca is not easy,
             Though of course less uneasy
             Than the wife of Agamemnon.
             That is why Clytemnestra
             Has taken her cousin
             Aegisthus into her bed.   (*)

CASSANDRA   Ai, Ai, Apollo…

             (*CASSANDRA begins to speak in Greek
             again. This time her words are from the
             'Agamemnon', lines 1125 & 1226-1232*)

AGAMEMNON   What is the matter?
             What is she saying?

POLYMESTOR   Some tale of a bull and a cow
             And how she horns her mate.

AGAMEMNON   Cows have no horns.

POLYMESTOR   Now she cries out of a lioness
             And a wolf who will kill you.

AGAMEMNON   A wolf?

POLYMESTOR   And now a hound
             Who licks your hand lovingly.

AGAMEMNON	What language is she speaking?
POLYMESTOR	The language of the oracles.
AGAMEMNON	It is hard to understand.
POLYMESTOR	Safer not to try.
AGAMEMNON	Tell me what she's saying.
POLYMESTOR	She is saying, Agamemnon, That your own wife will kill you.
AGAMEMNON	My wife? It is possible…

(CASSANDRA breaks off suddenly)

Tell me more.

POLYMESTOR	No, I must go now To the cave of Cheiron the Centaur: He will heal me of my wounds.
AGAMEMNON	You are blind, how will you get there?
POLYMESTOR	Maybe I'll find my way Sooner than you will.
AGAMEMNON	Before you go, tell me The meaning of your name That I may remember you.

(POLYMESTOR wipes the blood off his face)

FIRST MAN	My name is a simple one, 'Mindful of much': And so I leave your story.

(He goes into the cave) (*)

CASSANDRA	Why did you say that?
AGAMEMNON	What?
CASSANDRA	That you believe me.
AGAMEMNON	Why is that so strange?
CASSANDRA	You cannot believe me.
AGAMEMNON	Why should I not?
CASSANDRA	I am cursed by a god.
AGAMEMNON	Yes, I have heard that tale.

CASSANDRA   Then why do you lie to me?

AGAMEMNON   I do not believe you
               Because you are a prophet
               But because I know my wife.
               I killed her first child
               And she swore to be revenged;
               I killed her second also:
               If she were to kill me
               It would be just.

CASSANDRA   You do not believe me,
               You only pretend to.

AGAMEMNON   Why should I pretend?

CASSANDRA   Because you want to please me.

AGAMEMNON   Why should I want to?

CASSANDRA   You want to rescue women.

AGAMEMNON   Is that strange?

CASSANDRA   It is dangerous.

AGAMEMNON   To whom?

CASSANDRA   To the women.

AGAMEMNON   But I wish all women kindness.

CASSANDRA   Yes, on a rowing bench.

AGAMEMNON   That is not why I took you.

CASSANDRA   No, you thought that to take
               A prophet would be useful.

AGAMEMNON   And you've proved yourself a good one;
               Go on with your prophecy.

CASSANDRA   I have said it.

AGAMEMNON   Tell me more
               Of what is to come.

CASSANDRA   Must you ask the same question
               All the rest of them have asked?

AGAMEMNON   I like to hear stories
               Of the past and what's to come,

Why are you frightened?
Let Apollo speak through you. (*)

(*Pause*)

CASSANDRA Ai, Ai, Agamemnon…
She will kill me first
And Aegisthus in the house
Will take it as a signal
And kill you while you're bathing.

AGAMEMNON Will she strike me down also?

CASSANDRA That is not yet clear to me;
(*Quietly*) Some will tell it one way
And some will tell another…
I think I see Aegisthus
Thrust an axe into her hands
And make her go outside
To speak to the people.

AGAMEMNON That will be necessary:
What will she say?

CASSANDRA She will say she has punished you
For what you did at Aulis.

AGAMEMNON She will never say that;
She agreed with my decision.

CASSANDRA She will say you broke your oath
Never to harm our city.

AGAMEMNON It would be just if she said that
But I do not think she will.

CASSANDRA Easier words for a woman
Than confessing she was jealous.

AGAMEMNON Of whom?

CASSANDRA Use your wits.

AGAMEMNON Go on.

CASSANDRA When they have thrown
Our bodies on the rocks
And beasts have picked our bones

	She will marry Aegisthus And they will rule together.
AGAMEMNON	And the people?
CASSANDRA	Will respect Those who have the power.
AGAMEMNON	That is natural and sensible But there's always an avenger. Will it be my son?
CASSANDRA	If you already know it Tell the story yourself; But you do not believe me.
AGAMEMNON	Yes I believe you: It's as if you tell me something I've already heard inside me.
CASSANDRA	Now it's you who plays the prophet.
AGAMEMNON	No, but I know The history of our house.
CASSANDRA	Then you should be wiser. (*)
AGAMEMNON	But why does the curse go on?
	(*Pause*)
CASSANDRA	It is all in one word...
AGAMEMNON	What word?
CASSANDRA	The name Of the founder of your house.
AGAMEMNON	Tantalus?
CASSANDRA	All there.
AGAMEMNON	How can a name Given to a baby Define a man forever? That would mean we're as we are Before we know language.
CASSANDRA	Not if the name's a good one. Search it, go deep in: *Tantalou talanta...*

AGAMEMNON	That means as rich as I am Or I was before the war.
CASSANDRA	Go on, what is *Thallo*?
AGAMEMNON	'Flourishing'…
CASSANDRA	Go on.
AGAMEMNON	…Yet *Talas* means 'suffering' And *Talantatos* 'very wretched'; These are all contradictions.
CASSANDRA	Very good, Agamemnon. *Talanton*, what does that mean?
AGAMEMNON	It means 'a pair of scales', So perhaps it means 'justice' Or perhaps 'a balance'; I should like to find a balance. But it cannot mean all of them.
CASSANDRA	Why not?
AGAMEMNON	Yes, it's possible.
CASSANDRA	Then you've answered your own question.
AGAMEMNON	If our truth lies in our names Then everything is fated: I do not believe that.
CASSANDRA	Didn't Odysseus tell you If you took me back as a slave Your wife would not harm me?

(*She takes a brand from the fire*)

	If you take this and use it Your wife will not touch me.
AGAMEMNON	She would know you are not a slave; I will not touch you either.
CASSANDRA	No?
AGAMEMNON	I have chosen.
CASSANDRA	None of us can choose To be other than we are And as the gods made us.

AGAMEMNON   My daughter once said to me
               'Though the gods control
               Our beginnings and our endings
               The middle of a story
               Is ours and it's open.'

CASSANDRA   So?

AGAMEMNON   It's told that Apollo
               Put a curse on your tongue.
               When you refused to lie with him
               He raped your mind instead.

CASSANDRA   Take me to your ship.

AGAMEMNON   Does the god never leave you?

CASSANDRA   Yes, when it is winter
               And the birds fly to the South
               He loves to go northwards
               Among the Hyperboreans
               Until it is spring.

AGAMEMNON   Winter will soon be with us
               And he will leave you in peace.

CASSANDRA   For a while, but he'll be back.

AGAMEMNON   Then we will wait a while
               And eat and drink a little.

               (*He sits and she sits facing him*)

               When we reach Mycenae
               We will not cross the threshold
               As a conqueror and a slave
               But a beggar and a suppliant
               And then it must go as it will.

               (*Drops of snow begin to fall*)

               Look there in the sky;
               The cranes are flying to Libya.
               Palamedes told me once
               That it's a sign of winter.

               (*They eat*)

Let me see your face...
My words seem to frighten you.
Calchas told me that gods
Only speak through prophets
When they are masked or painted.
What are you afraid of?
The sea will wash it off
Long before we reach Mycenae.

CASSANDRA   Then wipe it off, War-King:
I cannot prevent you.

AGAMEMNON   I would never do that,
It would be a kind of rape.

CASSANDRA   You raped you own wife once.

AGAMEMNON   I know that, Cassandra.

(*She takes a sponge from the pool*)

CASSANDRA   Wipe it off, Agamemnon.

AGAMEMNON   Do you really believe
One dab of a wet sponge
Can wipe out all the god
Wrote in you as a child?

CASSANDRA   Maybe; try. One dab.

AGAMEMNON   Then wipe it off yourself.
What are you afraid of?
All your life you have longed
For someone to believe you;
Now one does, you reject it.
Why?

CASSANDRA   Ai, Apollo...
What are you doing to me?
Does this man speak truly?
I do not see clearly.

AGAMEMNON   Then drink and stop thinking.

CASSANDRA   Bad men bring more suffering
But good men make more sorrow.

(*She rises*)

AGAMEMNON
Easy now: your god
Is destroying you, Cassandra.

CASSANDRA
And you want to save me from him?

AGAMEMNON
Let Zeus free you.

CASSANDRA
Zeus?

AGAMEMNON
I believe Zeus rules his son
And that Zeus is just.

CASSANDRA
Justice,
Is a word, Agamemnon,
That sounds well in human mouths
But it's only a label
Men have tied to a something
Which does not exist
Either on earth or Olympus.
It is true that Apollo wishes
To usurp his father's power
Just as Zeus himself did
To his father before him
And Kronos to his.
Until the great rock falls
What has happened already
Will happen again:
That is god-law, Agamemnon,
As it's man-law on earth.
Epikou Kuklos leipsana...   (*)

(*A strange sound far-off. More snow falls*)

AGAMEMNON
What's that sound? It seems
To come from the air and the earth.

(*CASSANDRA laughs*)

Understood: the god has left you.
You are free of him.

CASSANDRA
Free...

(*She looks into the sky as the snow falls*)

For a while.

AGAMEMNON
Then it's time
To wipe him away.

CASSANDRA   Then wipe away, war-man.

                 (*She shuts her eyes as he wipes the paint off*)

AGAMEMNON   Now open your eyes and tell me:
                 Can you still prophesy?

CASSANDRA   No, I am in the Now,
                 Not in the past or the future.

AGAMEMNON   In the Now?

CASSANDRA   So I call it.
                 It is where all humans are.

AGAMEMNON   The sea is quiet now;
                 We must go to the ships.

CASSANDRA   Listen, can you hear them?

AGAMEMNON   I hear nothing but the waves
                 Lapping on the sea-shore.

CASSANDRA   That's because you're still listening
                 To what's past and what's to come,
                 Just like my father.
                 Look at me and listen.

                 (*The Muses are heard singing far-off*)

AGAMEMNON   I hear them and I feel them
                 As I did when I was a boy
                 And sometimes in the evening
                 When I watched the walls of Troy.
                 Maybe one day what's lost
                 Will be found again, Cassandra...
                 Did you bring them?

CASSANDRA   No:
                 You brought them to us.

AGAMEMNON   Let us go now to my ship.

CASSANDRA   Then take back your sea-cloak
                 You will need it more than I.

                 (*AGAMEMNON kneels to put out the fire. As
                 CASSANDRA puts the cloak on his shoulders,
                 she begins to sing in Greek from her opening
                 speech in the 'The Trojan Women'. The*

> (*CHORUS reappear singing in the distance. As she begins to dance, AGAMEMNON sees the dress*)

AGAMEMNON | That dress: you must not wear it!

CASSANDRA | But I put it on to please you.
What are you afraid of?

AGAMEMNON | It's not yours; take it off.

CASSANDRA | Let it out, Agamemnon:
Time to dance the wedding-dance!

AGAMEMNON | Why should I dance with you?
You are not my bride.

CASSANDRA | Yes, I am your slave-bride,
That is how it is written.

AGAMEMNON | By the gods?

CASSANDRA | No, within us
And in the Muses' songs.

AGAMEMNON | My wife must not see you
In that dress when we reach Mycenae.

CASSANDRA | Then you shall take it off me
When we are in your ship.

> (*She takes the brand from the fire again and dances*)

Burn, light, high!
Let it flame up to Olympus!
Hymenaeus, hear me!
Hymn my bridal and my bridegroom.
Muses, dance with me
And with all who are human
That ever were and will be,
I dance for this man!

AGAMEMNON | O all you gods that are,
Great ones and little ones,
Bless us in our journey
And take us safely home
That we may go on searching

And learn what we are born for.
Sing no more to us of sorrow
But let the good prevail.

(He covers CASSANDRA with his cloak and they both go. The sea sounds and dust falls from above)

PART III
The Homecomings

Play 8
HERMIONE

PHTHIA – THE HOME OF HOUSE OF PELEUS

CAST

First Woman	(–)
Second Woman	THETIS
Third Woman	ANDROMACHE
Fourth Woman	HERMIONE
First Man	PELEUS
Second Man	MENELAUS
Third Man	CALCHAS
Fourth Man	NEOPTOLEMUS/ORESTES
+ Boy	MOLOSSUS

CHORUS – Trojan Slaves

(*Phthia; the house of Peleus. The golden
armour given him by the gods at his
wedding-feast is hanging and clanks again on
the tree. The CHORUS of Trojan slaves are
working on household chores*)

CHORUS   Seven years... Seven years
                       Since the girl by Priam's side
                       Took up the sword and slew him...

                       Seven years since our master
                       Neoptolemus led the butchery
                       And the War-Kings broke the walls
                       And dragged the mooring cables
                       From the sea that was once ours
                       And took us to the West
        —   Seven years since Agamemnon
                       Was murdered by his wife
        —   It was just – Now Clytemnestra
                       Is punished like the rest of us
        —   The gods are still just
        —   If so, I'd like to know
                       Why we are still suffering.
        —   Hecuba used to tell us
                       That the gods love to test us:
        —   But how long will they go on testing?
        —   Until we all grow wise
        —   When will that be? – When we are
        —   But when will we know we are?
        —   Why ask stupid questions?

            (*Distant music*)

        —   Do you remember that morning
                       When we first saw the Horse
                       In the war-camp by the sea-side?
        —   We ran down and danced on the sands
                       And cried out 'It's over'!
        —   If Apollo had stayed with us
                       We would have won the war
        —   It is he, the Lord of Light,
                       Who has brought us into the darkness

	— Then perhaps if we still honour him He may bring us light again. (*)
	(*Enter PELEUS from a journey*)
PELEUS	'If' is a human word; The gods never use it.
CHORUS	Where have you been, Peleus?
PELEUS	Athens.
CHORUS	You went to Athens?
PELEUS	It is not the sort of place One went to in the old days, But I went to the trial of that boy; All the gods were there As they were at my wedding-feast.
CHORUS	What happened?
PELEUS	He got off.
CHORUS	Orestes was acquitted? — But he killed his own mother.
PELEUS	The Athenian legal system Leaves much to be desired.
CHORUS	But why was he tried in Athens And not in Mycenae?
PELEUS	It was thought that Athenian courts Would provide a fairer trial; All Athens really wanted Was to attract trade and travellers.
	(*He sees the golden armour*)
	What is this? Why have you not Polished your master's armour?
CHORUS	We polished it last week.
PELEUS	Take it down and get on with it.
	(*They do so*)
	Where is Neoptolemus?
CHORUS	At Thetis' shrine by the sea-side.

371

PELEUS   Menelaus is back with Helen...

CHORUS   Helen back?

PELEUS   They took their time:
Seven years... Theseus told me
He found his way to the Minatour
In precisely seven minutes.

CHORUS   He cheated.

PELEUS   He showed skill.

CHORUS   What will Menelaus do?

PELEUS   Try her.

CHORUS   Why?

PELEUS   To discover
If there were one or two of her.
But what does it matter?
We should hold a celebration
Of a lady and a war
That has made this land famous.

CHORUS   Don't say such things to us!
Hundreds of thousands
Died because of her.

PELEUS   What of that? It is well-known
There are too many people.
Mortals like you
Accepted their mortality.
Hercules, Theseus...dead...
And I have outlived them all.
Peace has made the West grow soft
And since Hermione your mistress
Ran away to Mycenae
You have all grown lazy:
Seven years of self-pity
Since the night that your master
Opened the door in the Horse.

(*Enter ANDROMACHE from the house*)

CHORUS   I've never understood how...
All the planks were sealed;

No cracks, no sign of doors
Wide enough for a warrior
To squeeze through in full armour
—   How was it possible?

PELEUS   How? *Hipposodomos.*

ANDROMACHE   What are you saying?

PELEUS   I am saying how it happened:
Hipposodomos.

CHORUS   Who was he? A god?

PELEUS   You missed a small trap-door
Just wide enough for a boy
To slip through unnoticed
And undo the bolts outside.

CHORUS   How do you know?

PELEUS   I suggested it.
Hipposodomos…!

ANDROMACHE   Stop saying that, Peleus.

PELEUS   Why d'you think the boy went wild
The night Troy was taken?

CHORUS   Because he was your grandson.

PELEUS   It was dark inside the Horse,
Tenebrous and terrible
And worst of all, tedious;
So to pass the time each warrior
Took his pleasure with the boy;
All thirty, even Calchas.

CHORUS   All thirty? Did he like that?

PELEUS   Of course he didn't like it
But if he had uttered a sound
He would have betrayed his comrades;
So he bit his tongue and endured
Till it was time to channel it
Into something noble: wrath.
Is it surprising
If it led to a few excesses?

CHORUS   Is it true?

PELEUS   Would I tell you
If it wasn't? *Hipposodomos*!

ANDROMACHE   Why do you speak such nonsense?

CHORUS   It makes a sort of sense
Of what happened afterwards
— When something bad is done to us
We take it out on others
— It is human — Only human.

(PELEUS rises)

PELEUS   Don't sit there talking:
Get on with your work.
I am going for a little walk.

(PELEUS goes)

CHORUS   Where's he off to now?

ANDROMACHE   Each month he goes down to the sea-shore
And waits for his lost love Thetis:
He says she will come for him.

CHORUS   Does he still go on hoping?

ANDROMACHE   Don't we all? Back to work.
I will fetch him when it's bed-time.   (*)

(A BEGGAR WOMAN comes in cautiously)

BEGGAR   Has he gone? Is it safe
To go into the house now?

CHORUS   Beggars not welcome here
— If you want some food and drink
You must wait till Hermione's back.

BEGGAR   But I am back: you must help me!
Is my husband here, Andromache?

ANDROMACHE   Hermione, is it you?

CHORUS   It can't be!

ANDROMACHE   Welcome your mistress, women:
Hermione has come home!

HERMIONE   Sh! Speak more quietly;
I'm frightened.

(*HERMIONE weeps*)

ANDROMACHE	So we see; I'm sorry your stay in Mycenae Was not a happy one.
HERMIONE	It was horrible, Andromache; But now I am terrified My husband will beat me Because I ran away.
ANDROMACHE	Then why are you dressed in rags? Neoptolemus won't like it.
HERMIONE	I have come home as a suppliant.
ANDROMACHE	Is that wise?
HERMIONE	I shall be safer; Nobody beats suppliants.
ANDROMACHE	Agamemnon came home As a suppliant; remember What happened to him, Hermione.
CHORUS	She must have seen everything That happened in Mycenae!

(*HERMIONE gasps and collapses*)

HERMIONE	It was terrible…
CHORUS	Orestes Is a monster – His own mother…
HERMIONE	*O Talas… Talantatos…*!
ANDROMACHE	Drink this and try to relax.
HERMIONE	Don't you want to know what happened?
CHORUS	We will know it when you've told us.
ANDROMACHE	Speak as clearly as you can.

(*HERMIONE drinks deep*)

HERMIONE	I loved Clytemnestra! She is…was…the only one Who has ever been kind to me.
CHORUS	You loved her, a murderess?

HERMIONE	She wasn't a murderess! She only killed a Trojan slave Who'd seduced Agamemnon.
CHORUS	But all the world knows –
HERMIONE	The world only knows What Electra told them afterwards.
CHORUS	There were other witnesses.
HERMIONE	They were in Aegisthus pay; He alone killed Agamemnon.
CHORUS	How do you know?
HERMIONE	I was there. When the war began they sent me To stay in Mycenae. When Agamemnon died Clytemnestra wept and told me She only killed Cassandra In a moment of jealousy Because she loved her husband.
ANDROMACHE	Jealousy is dangerous.
HERMIONE	So I stayed to look after her. She feared that Aegisthus Would kill her son Orestes So that he could go on ruling, So she sent him away to Phocis. When my husband came home from the war He claimed me as a war-prize And brought me here to Phthia.
CHORUS	Then what? Tell us!
HERMIONE	Then The letters came.
CHORUS	What letters?
HERMIONE	Beastly, dreadful letters From Electra to Orestes Saying he must kill his mother.
CHORUS	We heard it was Apollo Who commanded it.

HERMIONE   Him too;
                      He was cross about Cassandra
                      Because she'd once been his priestess.
                      Then Clytemnestra begged me
                      To go back to Mycenae,
                      Saying I should leave my husband
                      And marry Orestes
                      As Agamemnon had promised
                      To my father at Aulis;
                      She thought I could distract him
                      From Delphi and Electra
                      And control him.

ANDROMACHE   By marrying him?
                      You're at least ten years older.

HERMIONE   Speak for yourself.
                      So I went and when Orestes
                      Came home to kill Aegisthus
                      I told him I would marry him
                      If he would protect me
                      From the husband I had here.
                      But then Electra came
                      With her father's axe and screamed
                      He must kill his mother too
                      As Apollo had commanded.
                      When I naturally protested
                      They locked me in the watch-tower.

CHORUS   Then how can you know what happened?
        –   Did you see?

HERMIONE   How could I see?
                      I was locked up in the watch-tower.

CHORUS   But you heard what they said?

HERMIONE   How could I hear properly
                      When each of them was screaming?
                      I screamed too for three days
                      Till I heard my parents' voices:
                      They have both come back from Egypt.

CHORUS   What were they doing in Egypt?

HERMIONE	I don't know, don't interrupt!
	So I screamed till my father came
	And hid me in the house.
CHORUS	Why?
HERMIONE	Because the people
	Were throwing stones at my mother
	And one of them hit me.
	When my father tried to negotiate
	Orestes set the house on fire.
ANDROMACHE	His own house?
CHORUS	That is bad.
HERMIONE	What happened next was worse.
CHORUS	They cut Helen's throat?
HERMIONE	Don't interrupt me
	And leave my mother out of it!
	Calchas arrived from Delphi
	With a message from Apollo
	And told them they must stop it.
CHORUS	Good.
HERMIONE	It wasn't good!
	He said that Orestes
	Must be tried at Athens
	And that if he was acquitted
	I must marry him, a madman
	Who attacked his own relations
	With an axe.
ANDROMACHE	You did well
	To come home.
CHORUS	You are safe.
ANDROMACHE	Not if he sees you like this;
	You must put some proper clothes on.
HERMIONE	No, I am a suppliant;
	Put some ashes on my hair.
ANDROMACHE	Go in and don't be silly.

HERMIONE	Now the curse falls on me; O why am I a child Of the house of Tantalus? (*)

(NEOPTOLEMUS enters. He is now bearded)

NEOPTOLEMUS	Is it true what Old Peleus Has told me? Has Orestes Been acquitted?
CHORUS	It is true.
NEOPTOLEMUS	What's this woman doing here?
ANDROMACHE	It's your wife, be gentle to her; She is in great trouble.
NEOPTOLEMUS	Why is she dressed like that?
ANDROMACHE	She says she is a suppliant And asks you to protect her.
CHORUS	She says she has suffered.
NEOPTOLEMUS	Hermione, stop snivelling; Wash your face and change your dress; It disgusts me to look at you.

(HERMIONE runs in)

Has the girl gone mad?
Take her in and wash her;
Send my son to me and tell
My Myrmidons to arm.
Leave the armour where it is. (*)

(CHORUS go)

ANDROMACHE	Where are you going?
NEOPTOLEMUS	To Delphi.
ANDROMACHE	Then why do you need armour?
NEOPTOLEMUS	Last night I dreamed my father Came to me in my sleep And cried out 'Why have you not Avenged my death in Thymbria At the hands of the son of Zeus? Three times you have sent to Apollo Demanding compensation,

Yet you've lived here in idleness
For seven shameful years:
If you wish to be a warrior
Worthy to wear my armour
You must go now to Delphi
And outface him as I did
And destroy Apollo's shrine.'

ANDROMACHE It was you I heard cry in the night.
If you go, you know you will die.

NEOPTOLEMUS Maybe.

ANDROMACHE Then stay.

NEOPTOLEMUS For your sake?

ANDROMACHE To protect your wife from Orestes.

NEOPTOLEMUS I do not wish to speak to her;
Let her stay in the house till I'm gone.

ANDROMACHE If you go, the god will destroy you
As he destroyed your father.

NEOPTOLEMUS Zeus will protect me.

ANDROMACHE How can you say that?
He didn't protect Achilles.

NEOPTOLEMUS There are always risks
And warriors must face them.

ANDROMACHE But you have always told me
That you are not a warrior.

NEOPTOLEMUS I said I was not a true one.

ANDROMACHE The world believes you are.

NEOPTOLEMUS What the world believes is a lie.
I have not earned this armour:
True warriors achieve
That feat of arms they were born for.

ANDROMACHE Only the gods know
What we are born for;
You did what you had to do
As is natural to men.

NEOPTOLEMUS   What I did was evil;
               Everyone despises me.

ANDROMACHE   I do not despise you.

NEOPTOLEMUS   Then put my armour on.

ANDROMACHE   I will not.

NEOPTOLEMUS   Do you not fear my anger?

ANDROMACHE   Not any longer.

NEOPTOLEMUS   Do your duty, slave-wife.

ANDROMACHE   Then be still while I take your cloak off
               Or I cannot undo the clasp;
               Stay still. For our son's sake
               Stay here a little longer,
               And drink before you go.

               (*She begins to arm him. They do not see
               MOLOSSUS enter. He is 'practising' as
               ACHILLES did in Play 1, but stops and sits to
               watch them*)

NEOPTOLEMUS   He's a fine boy: he will make
               A better king than me.

ANDROMACHE   No, you must not say that.

NEOPTOLEMUS   I say it and I mean it.
               I have done evil
               And I have lost my way.

ANDROMACHE   Since you brought me to your house
               I have not found you evil.
               Men and gods have done evil
               To both of us. Drink this.

NEOPTOLEMUS   It was done to you by me.

ANDROMACHE   You were not yourself then.

NEOPTOLEMUS   That was the evil.

               (*He drinks*)

               I vowed when I was little
               To be true to myself
               But I let my truth be twisted:
               Now I must make good.

ANDROMACHE   While you're here our boy is safe
              And you and I are happy.

NEOPTOLEMUS   Do not speak as if you loved me.

ANDROMACHE   I have come to know you;
              Sometimes that serves as well.

NEOPTOLEMUS   Then what are you afraid of?

ANDROMACHE   Of being a slave again.

NEOPTOLEMUS   You are a slave already.

ANDROMACHE   You do not treat me as one.

NEOPTOLEMUS   Because you're a better wife
              Than Menelaus' puppy.

ANDROMACHE   She is young and she's unhappy
              Because she is barren.

NEOPTOLEMUS   She is noisy and petulant
              And she doesn't even know
              How to give a man pleasure.

ANDROMACHE   That's because she is afraid of you
              And it's why she ran away.

NEOPTOLEMUS   What is that to you?

ANDROMACHE   If you go it will be I
              Who will have to handle
              Her fear and her self-pity.
              She only dared to go
              Because she knew her aunt
              Would be kinder to her than you are.

NEOPTOLEMUS   Clytemnestra deserved all she got.

ANDROMACHE   Evil was done to her too
              As it was to Hermione
              When her father Menelaus
              Made her marry you.

NEOPTOLEMUS   Better if he hadn't.

ANDROMACHE   If she is hard to live with
              It's because she had no parents
              To help with her rearing.

NEOPTOLEMUS	Nor did I.
ANDROMACHE	I know that.
NEOPTOLEMUS	My father went to Troy Before I was born.
ANDROMACHE	Who was your mother?
NEOPTOLEMUS	Deidamia of Scyros; She died when I was born.
ANDROMACHE	You remember nothing of her?
NEOPTOLEMUS	No, the midwife sent me To be reared by Peleus.
ANDROMACHE	No father and no mother Makes for a lonely childhood.
NEOPTOLEMUS	Mine was like my father's And he was not lonely.
ANDROMACHE	No, he was reared by bears.
NEOPTOLEMUS	Peleus is a sort of bear.
ANDROMACHE	Yet you can be gentle. Leave your armour where it is And come into the house: I will refresh you.

(*She raises him up and he sees MOLOSSUS*) (*)

NEOPTOLEMUS Boy, come here and show me
If you know how to buckle armour.

(*MOLOSSUS goes to him*)

Your father is going
On a venture that is perilous.
The heart-blood of our land
Has grown thin and feeble
Since our greatest warriors died
Before the walls of Troy.
Yet the world still needs heroes;
That is why there are times
We must go on such ventures
As women think impossible;

	This is my time, my dear one.
(To Andromache)	You must send him to the mountains
	To make his sinews stronger
	And play with bears and mountain goats
	If he's to be a warrior.
	Do not let your mother
	Teach you Trojan songs
	Nor listen when these women
	Tell tales of Hector and Paris
	Who loved women more than war.
(To Molossus)	But now you must promise me
	Never to tell lies
	Nor pretend to be what you are not
	But rather to keep on practising
	All that I have taught you.

ANDROMACHE My lord, we understand you.
      Your Myrmidons are ready.

(The MYRMIDONS enter)

NEOPTOLEMUS Now Zeus, sky-lord, thunderer,
      If you still rule in heaven
      Help me now to destroy
      The destroyer that you loved once,
      Apollo, Lord of Light.
      You have let his deeds and prophecies
      Usurp men's minds on earth
      So that mortals have forgotten you.
      If you are still all-powerful
      And if you still love justice
      Uphold me with your thunderbolts
      And grant me your justice;
      Look kindly on this woman
      And this boy. Let us go.   (*)

*(NEOPTOLEMUS goes with his
MYRMIDONS. ANDROMACHE and her son
watch them disappear)*

MOLOSSUS Don't be frightened, Mother;
      Tell me a story.

ANDROMACHE Which one?

MOLOSSUS	The Apple one.
ANDROMACHE	Everyone thinks they know it.
MOLOSSUS	But you know it best;

(MOLOSSUS sits by her)

Tell it me again.

ANDROMACHE | Once upon a time
There were three great goddesses:
Hera offered Paris riches
And dominion of all Asia,
Athene offered wisdom
And victory in war,
But Aphrodite offered him
The fairest girl in the world.

MOLOSSUS | Helen?

ANDROMACHE | It is told so,
But only one person knows
What she really said to Paris
And Oenone is dead.

MOLOSSUS | Oenone
The mountain-nymph?

ANDROMACHE | Yes, they are different
From wood-nymphs and sea-nymphs
That splash about in the sea;
She was tender and gentle
And he made her so happy.

MOLOSSUS | How do you know that
If she lived on Mount Ida?

ANDROMACHE | When Paris came down to Troy
And brought Helen back from Sparta
He was struck down at last
By the great bow of Heracles;
So Oenone came and flung herself
On her lover's funeral pyre;
Before she died she told us
Aphrodite had never mentioned
Helen's name, but the love

Of the Fairest Girl in the World.
Since till then the only woman
Whom Paris had ever seen
Was Oenone herself
He naturally assumed
If he gave Aphrodite the apple
He would keep his love forever.

MOLOSSUS   That was stupid, Mother.

ANDROMACHE   What would you have said
If three naked goddesses
Suddenly appeared to you?
Wouldn't you have been shy too
And afraid of offending them?
Paris thought it wisest
To hold on to the girl
Whom he had won already,
So he gave Aphrodite
The apple for Oenone's sake.
I understand that;
I too have only had
One love all my life.   (*)

(Re-enter CHORUS)

CHORUS   Where's our master gone?

ANDROMACHE   To Delphi.

CHORUS   Just as well...

ANDROMACHE   Why are you laughing?

CHORUS   If he saw Hermione now
He would stay there for ever.

(Enter HERMIONE in an Egyptian dress)

HERMIONE   Father brought me this from Egypt!
Where's my husband?

CHORUS   Gone to Delphi.

HERMIONE   Why are they smirking?

ANDROMACHE   You have smudged your face
By painting it too quickly.

HERMIONE	It's because you stole my mirror. Why are you wearing my dress?
ANDROMACHE	Your husband gave it to me Because you never wear it.
HERMIONE	Take it off at once, It does not suit a slave. You were hoping, weren't you, That I would not come back?
ANDROMACHE	No, I'm glad you are back.
HERMIONE	Glad?
ANDROMACHE	Yes, I feel safer.
HERMIONE	Then you are very foolish: You must leave this house today.
ANDROMACHE	I am not your slave; Neoptolemus is my master.
HERMIONE	You're a slave, a prize of war, And such women are treacherous; Take that dress off and go.
ANDROMACHE	It is true, Hermione, That we've never liked each other But we've come to understand How each of us has her place. We should pray together now For your husband's safe return.
HERMIONE	When he's back I shall tell him All I've learned since my father Came back home from Egypt.
ANDROMACHE	You have never learned anything.
HERMIONE	O yes, I have, Andromache; I have learned the secret Of how your city fell.
CHORUS	It fell, do not talk of it.
HERMIONE (*To Chorus*)	Did you know that this woman Is sharing the bed of the man Who made Priam take in the Horse?

ANDROMACHE	No man persuaded Priam; We persuaded ourselves.
HERMIONE	But what of my husband's sister? What of her part in the story?
ANDROMACHE	I know what they made him do.
HERMIONE	You know it?
ANDROMACHE	He told me.
HERMIONE	And you still share his bed? It's unnatural and disgusting.
ANDROMACHE	You are easily disgusted.
HERMIONE	When you know what else I've heard You'll be glad to leave this house.
CHORUS	But how can you be sure What your father said is true?
HERMIONE	Because all the army knows it. It was not Odysseus Who threw her son from the walls But her lover-man, Neoptolemus.
ANDROMACHE	Do you think I did not know?
HERMIONE	You knew?
ANDROMACHE	In seven years One learns to know a man.
HERMIONE	Do you mean that he told you?
ANDROMACHE	His dreams have often woken me; Once he cried out in the night And then he wept and told me.
HERMIONE	You forgave him?
ANDROMACHE	I wept with him As I used to weep when Hector Told me of his night-fears Before he fought Achilles.
HERMIONE	I could not have forgiven him.
ANDROMACHE	Maybe that is why You are not a proper wife.

HERMIONE   You're despicable, an animal.

ANDROMACHE   A slave cannot afford
        To indulge in decent feelings.

HERMIONE   So I see.

ANDROMACHE   But it is sad
        That you have not yet learned
        How men in many ways
        Are more vulnerable than we are.
        A girl I loved once said to me
        'When a man shows a woman
        All his vulnerability
        That's when she starts to love him.'

HERMIONE   Do you love Neoptolemus?

ANDROMACHE   I might ask you the same question.

HERMIONE   I could never do what you have done.

ANDROMACHE   Perhaps that is why
        Your husband does not love you;
        You should have learned by now
        How to please a man.

HERMIONE   It is a husband's business
        To learn to please his wife;
        And I did not choose my man,
        My father gave me to him.

ANDROMACHE   As mine gave me to Hector.

HERMIONE   That is why most women
        Are wretched.

ANDROMACHE   If you say so.

HERMIONE   If I or my mother
        Or Leda my grandmother
        Had chosen their own husbands
        None of all this beastliness
        Ever would have happened.

ANDROMACHE   What do you do, Hermione,
        When it's your turn in his bed?

HERMIONE   That is not your business.

ANDROMACHE

Do you scold or shut your eyes
And wait for things to happen?

HERMIONE

I do as decent women do.

ANDROMACHE

Did your mother teach you nothing?

HERMIONE

Leave my mother out of it!

ANDROMACHE

But of course when you were little
Her mind was on other things.
Your best hope of a child now
Is for Peleus to rape you.

HERMIONE

You are more disgusting
Than my mother: sex
Is all you ever think of;
If you lay with a centaur
Or a goat you'd enjoy it.
How do you know what passes
Between me and my husband?

ANDROMACHE

I can guess it by what passes
Between him and me.

HERMIONE

You have given him some potion
To help you to seduce him.

ANDROMACHE

I have no witchcraft,
I am merely pleasant.

HERMIONE

So you let him kill your child
And enjoyed it when he raped you.

ANDROMACHE

Neoptolemus never raped me,
He was too ashamed;
So he took me as a war-prize
To feel more like a man.
It was I who persuaded him
To let me share his bed.

HERMIONE

Then you're worse than my mother!
You're a whore, a Trojan whore,
And you have wrecked my marriage.

ANDROMACHE

It is you who are the wrecker.
It is sad and I am sorry
You have never had a child.

CHORUS	Why not try the bullrushes Like Leda your grandmother? — If you lie down by the river Some god might pity you And even give you pleasure.
HERMIONE	Whores, you are all whores!
CHORUS	She may have a long wait.
HERMIONE	When I tell my husband What I heard you whispering To the boy, he'll kill you both.
CHORUS	What did you hear, Hermione?
HERMIONE	That this brat is not his son But the Trojan seed of Hector; Laugh at that if you can.
ANDROMACHE	I laugh at you, Hermione. Do you think your man will thank you For telling him it's his fault That your womb is still empty? If you do, you'll be the one Who is thrown out of the house.
HERMIONE	I will show you who rules here: Fetch my husband's men!
CHORUS	They have all gone to Delphi.
HERMIONE	Take that dress off her, women!
CHORUS	Which dress do you mean?

(*CHORUS laugh at her. HERMIONE snatches
a kitchen knife from one of them*)

HERMIONE	Give that boy to me!
ANDROMACHE	I will kill you if you touch him.
HERMIONE	No, everyone will honour me When they hear how a loyal wife Handled her and Hector's brat.

(*She goes for MOLOSSUS. CHORUS try to
stop her, but she breaks away from the
CHORUS and seizes MOLOSSUS*)

Now you shall learn
Who is mistress in this house.

CHORUS   Both of you be careful!

ANDROMACHE   Let her be and listen.
Do what you will with me,
But if you harm the child
Neoptolemus will kill you:
Think before you act.

(*HERMIONE screams*)

(*To Molossus*)   Listen to me, my darling:
It is my turn to die
So that you may go on living.
You must not be frightened.
I have seen Achilles
Drag my husband's heels
Round our dear city's walls
And I have been enslaved
By the son of the man who did that.
When such things happen
We have to make the best of it.
I have always known
That the life of a child
Is the first thing of all things;
Women who have no children
May suffer less than I have
But they are not so lucky,
Their luck is really loss.
Do take that dress off,
You look so ridiculous.   (*)

(*HERMIONE screams again. Enter
MENELAUS*)

MENELAUS   Hermione, be quiet!

CHORUS   It is the King of Sparta!

(*They fall silent*)

HERMIONE   Father, save me from these women!

MENELAUS   Put that down! In the West
We will never tolerate

392

Violence against women.
Do be quiet, Hermione.

HERMIONE   They tried to kill me, Father!

CHORUS   Your daughter, Menelaus,
             Was trying to kill the boy.

MENELAUS   Why should she try to do that?
             Why is your dress undone?
             And how dare you wear it?
             It's a present for my wife.

HERMIONE   Don't try to change the subject!
             You brought no gift for me.

MENELAUS   I should have thought at your age
             You'd have outgrown the habit
             Of wearing your mother's dresses.

HERMIONE   Why did you give me a husband
             Who is sterile?

MENELAUS   Sterile?

CHORUS   This boy is Andromache's.

MENELAUS   I understand the problem:
             Two wives in one house;
             It always leads to trouble.

ANDROMACHE   I am not his wife.

HERMIONE   Whip her and throw her out;
             Whip all of them, they hate me!

MENELAUS   Easy now; I fear
             Though to win a war is hard
             To keep a peace is harder.
             I of course understand
             That a mistress in one's home
             Is a tricky thing to handle
             But it can have advantages.

CHORUS   That's what we've been telling her.
             It's because of Andromache
             That he's let Hermione stay.

MENELAUS   I think I understand you.

HERMIONE   Why have you come here?
                  I don't want you in my house.

MENELAUS   I am troubled by Apollo:
                  He says you must marry Orestes.

HERMIONE   You want me to marry
                  A murderer and a madman?

MENELAUS   I did not say I wanted it:
                  I wish to protect you.

HERMIONE   What does that mean? Speak plainly.

MENELAUS   In speaking of Apollo
                  We must use words with care:
                  We all know what happened
                  When poor Marsyas offended him
                  And those girls who were coy
                  And refused to give him pleasure,
                  But if you act sensibly
                  You will be safe enough.

HERMIONE   Why did you ever give me
                  To a man who does not love me?

MENELAUS   How could I know that beforehand?
                  I admit I was wrong
                  When I broke my first promise
                  To my poor brother at Aulis.
                  But when we conquered Troy –

HERMIONE   It is easy to admit things
                  But that does not excuse them.

MENELAUS   I accept that; I'm ashamed
                  That it led me into a quarrel
                  With my brother whom I loved.
                  It was the last time I saw him.

HERMIONE   I don't want apologies,
                  I want you to save me
                  From Apollo and Orestes!
                  Do you think I will marry
                  A man who not only
                  Murdered his own mother

	But set fire to his own house?	
	How could I enjoy	
	A single moment's peace	
	In the bed of an arsonist?	

MENELAUS   There are two sides to that question;
He will have to live with you.
Shut up and trust in Zeus;
You're becoming hysterical.

HERMIONE   You are making me hysterical!

MENELAUS   You know it is bad for you
To get over-excited.
Go in and take that dress off.

HERMIONE   I will never, never marry
A man who's killed his mother!   (*)

(Enter CALCHAS)

CALCHAS   From afar I have heard
The sound of Spartans quarrelling;
Their voices are unlovely,
Their arguments confused
And their wishes irrelevant.
Quiet, Hermione…Menelaus,
Why have you come here?

MENELAUS   To speak with my daughter
And tell her Apollo's will.

HERMIONE   I won't do it, Calchas!
I am staying here with my husband.

CALCHAS   But your husband is dead.

MENELAUS   How can he be dead?

HERMIONE   I do not believe you.

ANDROMACHE   I feared this, Hermione.

CALCHAS   He asked Zeus for justice
And he got what he asked for.

HERMIONE   No! I cannot bear this!

MENELAUS (*To Hermione*) I do not understand you.
Be quiet and listen to him.

CALCHAS

Her husband tried to burn
The sacred shrine at Delphi.
When our priests resisted
He would have killed them all
If Orestes himself
Had not come with a libation
To the god who had saved him:
When he saw what was happening
He killed the intruder.

MENELAUS

My nephew killed Neoptolemus?
But he is on trial in Athens!
Do you mean the gods acquitted him?
The boy is as mad as Ajax.

HERMIONE

This can't be true, it can't be!

CALCHAS
(*To Hermione*)

With the gods all things are possible.
Since your husband has been murdered
Apollo has given you
Orestes as compensation.

MENELAUS

If the compensation's mad
I doubt if it is valid.

HERMIONE

I would rather lie with Typhon
Or one-eyed Polyphemus.

CALCHAS

You wouldn't; speak more wisely
And honour the gift of the gods.

HERMIONE

You that are powerful
Think you can do anything.

CALCHAS

That statement is accurate.

HERMIONE

I would rather throw myself
From the rock of poor Niobe.

CALCHAS

That statement is foolish:
The rock is in Asia.
It was to Orestes
That your father first promised you.

HERMIONE

Why should I suffer for it?

CALCHAS

Many have suffered here;
The god himself is grieving
For the damage to his shrine.

HERMIONE	I will not! I will not!
	I will tear my hair, Father,
	If you do not stop him.
MENELAUS	Be careful with her, Calchas;
	She has had such attacks
	Ever since she was a baby.
CALCHAS	I am all too aware
	That there's madness in your family.
MENELAUS	I am not easy, Calchas:
	We may be doing her wrong.
CALCHAS	I am not easy either;
	But this is not the matter
	That has brought me to this house.
	Why have you not yet brought
	Your wife to be tried at Delphi?
MENELAUS	I've explained to you already
	Helen never went to Troy:
	She was victim of a god-trick.
CALCHAS	Gods do not play tricks.
MENELAUS	But you know there were two Helens,
	The Trojan one, an image,
	And mine who is the true one.
CALCHAS	I know, so it is surely
	In your interest to prove it?
MENELAUS	I have already done so
	By showing you the hieroglyphs
	I brought home from Egypt
	From the priestess Theonoe.
	She has sworn that my wife
	Never went to Troy
	But spent the war in Egypt.
	If you want further evidence
	I will send for further hieroglyphs.
CALCHAS	That will not be necessary;
	I am speaking of witnesses
	Of what went on in Sparta
	Before Helen went to Egypt.

MENELAUS   Everybody knows that:
                          Paris abused our guest-laws.

CALCHAS   Then it's surely in your interest
                          To determine the true blame.   (*)

HERMIONE   I know who are to blame:
                          I know the guilty ones!

CALCHAS   If you were there in Sparta
                          You are needed as a witness.

HERMIONE   You should first arrest my grandfather.

MENELAUS   What has Tyndareus
                          Got to do with it, Hermione?

HERMIONE   He married you to mother
                          Though there have never been
                          Two people less compatible;
                          He filled your greedy mind
                          And all the war-kings too
                          With the nonsense that has ruled
                          The lives of all the West,
                          Saying that power and riches
                          And pride in one's country
                          (Whatever that may mean)
                          Is the greatest thing since Cadmus
                          Invented the alphabet.

MENELAUS   Palamedes invented it.

CALCHAS   No, he only finished it.

HERMIONE   But for Tyndareus' obsession
                          There would have been no war.

MENELAUS   Not true.

HERMIONE   He made the suitors
                          Swear to protect mother
                          And held them to their oaths
                          With promises of gold.

CALCHAS   He merely tried to prevent war
                          With a sensible plan that went wrong
                        Like most human ventures.

HERMIONE (*To Menelaus*)	Then I'll tell you who's really to blame. Before you married Mother Did you not promise Tyndareus A large dowry?
MENELAUS	Naturally.
HERMIONE	But did you ever pay it?
MENELAUS	My debts and obligations Led to a certain delay.
HERMIONE	But when Paris seized her You could not pay it at all.
CALCHAS	Why was that, Menelaus?
HERMIONE	Because Paris seized his treasure.
MENELAUS	Yes, my wife is my treasure.
CALCHAS	But you also had a gold-hoard?
MENELAUS	Yes, but he seized that too.
HERMIONE	So you wanted it back?
MENELAUS	Of course, it was my property.
HERMIONE	So you had to pay the War-Kings To hold them to their oaths, But they said it did not apply To rescues in foreign countries Since they'd only sworn to protect her From each other in the West.
MENELAUS	They made no such conditions But were happy to take part In a rescue operation.
HERMIONE	But the war went on for years And they would have all gone home If you had not made fresh promises.
MENELAUS	Who told you this nonsense?
HERMIONE	My husband: he said my dowry Has still not been paid either.
MENELAUS	How could I have paid it When I was lost at sea?

HERMIONE   How could you be lost
            For seven years?

MENELAUS   Because
            The gods were unkind; it is said
            That even Odysseus
            Has had problems with Poseidon.

HERMIONE   You began this war
            With promises of gold-hoards
            Which you have not fulfilled.
            If the war was a crime
            It is you who are the criminal.

CALCHAS   Such judgements are the business
            Of gods, not hysterics.
            Ask yourself one question:
            Would you rather die barren
            Or make a bad marriage
            But find your womb is fruitful?

HERMIONE   Not with the seed of Orestes:
            It would be one more rape
            In the story of our house:
            First Leda, my grandmother,
            Then this man's wife, my mother,
            And now me, his daughter.
            My father is a raptor.

CALCHAS   Do not misuse words.

HERMIONE   I know what 'raptor' means:
            'To seize another's property,
            Treasure or land or cattle
            Or fishing rights or women;'
            It's the same word as 'rape'.

CALCHAS   Not these days, Hermione.
            And yet she is right
            To remind us that rape
            Is an offence against property,
            The right to dispose of which
            Belongs to the father.
            We are grateful for your counsel.

HERMIONE	I will not be the victim Of your man-laws and customs!
CALCHAS	Speak to her, Menelaus.
MENELAUS	Apollo surely understands My position is not an easy one.
CALCHAS	No one's ever is.
MENELAUS	It is true that I owe: I owe all to my brother. I promised him at Aulis That Orestes should marry you When we brought Helen home, But I broke my word and gave you To the man who won the war And I bitterly regret it. Now I must repay my debt To the brother whom I loved.
HERMIONE	So I am to be the victim Of his hopes to be ruler Of both Sparta and Mycenae.
MENELAUS	I'm afraid we are all victims. I understand your feelings, But if we try to prevent Something unpreventable We will suffer much more sorrow Than if we make the best of it: I am thinking of Andromache Who understands these matters. Do not shun a god-gift: I will give you a new wedding dress.
CHORUS	There's no time; don't you see? Orestes is coming Dragging something up the roadway.
CALCHAS	He has come to claim his god-gift.
ANDROMACHE	She's in no state to see him.
CALCHAS	Go in and put on your wedding-dress.
HERMIONE	I will go in and kill myself.

(*She still has the knife*)

MENELAUS You won't: you're a survivor.

HERMIONE I don't want to survive!

CALCHAS (*To Chorus*) Take her in: if she resists
Gag her and bind her.

ANDROMACHE How can they dress her
If she is gagged and bound?

HERMIONE *Talas Talantatos*!
Weep with me for your master.

CHORUS Why should we weep?

HERMIONE We are all going to die!
See, I beat my breast
And tear at my soft cheeks;
Now I lead the dirge

(*She beats the ground*)

With drumbeats of anguish
For my house that is destroyed.
See how the long procession
Of generations passes;
Pain, decay and sorrow
Makes up the life of man.
Take me to the doom-rock
And when I have spat upon
The founder of our house
Who began all this horror
Let it fall down on me!

ANDROMACHE If you both leave her alone
She will pull herself together.

MENELAUS Necessity, Hermione:
Remember that word.   (*)

(*HERMIONE looks at them and goes in. The CHORUS follow her*)

CALCHAS I'd have found her words more touching
If I had not heard Electra
Say them all in Mycenae.

402

MENELAUS Look at him, I pity him.
But this is no fit husband
For my daughter, Calchas.

(*ORESTES enters, dragging the body of*
NEOPTOLEMUS and his armour trailing after.
He is filthy and sick and speaks brokenly)

ORESTES See, the rock is falling.

CALCHAS Why have you come here?

ORESTES To claim what you promised me.

MENELAUS Do you think I will let my daughter
Marry this creature?

ORESTES (*To Calchas*) You promised me a wife
And to heal me of my madness;
You swore if I came to Delphi
And made the god an offering
Apollo would heal me.

CALCHAS When you came you committed murder.

ORESTES I saved your shrine from burning
And I helped the priests defend it.

CALCHAS The priests had already
Contained the conflagration
Before you interfered:
You are not yet fit for healing.

ORESTES It was Apollo's promise!
Yet since my trial I have had
Three more fits of madness.

CALCHAS You must help to heal yourself.

ORESTES How can I as I am?

CALCHAS Stop whining and listen.

ORESTES Where's my wife?

CALCHAS You shall take her;
But then you must leave this land
And go on a perilous quest.

MENELAUS Do you mean he must find Odysseus?

CALCHAS   You shall fetch one from the dead.

MENELAUS   Charon rarely offers
Return trips to travellers.

CALCHAS   You must fetch something precious
To the god and to you:
You shall bring back from Tauris
The Image of Artemis,
Apollo's twin sister.

MENELAUS   Careful: it is told
That no one comes back from Tauris.
And who will protect Electra
From the children Clytemnestra
Has born to Aegisthus,
Aletes and Erigone?

ORESTES   Erigone hates me
And would kill me if she could.
She made them try me in Athens.

CALCHAS   Then you should be grateful:
Mycenae would have stoned you.
Take heart; your friend Pylades
Shall go too and when you're back,
He will marry Electra.

MENELAUS   She will never marry:
No one will take her.

CALCHAS   She will do as the god commands
As you all will. Where's Hermione?

ORESTES   I know now that the Furies
Will never go away.

MENELAUS   I pity you, Orestes.

ORESTES   Yes, I am loathsome
But I do not want your pity.

MENELAUS   Let me speak to him. Suppose
It is Zeus and not Apollo
Who has put this curse upon you
As he has with all our house:
Pelops, Thyestes, Atreus

Aegisthus and perhaps
Your sister Iphigenia
Who died when you were born:
Zeus the just, Zeus the moody,
Said by some to be
As full of doubts as we are.

CALCHAS   You are rambling, Menelaus.

MENELAUS   Tantalus our fore-father
Sought to learn the gods' secrets
For the sake of mankind.
Our family has strived
To rule well by distinguishing
Between good and ill
And sometimes we have managed it.

CALCHAS   The mixture of high crimes
Committed with good intentions
Has been characteristic
Of your House since the moment
That Tantalus began it.

MENELAUS   All rule is patchwork.
How can we know better
Than gods?

ANDROMACHE   And why suppose
That they know better either?

MENELAUS   If you wish to rule, Orestes,
Where your father ruled before you,
Trust in Zeus and fetch that Image
And you shall have my daughter
And help to rebuild our house.

ORESTES   See, don't you see?
The great rock is falling.

MENELAUS   The rock is where it always was,
No higher and no lower.
Have courage and go on.   (*)

(Re-enter CHORUS with torches)

CHORUS   My lord, she is coming.

405

CALCHAS

Then raise the wedding-hymn
And sing it as it's always sung
Among all human people.

CHORUS

Hymen, Hymenaeus...

(As the CHORUS sing, ORESTES has another fit of madness)

CALCHAS

Come forth to him, Hermione.

MENELAUS

Let the wedding-dance begin!
Come girl, don't be shy.

(HERMIONE enters in black)

This is no wedding dress.

HERMIONE

How can I wear a wedding-dress
While my husband lies unburied?

MENELAUS

The point is a fair one.

HERMIONE

Stop slobbering, Orestes,
And come with me to the river.
Try to show a little dignity;
Neither of us are either
Likeable or lovely
To the world or to ourselves,
But my father is hoping
That once we are married
We will trouble no one
But each other. To my father
I have always been a bitch-dog
Convenient to breed with;
It is now my wish also
Since I shall soon be
Past child-bearing age.
Get up, Orestes;
We must go to the river
And there make a child.
We are monsters and monsters
Must do as they must.

CALCHAS

That is well said, take her:
May your quest thrive
And you be healed and purified.

MENELAUS   When you're back, I will help you
             To win back your kingdom.

CALCHAS   Go now and multiply
             According to the custom:
             It is sweet by the river.

CHORUS   Do as your grandmother
             And mother did before you:
             Go down to the river
         —   Lie on your back
         —   Feet in the water
         —   Head in the bullrushes
         —   Undo your girdle
         —   Try not to tense up
         —   That is never helpful
         —   Open your legs and wait
             And hope for the best.   (*)

             (HERMIONE leads ORESTES away)

CALCHAS   Now she has let it out
             She will soon feel much better.

MENELAUS   Your treatment of my daughter
             Is a grave breach of our guest-laws.

CALCHAS (*To Andromache*) Now tell us, Andromache:
             Was Paris to blame
             For what happened at Sparta?

ANDROMACHE   No, the human blame belongs
             To Priam and to Hecuba;
             They sent Paris to seize Helen
             As a hostage for Hesione.
             They thought he was Helen-proof
             Because of his love for Oenone.

CALCHAS   But how did Paris bear himself
             When he brought her back from Sparta?

ANDROMACHE   He was ashamed and sorry
             For Oenone and his city.

MENELAUS   I have no doubt Andromache
             Believes what she says,

But naturally her words
Are coloured by her suffering
And scarcely sound as evidence.

CALCHAS
I was there and can confirm them.
You have spoken well, Andromache,
And the god will reward you.

ANDROMACHE
I don't want to be rewarded.

CALCHAS
What do you want, then?

ANDROMACHE
For my son to live in safety.

CALCHAS
Then you need a proper husband.

ANDROMACHE
Hector was and is my husband.

CALCHAS
You shall take another Trojan
For the sake of your son.

ANDROMACHE
But all our men are dead.

CALCHAS
Cassandra's brother Helenus
Lives in quiet by Zeus' oracle
At Dodona in the northlands.

ANDROMACHE
Helenus was a traitor
Just as you are, Calchas.

CALCHAS
What is a traitor?
One who sees through Kings' mistakes.

CHORUS
What mistakes, Calchas?

CALCHAS
The worst mistake of all:
Believing one is right
Or, as men like to word it,
'In the right': what does that mean?
A morass of self-delusion.
When combined with the sense
That the land you were born in
Is the centre of the world
You all believe it right
To destroy the lands and cities
That belong to other people
Born in less happy lands.
But the centre of the world

	Is Delphi which belongs To Apollo and him only. That is why I left Troy: Call me traitor if you will.
CHORUS	You are contemptible.
CALCHAS	No man is contemptible If he is useful. Take my offer for your son's sake; Think clearly and act wisely.

(ANDROMACHE looks at her son)

CHORUS	Why should any of us Trust the words of a god Who betrays his own people?
MENELAUS	A reasonable question.
CALCHAS	The question is impertinent.
MENELAUS	But don't you see, Calchas, That some curse is at work here?
CALCHAS	Apollo is weary Of men offering the excuse That their own ineptitude Was due to some curse Being laid on their house, And you and your brother Have been the worst offenders. The cause of a curse Is always particular, Greed and stupidity: That is the curse of Tantalus.
MENELAUS	All I ask for is justice.
CALCHAS	You shall have it at Delphi. (*)

*(CALCHAS goes. ANDROMACHE is by
NEOPTOLEMUS' body)*

MENELAUS	The gods are not kind today. Andromache, I am sorry Both for you and your man.
ANDROMACHE	Go away, Menelaus.

MENELAUS   Understood; you must bury him.

ANDROMACHE   That is not what he'd have wanted.

MENELAUS   Understood: a funeral pyre.
In the beginning he was noble.

(*CHORUS lay the body on the fire. Flames rise from the fire*)

ANDROMACHE   This man was not noble;
He wanted to make good
And he wanted to be punished.
When we know a man's truth
It is time for us to pity him.

MENELAUS   You have made the best of things;
I honour you, Andromache.

CHORUS   But what of us, my lord?

MENELAUS   You?

CHORUS   What of us?

MENELAUS   When my daughter is married
You will be fetched to Sparta.

CHORUS   Not with her, we beseech you!

MENELAUS   Do not be afraid;
My daughter will be living
With Orestes in Mycenae.
I know what it is to suffer:
It has all been a mistake.   (*)

(*He goes. ANDROMACHE and her son kneel by NEOPTOLEMUS' smoking body. MOLOSSUS picks up the helmet of ACHILLES and puts it on*)

ANDROMACHE   Put it down; it is not yours.
You shall have a new father
To protect us in Dodona.
You are a brave boy
But it's time for you to learn
That this longing to be noble
May make men of boys
But it makes men into monsters.

No-one ever learns anything
Except when they are little.
There is only one way
To heal human pain:
Forgive but don't forget.
It takes time but it is worth it.

MOLOSSUS   Does it take very long?

ANDROMACHE   A long, long time, my darling,
Perhaps many ages.

MOLOSSUS   How many ages? A hundred?
A thousand? Or even longer?

ANDROMACHE   Rather longer, my darling.
What we think will happen
Almost never happens
And what cannot happen
Very often does.
There is no happiness,
There is only what happens.
All of you, remember that.   (*)

(*ANDROMACHE goes with her son*)

CHORUS   Now our mistress has gone
Why don't we run away?
— This house is dead and empty
— No it's not, it's full
— Of what? – Hermione's things!
— Risky – Her dresses!
If we wore them nobody
Would know we are slaves
— Old Peleus would see us
— He's asleep at Thetis' shrine
— Come on then, let's do it!

CHORUS A   Don't shout, but do it quickly.
I'll keep watch... Quietly.

(*ALL but one of the CHORUS go in. Enter
PELEUS from the shrine*)

PELEUS   What was all that shouting
And this stench of burning flesh?

CHORUS A	Menelaus and Calchas Were here; they've gone to Delphi.
PELEUS	Why is my grandson's armour Still here?
CHORUS A	He is dead.
PELEUS	Don't be stupid, he's at Delphi.
CHORUS A	That is why he is dead. Your house is over, old one; Your last lord is ashes.

(*PELEUS looks into the fire*)

PELEUS

Ashes... All my life,
All my living ends in ashes.
I thought I was too old
For Fate to bother with me.
'Want some drink... I am nothing
But a stupid, weak old man.
It is time for me to follow
My brood into the fire...

(*He drinks and weeps*)

It's time now for all of us
To take the boat to Asphodel.
There's something in the cup.   (*)

VOICE	Don't be so stupid: Stop weeping and get up.
CHORUS A	What is that?
PELEUS	I hear her!
VOICE	Zeus has other plans for you.
PELEUS	Where are you?
VOICE	In your cup Until you spat me out.

(*THETIS emerges*)

CHORUS	Look, it is your sea-nymph!
PELEUS	Why have you come back? Go away, I am unhappy.

THETIS	Have you forgotten The great jars of Zeus?
PELEUS	I know what jars I've drunk from.
THETIS	He has given you the mixture That he gives to most men; Those who deserve happiness Do not always get it And those who don't, do.
PELEUS	Do what?
THETIS	Get it.
PELEUS	Go away! I have not been treated fairly.
THETIS	Why should you look for fairness? Is the sea fair? Or the wind? Or the rain or the sun or the lightning? When Zeus sees a man like you His mind is more mixed than usual. He has given out so much From the great jar of sorrows While the other jar of blessings Is still full of gifts That he has decided It is time to give a gift To one who least deserves it.
CHORUS	Why should he do that?
THETIS	Why? Because he loves me And wants to restore the balance While there is still time: God-time can run out.
PELEUS	How? Gods are timeless.
THETIS	That is not certain.
PELEUS	What has Zeus to give me?
THETIS	Me. When you were young You were fair and I was foolish.
PELEUS	You still are.

THETIS   That perhaps
                  Is why I still love you,
                  You horrible old man.
                  So I have made Zeus promise
                  That we shall live together
                  Down in the purple sea-deeps;
                  We shall tread the foamy ocean
                  And you shall see our son
                  Achilles in the Happy Isle
                  Of Leuce that's all light.
                  We must go back to our love-cave
                  Where you wooed me long ago
                  And where for a moment
                  We made each other happy;
                  And there I will turn myself
                  Into a thousand creatures,
                  Fishes, serpents, sea-beasts
                  That wriggle and roll and revel
                  And you shall be lord of them all.

PELEUS   What are you saying?

THETIS   I want you: I am lonely.
                  When we have danced the wedding-dance
                  We shall dive into the deeps
                  And we'll wrestle there together
                  As we did when the world was young.
                  Mother Earth's an old whore,
                  Tired, grimy, noisy
                  But the sea-deeps are still silent
                  And secret as the stars.
                  Come with me, cave-love.

PELEUS   No, I cannot go;
                  My armour would rust there.

THETIS   You will not need armour
                  When we are in our sea-bed.

PELEUS   But it was a wedding-gift
                  Made for me by Hephaestus.

THETIS   Then he will keep it polished
                  In case you ever came back.

414

PELEUS	Yes, I might do that When the world has need of me.
THETIS	Hang it up and in time He will give it to some other.
PELEUS	Many ages will pass Till another is fit to wear it.

(*He hangs up the armour on the tree again*)

THETIS	Now wash before you go.
PELEUS	Why?
THETIS	Because you smell.
PELEUS	I am old, I cannot help it; But now I have wept I feel myself again.
CHORUS A	Go and wash, Peleus.
PELEUS	Going. (*)

(*He goes*)

CHORUS A	Tell me one thing, sea-nymph; If the jars of Zeus Are still so brim with blessings Why does he only Dish them out to heroes?
THETIS	Do you think he even notices Creatures such as you are?
CHORUS A	I'm a human-being, sea-nymph.
THETIS	Why do you think that so special? Your kind will die out As the Titans did before you And those that came before them.
CHORUS A	But you are immortal.
THETIS	I am not quite immortal. It is true I have been here Since the very beginning But when the world dies I shall die also.

CHORUS A	When will that be, Sea-nymph?
THETIS	Perhaps when the ice melts And the ocean swamps the land again; But if it does so this time It will pollute the water That has given me life so long; Or perhaps when some star falls And turns the sea to steam Or perhaps when the rock falls... But you do not need a prophetess To tell you what is obvious. You are all so small And see less than ant-men. I shall fly now to some mountain Where the air is clean and fresh And there I will renew myself. Pebbles, you're all pebbles. (*)

(She vanishes. Thunder far off. Then music and laughter in the house. The CHORUS re-enter, finely dressed)

CHORUS	Now we look like Trojans! – Put this on, my darling.

(One of them offers HERMIONE's wedding-dress)

CHORUS A	It is never wise To wear another's wedding dress.
CHORUS	Then try this – Or this.

(Distant thunder again)

CHORUS A	Quiet: Zeus is angry.
CHORUS	Not with us but with the West – Thunder's the same wherever it is – Hurry up.
CHORUS A	Before we go Let us pray to the god again.
CHORUS	The Destroyer?
CHORUS A	And the Healer.

CHORUS	Why should we trust him?
CHORUS A	Because it's worth a try.

(*They invoke Apollo*)

ALL   Apollo, Lord of Light
God of many names
Apollon... Apulunas...
Appellazo... Appleman...
Sun-god that warms us
Sun-god that burns us
Knower of all things
Show us your light!   (*)

(*A faint flash of light. CHORUS go in: Bright music. The armour clanks again*)

Play 9
HELEN

DELPHI

CAST

First Woman	AETHRA
Second Woman	PYTHONESS
Third Woman	HELEN
Fourth Woman	(–)
First Man	PELEUS
Second Man	MENELAUS
Third Man	CALCHAS
Fourth Man	(–)
	CHORUS of Nine Women

(Delphi. The shrine is still smoking but the Castalian Spring bubbles freshly. CHORUS enter. To them comes MENELAUS with HELEN and then CALCHAS. HELEN is veiled and simply dressed)

CALCHAS

Here in sacred Delphi
The truth shall be known.
Though the shrine of Apollo
Is burned and defiled,
Here the Spring Castalia
Still bubbles from the rock-face,
Pure, fresh, serene,
And beneath us the Pythoness
Sits in her secret chamber
Beneath the charred earth
Waiting for the god
To breathe truth into her nostrils
For her to shape and sound.

We are told a man has come to us
To learn about his wife
And sift true things from false things.
All this winter the God
Has been with the Hyperboreans,
An uncouth unlovely people
That dwell in lands of ice;
Now it is springtime
And he is back among us
To pierce us with his light.
But before he gives judgement
He will hear what is said of Helen
Both for and against her.
Whoever would speak here
Must drink first of Castalia.

(MENELAUS drinks of the spring)

Is your name Menelaus?

MENELAUS

You know it is my name.

CALCHAS

And have you sworn to bring
Your lady to this oracle

420

	To learn the very soul of her Whether for good or ill?
MENELAUS	We've discussed this already.
CALCHAS	Is she your wife?
MENELAUS	Who else's?
CALCHAS	That's what we're met to determine.
CHORUS	Let us see her – Why is she veiled?
MENELAUS	She's in mourning for her sister.
CHORUS	Then how can we be sure That she is really Helen? We hear there are two of them
–	How can we be certain That this is not a third?
–	Let us all see her face!
–	She is ashamed to show it.
MENELAUS	Her sufferings have wasted her; She does not want the world To look upon her sorrow.
CALCHAS	Who are her accusers?
CHORUS	The Women of the West.
CALCHAS	What is she accused of?
CHORUS	War-crimes.
CALCHAS	What is a war-crime?
CHORUS	Helen is a war-crime.
CALCHAS	How is that possible? How can she be accused Of a crime that neither I Nor the gods have ever heard of? If war became a crime There would never be enough Divine or human courts Ever to try the criminal.
CHORUS	– Because of this one woman All our men are dead – Their blood cries out against her.

CALCHAS

That is much, but is it possible
One woman could kill them all?

CHORUS

She alone began the war
— We demand that the god
Should punish her with death.

CALCHAS

Never make demands of a god;
They don't like it. Remember
You accuse a child of Zeus
And that it is not you
Who have brought her to this oracle
But her husband, the King of Sparta.
Drink, Menelaus;

(*To Chorus*)

Mark his words with reverence.   (*)

MENELAUS

Now, great Apollo,
Let your light shine like starlight
On the dark vale of this world.
The truth has been found in Egypt,
A great and ancient land
Where for seventeen long years
My wife has been held prisoner:
Helen never went to Troy
So there is no need to try her
And we can all go home.

CHORUS

What is this?

CALCHAS

Have you evidence?

MENELAUS

Look upon these words
Carved in stone by Theonoe,
The King of Egypt's sister.

(*He presents hieroglyphs*)

CHORUS

What wonder is this?

MENELAUS

Theonoe is a prophetess.

CALCHAS

I know her and honour her.

CHORUS

Read it for us, Menelaus.

CALCHAS

I know what is in it.

MENELAUS

How is that possible?

CALCHAS   Prophets know the minds
                 And words of other prophets
                 Through the sacred web and net
                 Of priestly transmission.
                 Tell these women what is in it;
                 If you twist one word
                 The god and I will know it.

MENELAUS   And the world shall know it too.
                 When we finally took Troy
                 And set sail for home
                 A great storm overtook us
                 And blew us to the South.
                 For many long sea-days
                 Helen slept and said no word
                 Till we entered tranquil waters:
                 I saw land, flat and fertile
                 And I knew we had reached Egypt.
                 Suddenly my wife
                 (Or perhaps I should say the woman
                 I had rescued from Ilion)
                 Cried out amazing words:
                 'Father in Heaven,
                 I have fulfilled my purpose
                 And am coming back to you!'
                 Then she flung herself overboard
                 And vanished beneath the waves.
                 Of course I dived in after her
                 But the ocean had swallowed her.
                 I wept, but my men demanded
                 That since I was in the water
                 I should swim ashore to find
                 Fresh fruit and herbs and olives
                 Instead of Phrygian biscuits.
                 So after a long day's swimming
                 I came to the mouth of a river
                 Wider than twenty roadways
                 And hid among the bull-rushes
                 To find out if the natives
                 Were friendly or hostile.
                 But as I lurked I saw my wife

Asleep on the silver sands
Bathing naked in the sun.

CHORUS   What did she say when she saw you?

MENELAUS   She screamed 'Another rape!'
And hid behind an obelisk.
When I approached her cautiously
She cried out 'O my darling,
I have waited twenty years
For you to come and find me.'
Thinking her mind dazed
By lying too long on the beach,
I told her to put a dress on
So that I might question her
More closely; so she did
And put on the very same dress
That I gave her twenty years ago
Before I left Sparta
To visit a friend in Crete.
I held her very gently
And she began to tell me
How the gods had sent an image
To Troy to take her place
And that it was this image
Who had been there with Paris
While she was in Egypt, weeping.

As we lay there on the sand
Theonoe came to us
And told us to go quickly
Before the king her brother
Forced my wife to marry him;
I killed a dozen guards
And we set sail for Sparta.
So you see that I am speaking
Of a rape that never happened
But of one that might have happened
If I had not brought her home.

CHORUS   Is all of this set down
In Theonoe's letter?

MENELAUS   All.

CHORUS	Then she never went to Troy?
MENELAUS	Never.
CALCHAS	It would seem so.
MENELAUS (*To Chorus*)	Then may we both go home now? All of you, go home. (*)
CALCHAS	We must surely first establish When the crucial substitution Of one Helen for another Actually took place: Egypt? Troy? Or Sparta? When he came and stayed with you Did the Trojan seize her Or did she perhaps encourage him?
CHORUS	We need witnesses of that.
MENELAUS	I have three.
CALCHAS	Then produce them.
MENELAUS	First, my daughter Hermione...
CALCHAS	I have spoken with her already And found her unreliable.
MENELAUS	Then wait till Peleus comes: He was there when it happened.
CHORUS	Where is he?
CALCHAS	Gone for good.
MENELAUS	How can you be certain?
CALCHAS	Because I'm Apollo's prophet.
MENELAUS	But I have one other witness Whose knowledge of the past Exceeds your own.
CALCHAS	Then name her.
MENELAUS	Theseus' wife Aethra.
CALCHAS	Aethra of Athens.
CHORUS	But she is an ancient Who died long ago.

MENELAUS   No, she lives and was in Sparta
                    When Paris seized my wife.
                    So he seized Aethra too
                    As a prisoner in Troy
                    Throughout ten years of war
                    Till her grandsons rescued her.
                    True, Calchas?

CALCHAS   It is true;
                    It is in the sources.
                    We shall be glad to hear her.
                    Bring her to us, Menelaus.   (*)

                    (Enter AETHRA, supported by women)

                    Now, Lady Aethra,
                    Aethra, 'Clear sky',
                    Aethra, 'Fair weather'.
                    Since some minds here are cloudy
                    Speak winged words now
                    That may bring us all to light.

AETHRA   I was watching the trial
                    Of the son of Agamemnon,
                    Hearing gods themselves
                    Debating good and ill.
                    Why have you brought me
                    To this secondary site?
                    The journey was tedious
                    And the food here is execrable.

CALCHAS   Drink from this stream:
                    It will very soon refresh you.

AETHRA   This spring has been polluted
                    Ever since the day
                    That Apollo slew the Python
                    And left it here to rot.
                    When my father was living
                    He sent it to be tested
                    As a health-risk to suppliants.
                    Ever since this shrine became
                    A lure to nosy travellers
                    The slobberings of the curious
                    Have made it a death-trap.

CALCHAS	I will speak to Apollo.
MENELAUS	All of us have drunk from it And it has harmed none of us.
AETHRA	How can you tell with pollution? But when you are my age What does it matter? Women, fill me a cup.

(She drinks)

MENELAUS	My wife has been fortunate To have had you for company Through the long unhappy years.
CHORUS	But was it her or wasn't it?
MENELAUS	We must know the truth.
AETHRA	Men like to say that But in my experience All they want is a sense of truth Which is something very different. When a man dotes on a woman He is apt to confuse The image he first meets With the one he learns of later.
CALCHAS	Simply tell us what happened When Paris came to Sparta.
AETHRA	I will not speak in public Of matters that are private; What goes on within human families Is no-one else's business.
CALCHAS	Such a code is admirable But a god bids you speak here.
CHORUS	We want to know the truth!
AETHRA	No you don't; you are like The hordes that throng Olympia To gape at the games And goggle at the muscles Of large men hurling javelins And punching each others' faces. Why have you brought me here?

MENELAUS   To prove that my wife
             Is guilty of no war-crime.

AETHRA   A War-crime? The word,
             Like most recent coinages,
             Is not only unnecessary
             But plainly contradictory
             In its terms. The only crime
             Recognised through all the world
             Is losing a war;
             Then as is natural
             The losers are punished.

CALCHAS   Answer us one question:
             What was Helen's state of mind
             Before Paris seized her?

AETHRA   Neither god nor mortal
             Can read a woman's mind.
             Try to speak more plainly, Calchas.

CALCHAS   What happened when Menelaus
             Went to Crete?

AETHRA   It was boring. Nothing happened.

CHORUS   Why?

AETHRA   The Trojan
             Had done no high deeds
             He had no good stories,
             So Helen yawned and set to work
             On a tapestry.

CHORUS   Of what?

AETHRA   The rape of her mother Leda;
             Paris held the spindle
             While she worked on the swan.

CALCHAS   So who began the war?
AETHRA   Zeus, of course.

CALCHAS   Zeus?

AETHRA   With a swan's egg; who else?

CALCHAS   We are not trying Zeus.

AETHRA	No, I would not advise it.
MENELAUS	Was my wife raped Or did she go willingly?
AETHRA	Why drag me from Athens To ask stupid questions?
MENELAUS	Was she raped against her will?
AETHRA	That is still the meaning Of the word in current usage.
CHORUS	Do you mean she is innocent?
AETHRA	Of course she is innocent: Very few girls like it.
MENELAUS	Apollo be praised!
CHORUS	If that is true we have all Been gravely misinformed — If that is true I pity her — If she is innocent We had better all go home.
MENELAUS	Let the god give the judgement!
AETHRA	Of course she was innocent: She was only nine years old.
MENELAUS	Excuse me, she was seventeen At the time of our marriage.
AETHRA	I remember quite clearly She was nine when he had her.
CALCHAS	You have drunk of the stream So be careful what you say.
AETHRA	I invariably speak carefully; I have always found it best.
MENELAUS	Yet you say she was nine; Are you sure that is accurate?
AETHRA	Nine, only nine, Or ten at the most.
MENELAUS	How is that possible?

AETHRA	You ask me how he did it? By hiding in the bull-rushes.
MENELAUS	There are no bull-rushes In the Spartan royal palace.
AETHRA	I never said there were.
MENELAUS	But you just said so.
AETHRA	Why don't you listen? I told you she was raped On the bank of the river; You surely have a river Known as the Eurotas?
MENELAUS	Not inside my palace.
AETHRA	This young man is a fool.
CALCHAS	Let her go on, Menelaus.
AETHRA	It was by your fair Eurotas That my great son Theseus Seized and enjoyed her And took her home to Athens.
CALCHAS	This is scarcely relevant To our purpose here today.
AETHRA	Of course it is relevant. I have travelled many miles And drunk your repulsive water And all you do is interrupt And ask impertinent questions.
CALCHAS	Did you know this, Menelaus?
MENELAUS	Yes, I knew; Helen told me But she soon recovered When her brothers brought her home.
AETHRA	So they did, and with another.
MENELAUS	No-one saw another.
AETHRA	How could they see it If it was inside her?
MENELAUS	What is this? Tyndareus Never told me of a child.

AETHRA
Of course he didn't tell you;
It would not have been suitable
In front of prospective suitors.

MENELAUS (*To Helen*) Why did I not know of this?

CHORUS
What happened to the child?

AETHRA
I presume that Tyndareus
Dealt with the matter
In the usual way.

MENELAUS
What's that?

AETHRA
It is normally the business
Of the Nurse of the child
To take it into the mountains
Where the royal shepherd lives,
Though they say that young Aegisthus
Was taken to a wood
And suckled by a goat.

CALCHAS
To the point, Lady Aethra.

CHORUS
Was the child ever found?

AETHRA
I expect so.

MENELAUS
Why do you say that?

AETHRA
Because they usually are
And it always turns out badly;
Mountain shepherds are kind-hearted
But much too interfering.
One or two are lodged with nymphs,
But if their nurse is sensible
The lucky ones are lodged
With some female relation.

MENELAUS
Is that so? This is strange.

AETHRA
It isn't strange, it's normal.

MENELAUS
But how can we tell if it's true?

CHORUS
By seeking out the Shepherd
– Or the Nurse – If they're still living.

MENELAUS
I do not believe a word of this.

AETHRA	If you'd had my experience You would be more open-minded.
CHORUS	Were you left on a mountain?
AETHRA	No, it happened by the sea-side.
CALCHAS	Aethra, not now.
AETHRA	Grieving at my virginity, My husband-to-be, Aegeus, Got drunk one night and lay with me. At length I fell asleep And dreamed that Athene Bade me offer a libation On the island of Sphaeria. You remember Sphaerus, Your grandfather's charioteer?
MENELAUS	I remember.
AETHRA	When I got there The god Poseidon raped me.
MENELAUS	How can you be certain?
CALCHAS	It too is in the sources.
CHORUS	So a god enjoyed you also?
AETHRA	I enjoyed it too; But when Theseus was born He and I were never certain Who his father really was.
MENELAUS	I fear that our house also Has had similar experiences.
AETHRA	It's presumptuous to assume We can ever know for certain Who our parents really are.
CALCHAS	Then try to turn your mind back To when Paris came to Sparta. Was Helen raped a second time Or did he seduce her Or in any way provoke her?
AETHRA	I did not come here To answer stupid questions.

CALCHAS	Then tell us what happened On the island of Cranae Where Paris and Helen stayed The night before they sailed.
MENELAUS	Trojan traces have been found there.
AETHRA	The journey was long, So as soon as we arrived –
CHORUS	Yes?
AETHRA	I fell asleep. I am tired, can I go now?
CALCHAS	Drink again of the spring And the water will refresh you.

(They give her a drink. AETHRA changes)

AETHRA	Starlight…!
MENELAUS	Take us with you.
AETHRA	I woke up into starlight: I heard singing in the sky And all the orbs were dancing! And on the sands I saw –
CHORUS	What? Who?
AETHRA	I saw footsteps Disappearing into the water.
CALCHAS	Male feet or a female's?
CHORUS	One pair or two?
AETHRA	A man's and a woman's And a few drops of blood.
MENELAUS	Ravishment.
AETHRA	No, sea-shells; My feet were bleeding too. The sea was serene and purple As the wine we drank in Ilion Except for one spot Where I saw the water frothing As it did when Aphrodite Arose glistening from Cythera.

Then a sea-mist rose over me
As the thick Dardanian battle-dust
Used to rise up from the war-plains
And stung our eager eyes
As we looked down from Ilion
And watched young Achilles
Chase Hector around the walls.
Then I heard more singing
As the Muses used to sing
When I was a little girl
And I fell in a deep slumber.
When I woke I was on a ship
And the oarsmen were smiling.
Their backs as they rowed
Were facing the stern
So they could not see the prow
But I saw it: the two of them
Were lying there in love.

CHORUS | Do you hear that, Calchas?
— There's your truth, Spartan!

MENELAUS | Yet this does not tell us
When the exchange took place
Between Helen and the image.

CALCHAS | The question is a shrewd one.

MENELAUS | Tell us more, if you can.

(AETHRA recovers)

AETHRA | I am weary of your questions;
You will only twist what I say
Into what you want me to say.
May I go now?

CALCHAS | You may.
We are grateful to you, Aethra.

AETHRA | Then provide me with an air-horse
To take me back to Athens:
Pegasus will serve
Or else Perseus' sandals.

CALCHAS | If you go into the shrine
And offer a libation,

I will speak to the god
And I'm sure he will assist you.

AETHRA   Whatever Paris did
To your wife, Menelaus,
One thing is certain:
My son did it better;
That is how it used to be.   (*)

(AETHRA goes)

MENELAUS *(To Helen)* My dearest, I am troubled.
You told me in Troy
You'd been raped when you were little
But you did not mention
That you had a secret child.
Since you hid this from me
How may I trust
Anything you say?

CHORUS   Let her be, she is weeping.
—   I want to see her face!
Take your veil off, Helen
—   Let us see if you are still
As fair as they sing of you.

(HELEN shakes her head)

CALCHAS   You must take it off now
To drink of the stream;
There is no avoiding.

(HELEN lowers her head and drinks)

Drink deep and answer
The charges made against you.

CHORUS   —   Whore! — Boat-destroyer!
—   Let us see how many ships
Your face could launch today.

(HELEN takes off the veil. She is unpainted and aging)

This is not Helen
—   What game is this?

435

MENELAUS   She is fairer to me still
            Than all the gods in heaven.

CALCHAS   Speak, Helen, and tell us
            Why did you hide this secret?

HELEN   Because my earthly father
            Made me swear not to reveal it.

MENELAUS   Tyndareus?

HELEN   He,
            He said the child was dead
            And buried on some mountain;
            I knew that such things happened.

MENELAUS   Yes, such things happen;
            Tyndareus should have told me
            But you are not to blame.

HELEN   Then why do you blame me?

MENELAUS   I do not blame you:
            I wish to prove you innocent.

CALCHAS   You must tell us what happened
            When Paris came to Sparta.

HELEN   What is the point of telling you
            How it was in Sparta
            All those years ago
            When I'm already god-cast
            In the minds of all the world?

MENELAUS   Yet tell us what you can.

HELEN   When you left me there as hostess
            All Paris did was talk for hours
            About a girl called Oenone
            He had left at home on some mountain.
            When Hermione tried to flirt with him
            And Peleus pinched her bottom
            And Aethra got asthma
            I decided we all needed
            Some fresh air by the sea-side.

CALCHAS   But did Paris rape you
            Either there or at Cranae?

CHORUS	Or did you seduce him?
HELEN	Nobody raped me In any of those places! The only rape I know of Is in your own sick minds. I have done nothing wrong; It has all been done to me Because a god begot me And because I have big eyes.
CHORUS	Other mortal women Have had gods for their fathers But they managed to live lives That were sensible and seemly.
HELEN	But I did not choose To be raped by Theseus Nor to marry Menelaus, Nor be left alone with Paris; I was chosen by Hera To be air-dropped into Egypt. You call me a war-crime But I am a victim.
CALCHAS	All women say that.
CHORUS	I don't – She's a victim Of her own lust – Who isn't? – That is not the point; We are talking about Helen.
ALL	Tell us the truth of it!
HELEN	This is my truth: I don't know who I am But I do know who it was Who committed your war-crime: I know, I have experience.
CALCHAS	Names would be useful.
	(*She does so*)
HELEN	Then I name Aphrodite, So coarse and pink and vulgar;

She does not understand
Real human love.
She rose naked from the sea
Covered only in the foam
From which she was engendered,
Not sea-foam, but blood-froth
From the bleeding genitals
Of some fallen sky-god.
The fable is nauseous
But it is characteristic
Of the tales of male poets.
When she emerged from the ocean
She hopped onto a scallop shell
And sailed about the ocean
Exposing her naked body
And smirking at sailors.

Thousands of years later
She came to Mount Ida
With Athene and Hera,
But Paris did not choose
To give her the apple
(He at least had manners):
Aphrodite chose him.
This did not please the others
So Hera decided
To thwart the poor boy's lust
By giving him not me
But an image made of air,
And Athene in her wisdom
Sent me to Egypt
To learn wisdom if I could.

So they left me beneath a palm-tree
Lonely, wretched, yearning
For my husband to take me home.
And at last he did so
Though I am bound to say
He took his time about it.
Don't you believe me, love?

CHORUS	Don't answer, Menelaus,
	Or she'll twist you round her finger. (*)
MENELAUS	My love, I believe you
	And I want to take you home
	But we must first establish
	The truth of who you are.
HELEN	You have made a myth of me:
	That is your mistake.
MENELAUS	What is a myth?
HELEN	What we make out of other people.
	What did you make of the other me
	That you rescued from Ilion?
	Which of us pleased you better?
MENELAUS	I hated her, she frightened me;
	On the ship I never touched her.
	She lay in the stern asleep
	While I stood at the prow
	Thinking and searching.
CALCHAS	For what?
MENELAUS	When one's heart is troubled
	And one searches in one's mind
	We may not always know
	What it is we search for
	Until the day we find it;
	That's why I go on searching.
CALCHAS	That is a good answer.
HELEN	I too am searching.
MENELAUS	What for?
HELEN	For the answer
	To one simple question.
CALCHAS	Then ask it.
HELEN	Menelaus,
	Drink again of the spring.
MENELAUS	As you will.

(He drinks) (*)

HELEN
                         Now tell me:
Why did you go to Crete?

MENELAUS   I had to go on business.

CALCHAS   What business?

MENELAUS   A meeting.

CALCHAS   Some matter of state perhaps?

MENELAUS   My friend Idomeneus,
The great King of Crete,
Lord of a hundred warships
And as rich as he is wise,
Hearing that the son
Of King Priam was with me
And fearing I meant to trade
With Troy and not with Crete,
Asked me to visit him:
One does not refuse such men.

HELEN   Take me with you, husband.

MENELAUS   Yes, I wish I could have done so.

HELEN   Was it so important?

MENELAUS   Yes, the Cretans were threatening
To cut off our oil supplies.

HELEN   You went there for oil?

MENELAUS   Our olive trees were withering;
It was either due to insects
Or some sickness in our soil.

HELEN   So you left me at home with Paris
To get oil?

MENELAUS   No kingdom
Can ever thrive without it;
I had to make a choice
And it was not an easy one.

HELEN   It would seem you were confused
With the same choice as Paris.

MENELAUS   I fear I don't quite follow you.

HELEN   Wisdom, Love and Power.

MENELAUS	Forgive me, but I do not Understand your analogy.
HELEN	Say which you hold greatest.
MENELAUS	My brother once told me If one tries to choose one thing At the expense of another So he loses his sense of the whole.
CALCHAS	Your brother, Menelaus, Was not altogether foolish.
HELEN	Answer me, Menelaus.
MENELAUS	For me love is greatest; That is why I am here. I have power already But it frightens and confuses me, So I'd like to be wise Or at least to act wisely. That is why I consulted Another of my guests, Nauplius's son, Palamedes, The wisest man in the West. He said he would give me A device he had invented To improve my sea-skills, But I was not quite clear How to use it correctly And so I was delayed. I regret it deeply.
CHORUS	What was this device?
MENELAUS	He called it a sextant; I believe that he gave one To Odysseus as well.
CHORUS	No wonder he also Has not yet reached home.
HELEN	So because of that device I spent seventeen long years Underneath a palm-tree.
MENELAUS	But when were you air-borne?

HELEN	I think that it must have been On the island of Cranae.
CHORUS	Proof: can you prove it?
CALCHAS	Speak, lady.
HELEN	I remember That Paris' men were weary From carrying the treasure...
CHORUS	Your gold-hoard, Menelaus.
MENELAUS	Go on.
HELEN	... It was hot and dusty So at sun-down everybody Went for a bathe in the sea.
CHORUS	And you? You bathed with them?
HELEN	I know who a queen Does and does not bathe with; I found a little cave Behind the next headland Where no-one could see me And slipped off my dress.
CHORUS	Doubtless there were bull-rushes?
HELEN	Only sand, burning sand But the sea was cool and lovely.
MENELAUS	Aethra told us that she saw Two sets of footsteps.
HELEN	So there were.
CHORUS	Yours and Paris'!
HELEN	The footsteps belonged to Hermes.
CHORUS	Did Hermes have you too?
CALCHAS	Be silent!... Continue.
HELEN	Hera sent him to carry me Through the wanton air to Egypt.
MENELAUS	That explains the other feet.
HELEN	I was swimming on my back And playing with a friendly dolphin –

442

MENELAUS	I have often warned you About playing with strange animals.
CHORUS	It might have been her father In disguise.
CALCHAS	Quiet. What happened?
HELEN	That is all I remember Till I found myself alone Lying beside a sarcophagus They were making for some bull.
CHORUS	Ha! A bull? – Was it Zeus?
CALCHAS	Be silent!
HELEN	I have done. O my love, I pity you. You are blind, you all are. I am a child of Zeus, Half mortal, half divine, So I see more than you do. Why should I waste my breath When I know that the world Never, ever will believe me Even if the blessed gods Spelt out the truth to you For five thousand years? Free me from their folly, Father! I am as you made me And I do not know why!

(She turns away)

MENELAUS	Where are you going?
HELEN	To offer a libation As a suppliant to Apollo: I appeal to him! Listen, Father's angry…

(Distant thunder)

MENELAUS	Stay, we have not finished.
HELEN	My story is finished But the gods have not finished.

443

Time to go in, my love:
It must be as it must.   (*)

(*HELEN goes into the shrine. Thunder. The
earth shudders a little*)

CHORUS   What's that rumbling in the earth?

CALCHAS   Merely an after-quake
Of some blasture long forgotten
That loosens and releases.
When there's star-fire in heaven
Mother Earth has qualms;
But the light of Apollo
Burns brightly down the ages.
Be silent and perpend.

(*Pause*)

CHORUS   Calchas, while we wait
May we ask you a question?

CALCHAS   Ask.

CHORUS   You said in Phthia
That Orestes must go to Tauris
To fetch some Image.

CALCHAS   So?

CHORUS   Will he find it?

CALCHAS   Ask Apollo.

CHORUS   But what is an image?
        —   Is it an imagining?

CALCHAS   Sometimes, not always.

CHORUS   How can one fetch an image?

CALCHAS   What's your problem?

CHORUS   You said he must fetch it
From the dead.

CALCHAS   That is where
All that is imagined
Usually ends up.

CHORUS   Then how will he find it?

CALCHAS	One that is lost will be found And one that is found will be lost.
	(*Pause*)
CHORUS	What would have happened If Paris had given the apple To Hera or Athene?
CALCHAS	The result would have been the same.
CHORUS	Then why give a choice at all?
CALCHAS	Gods like to watch men choosing.
CHORUS	So it's true that all is fated — I would say that it is rigged.
CALCHAS	Your verbiage is vulgar But it shows you are learning.
CHORUS	We wish to. Is it true That Atlas holds up the earth?
CALCHAS	Can you offer an alternative?
	(*Pause*)
CHORUS	May we ask one more question?
CALCHAS	If you must.
CHORUS	We have heard Clytemnestra did not kill Her husband Agamemnon.
CALCHAS	Who said so?
CHORUS	Hermione.
CALCHAS	Never quote unsound sources.
CHORUS	We are asking at the true source, This sacred spring Castalia — But the waters seem muddy now.
CALCHAS	That means the god is thinking.
CHORUS	If you know his thoughts, tell us.
CALCHAS	One day a Blind Poet Will tell of two versions: One where Clytemnestra

	Helped her lover kill her husband And one where Agamemnon Was killed by Aegisthus only.
CHORUS	Two versions of one tale?
CALCHAS	And in time rather more.
CHORUS	We're confused – We want to know The true answer now.
CALCHAS	Why cannot humans take A longer view of gods? Why do they all expect Quick answers to their questions? Gods laugh when mortals say They exist to provide them With a sense of understanding The meaning of all things. When will men and women learn That they live in a world Of brutal and blind chaos?
CHORUS	But is human life worth living If we have no sense of meaning?
MENELAUS	How can kings keep order?
CALCHAS	How can they keep something Which they have never had?
CHORUS	You speak darkly.
CALCHAS	No! Apollo is all Light, All Reason and all Truth, Perplexive to pretty girls But palpable to prophets; Purposive, yet random, Inscrutable, irrefutable, Invisible yet imminent: Such are the words of god.
CHORUS	Your words are hard to follow. – We've been waiting here all day.
CALCHAS	What is a day in god-time? All that's past is infinite,

446

Immemorial, inaccessible,
The Now is infinitesimal,
But the future hurtles on.
Yet gods cannot untangle
All the muddles of mankind
In a moment. It takes time,
Not long in god-time
But long in mortal reckoning.

CHORUS   But...

CALCHAS   No more questions: wait.

(*A cry below*)

CHORUS   What's that cry?

CALCHAS   It is the Pythoness
Who sits on the sacred tripod
Underneath the earth.

(*Pause. Bubbles begin to appear in the spring
and vapours creep from the shrine*)

CHORUS   What is this mist
Rising from the ground?
—   Is that truth?

CALCHAS   Yes, god's truth.

(*Cries are heard within or below*)

MENELAUS   That is not my wife's voice;
These are cries of pain.

CHORUS   It is a woman's voice;
—   What is Apollo doing?

CALCHAS   Speaking through the Pythoness;
She is breathing in his words
From the vapours of a chasm
In the centre of the world.

(*The PYTHONESS comes out of the shrine.
She makes wild sounds for a few seconds and
then collapses on the ground*)

PYTHONESS   ! *! *!

CHORUS   The voice of the god
Is harsh and fearful to me.

CALCHAS   Yet to me his words are plain
                 And as clear as the day-sky.

MENELAUS   Then tell us their meaning.

CALCHAS   You know it already
                 But you do not know you know it.
                 There were and are two Helens:
                 One is Zeus' daughter
                 And as such should be held
                 In more respect and honour
                 Than you have shown today;
                 The other is a woman
                 As stupid as the rest of you.
                 It was the will of Zeus
                 To create and use her loveliness
                 To purge the tired earth
                 Of the sad superfluity
                 Of human mortality.
                 Helen never went to Troy:
                 The gods set her image
                 To dwell there in her place;
                 What she did inside Ilion
                 Is irrelevant though resonant.
                 Zeus will not let her die.

MENELAUS   Then she shall live with me!

CALCHAS   I did not say that;
                 She shall live for eternity
                 In the minds and hearts of men.

MENELAUS   That is how it should be.

CALCHAS   She shall be enfolded
                 In the endless vasts of space,
                 Unsullied and immortal
                 And shining in the Heavens,
                 A light, a flame, a star…

CHORUS   A wonder! – Apollo,
                 We honour you! – Forgive us
                 If we have sometimes doubted

MENELAUS   How can you all believe him?
                 You yourselves have heard the voice

Of this unhappy woman
Imprisoned beneath the earth.
She was crying out her wretchedness
As we all will when it's our turn
To go down into Asphodel;
She is Apollo's prisoner
As my wife is and I am.
What Calchas tells us
Cannot be Zeus' justice.

CALCHAS   Men always find God's justice
Hard to understand.
If you'd wanted human justice
You should have taken Helen
Before a civil court
Though I would not have advised it.

CHORUS   Is it true that she shall be
A star in the heavens?

CALCHAS   Search the skies tonight.

MENELAUS   No! I'm taking her home.

CALCHAS   The Image is still available.

MENELAUS   That is not what I want!

CALCHAS   What men want they seldom get.

CHORUS   We want to see the star!

CALCHAS   When a new star is born
Or when a lost one's found
It takes some time for humans
To perceive its true nature.

CHORUS   He is right, Menelaus,
We know the mind's limits
—   I fear to learn too much
Lest it blasts my human mind.

CALCHAS   There is little risk
Of your minds being god-blast,
And so ends your story.
Come into the shrine
With libations to Apollo.

Now Helen's earthly mould
Must decline to clay and dust
But she in her true image
Shall ascend the shining pathway
That mounts up to the stars
And there she shall live for ever
And be a star for sailors.

(CALCHAS leaves. CHORUS start to go)

MENELAUS But here all is dark again
As it was for all those years
That I toiled on the beach-head
Yearning for my lost one,
Doubting and not knowing.
Now I know.

CHORUS   Is it better?

MENELAUS Is it better for her?
O Helen, my star-girl,
You will be so happy
Up there among the stars.

(Music far off. CHORUS pause)

CHORUS Listen, do you hear?
  — I can hear the Muses singing.

MENELAUS Go home and tell this story
To your children; make libations
To whichever god you will.

*(CHORUS go. The PYTHONESS goes back
into the shrine, mumbling)*

I will weep tonight
For I am full of sorrow
But I will learn to live with it
When I awake tomorrow.
Whether the god is evil
Or whether he is just
I do not wish to know now;
Time for me to go now:
It must be as it must.

(He goes)

Play 10

ERIGONE

MYCENAE

CAST

First Woman	NURSE/ HESTIA
Second Woman	PYTHONESS
Fourth Woman	ELECTRA/ HERMIONE/ IPHIGENIA/ ERIGONE

First Man	POET
Second Man	MENELAUS
Fourth Man	ORESTES

CHORUS

Herein cast as:

CALLIOPE	(Epic Poetry, Story-telling)
CLIO	(History)
URANIA	(Astronomy)
ERATO	(Personal and Erotic Lyric)
MELPOMENE	(Tragedy)
THALIA	(Comedy)
POLYHYMNIA	(Hymns in honour of the gods)
EUTERPE	(Pipe and Musical Instruments)
TERPSICHORE	(Choral Dance and Song)

(*Mycenae desolate, wan and dusty. There is smoke in the air. The CHORUS enters as they were dressed in Play 2*)

CHORUS   Delphi is still burning
–   So much for oracles
–   We had just left the shrine
     When we saw the Earth split open
     And rocks crash down from the mountain
–   Calchas fell into the chasm
     And was impaled on the tripod
–   Mother Earth is angry
–   There are flames in the night sky
–   There are fires in the forest
–   They say that the ocean's gorging
     On the verges of the West
     And the corpses of sea-beasts
     Are rotting on the beaches

–   They must all be signs:
     It is said if Delphi dies The world will die also
     As that tree there is dying
–   Not if the shrine is purified
–   Only Apollo can do that
–   It is over eight months
     Since he went into the North:
     He will not come back now.

–   Where is our Poet?
     If he doesn't come back soon
     We shall never know
     The ending of our story
–   If he did it wouldn't help;
     He will tell us some other version
–   Then why don't we make our own?
–   How, if we don't know it?
–   We might make a mess of it
–   We couldn't make a worse one
     Than he has made so far.

–   Didn't someone say something
     About Memory and the streams?

–   Yes, at Delphi – No, before that:
    Two streams to drink from...
–   One was of lost things hidden
    And one, I think, of finding
–   Which was which? – We were never told.

    Who is to blame for our sorrows?
    Is it god-work or man-work?
    Or some cause as yet unknown?
–   Or is it just possible
    It might even be someone
    Just like us? – How could that be?

–   It is told in the beginning
    The first human girl
    Like us, fair and intelligent,
    Was made by Zeus himself
    Out of clay, earth and mountain snow.
    So Zeus gave her a pot
    As a wedding gift for her husband
    He told how all truth
    Was hidden inside it
    But she must never open it.
–   So of course Pandora did –
–   I remember – It was natural
–   Then out tumbled Toil
–   Old Age and Sickness
–   Despair, Passion, Madness
–   Confusion, Chaos, Dread
–   Pandora's the one to blame...

–   But it's said Hope was left
    At the bottom of the pot
–   Hope? – Yes, she lingers...

    (*Moaning is heard in the house*)

–   What's that? – It's only Hermione
–   Menelaus wouldn't have her in Sparta,
    So they brought her to Mycenae
    For the birth of Orestes' child.   (*)

–   Look, there he is:
    Each year he comes with an offering

453

	To Agamemenon's grave
	— Some beggar girl has brought him
	— It's the Pythoness from Delphi
	— Sh, I think he's blind.

(The PYTHONESS, burned and grimy, leads MENELAUS to his brother's grave)

MENELAUS

Brother, what shall I say to you?
I live, you lie in the earth
But I alone am to blame
For all you endured and suffered.
If I had not gone to Crete
There would have been no war;
If I had not persuaded you
To take command at Aulis
The walls and towers of Troy
Which you loved would still be standing
And your wife would not have killed you.
The last time we met
I struck you in anger
Because I was in the wrong.
When I gave my own daughter
To Achilles' son, not yours,
I broke a sacred oath
And I am still ashamed.

(He rises)

I hear singing in the house.

CHORUS It's Erigone.

MENELAUS   Clytemnestra's child.

(Moans heard again in the house)

What's that?

CHORUS   It's your daughter,
Giving birth to her husband's child.

CHORUS Stay by the fire and warm yourself
    — You will soon be a grandfather.

MENELAUS So; another rape-child.

CHORUS Stay with us till she wakes.

(*They give him a hot drink. More singing in the house*)

— It's not good for a man
Who grows old to live alone
— You should take Hermione
And her child with you to Sparta.

MENELAUS   No, I am not strong enough.

CHORUS   You have done her much wrong.

MENELAUS   So it's better not to see her.

CHORUS   You can't go till you've seen her.

MENELAUS   O yes I can.

CHORUS   First tell us:
Is there any news of Odysseus?

MENELAUS   It is said he is still at sea.

CHORUS   Diomedes?

MENELAUS   Dead.

CHORUS   Idomeneus?

MENELAUS   Dead.

CHORUS   And old Nestor?

MENELAUS   Burned to death
In his palace at Pylos.

CHORUS   Who did that?

MENELAUS   It is said
Some People from the Sea.

CHORUS   And Orestes? Do you think
He will ever come back from Tauris?

MENELAUS   Nothing would surprise me.

CHORUS   And with the image?

MENELAUS   What image?

CHORUS   Weren't you there when Calchas
Commanded him to fetch it?

MENELAUS   I have often been present
When Calchas gives instructions.

CHORUS   But an image, what is it?
        —   What's an image?

MENELAUS   An imagining.

                *(He looks sykward. Some drops of snow or
                rain fall)*

CHORUS   Is Helen up there happy?

MENELAUS   Palamedes used to say
                Stars are neither happy
                Nor sad, they are just stars.

CHORUS   Is it true you've made a statue
                Of your star-wife all of gold?
        —   Do you kiss it? — Do you fondle it?
        —   Do you take it into bed?

MENELAUS   If I did it would crush me.
                When the sky clears I shall see her.

CHORUS   How will you know if it's her?

MENELAUS   Palamedes once gave me a star-map
                To improve my sense of direction;
                Yet my mind's eye and heart
                Are truer than my sextant.
                When it's dark I shall see her.

CHORUS   How, if you're blind?

MENELAUS   Sometimes in the night-time
                I see a little better
                Than I do in the day-sky;
                The light of Apollo
                Blinded me at Delphi.

CHORUS   It will soon be night again.

MENELAUS   'Want an apple.

CHORUS   Go to sleep
                Or go back to Sparta
        —   There will be no fruit till summer-time
        —   And there will be no summer
                If there is no spring
        —   Let him rest by the fire
                And let the girl warm herself.

(MENELAUS falls asleep)

  — There will always be spring
  — How can we be certain?
  — I remember when the Lord of Death
    Took Persephone down into Hades
    The world was wan and sunless
    Yet at last she came back
    And spring came back with her
  — That is only a story
  — What else have we got?

  — Come back, Persephone
  — Come back, Apollo,
    That all of us may know
    The end of our god-game.   (*)

(ELECTRA, still dressed in black, runs out of the house with AGAMEMNON's axe)

CHORUS	Look, there's Electra
—	Nurse told me that last night She wet her bed again Just to get attention.
ELECTRA	Here is my father's axe: The axe which Clytemnestra Split open his skull with!
CHORUS	Put it down, Electra.
ELECTRA	When I brought my brother home She and Aegisthus paid for it.

MENELAUS *(Half asleep)* Put it down.

ELECTRA	No, it's needed Now Orestes and my husband Pylades are dead I must be avenged On the incest-brood who rule here, Aletes and Erigone.
CHORUS	How do you know they're dead?
ELECTRA	Oeax told me who killed them And where I can find her.

CHORUS   Her?

ELECTRA   A priestess sacrificed my brother
                   On an altar of blood in Tauris.

CHORUS   Who is this Oeax?

MENELAUS   Palamedes' brother.

CHORUS   Then why should you believe him?
                   Oeax hates this house;
                   He wants to avenge some crime
                   Committed by Agamemnon
                   Long ago against his brother
               –   You're a married woman now
               –   You should go back to Phocis
                   And wait for your husband Pylades
                   Like any decent wife.

CHORUS   How do you know this is true?

ELECTRA   I will learn the truth at Delphi;
                   Apollo will reveal it.

CHORUS   Delphi is still burning
                   And Apollo is not there.

ELECTRA   Fire does not quench truth:
                   It often reveals it.

CHORUS   Then dig for it at Delphi
                   But first wash your face
                   And change that filthy dress
               –   If you go there in black
                   The Lord of Light won't like it
                   And he won't heal your brother.

ELECTRA   Before there can be healing
                   Blood must be spilt...
                   When it's done I will come home
                   And my pyre will be this hearth-fire.

                   (*She takes a brand from the fire*)

                   Truth-fire, Apollo:
                   The story of our house
                   Will not end till it has seen
                   Some high deed of Electra's.

MENELAUS (*Murmurs*) Zeus, defend us from all daughters... (*)

(*She goes. The CHORUS call after her. The wind rises*)

CHORUS   Beware of after-quakes!
— If Orestes does come back
    He will kill Aegisthus' children
— But Aletes is only a boy
— And why should he kill Erigone?
— Ever since her mother died
    She has hated Orestes
— It was she who sent him
    To be tried by the gods in Athens.

(*ERIGONE is heard weeping in the house*)

— She still mourns Clytemnestra;
    Ever since she has locked herself in
— If she does not stop weeping
    She will turn to stone like Niobe.

(*Distant screams within*)

— That doesn't sound like Hermione
— Remember the tales of dead babies
    Tortured in this house?
— *Talantos, Talantatos...*
— I have heard it said
    Talanton means a 'balance'
— There is no such thing.

PYTHONESS — If there wasn't, Atlas the Titan
    Would have dropped Mother Earth
    From his shoulders long ago.

CHORUS   She can speak our language!
— Calchas must have taught her.

PYTHONESS   I do not need
    To learn what I remember.
    When I was an infant
    He took me from my father,
    Bound me by the tripod
    And forbade me to utter

Any sound but the pangs
Earth's vapours breathed into me.
What I sounded Calchas
Worded as he willed.
Now the great Articulator
Is silent I am free of him.

CHORUS — We are glad – You are welcome
Are you saying that what he spoke
All came from what you sounded
And we trusted what he said?

PYTHONESS It's always hard to distinguish
An oracle from an orator.

(*Screams from inside the house*)

CHORUS — It's Hermione again
Her pangs, like yours, are wordless.

(*Pause*)

Did our Poet send you
To tell us the ending?

PYTHONESS While the rock holds
Your story will not end.

CHORUS Do you know what the ropes are tied to?

PYTHONESS That is not yet known.

CHORUS But will it ever fall?

PYTHONESS That depends on how strong the ropes are.

CHORUS But they were made by Zeus.

PYTHONESS That may be the problem.
They are not as strong as they used to be;
Since men have begun to try
To find out what they're made of
The wise have begun to doubt
If they will bear the strain.

CHORUS So it will fall one day?

PYTHONESS I can only see what's past…
I cannot see the future

Till it's over and done with:
Be patient and wait.

(*More screams in the house*)

-   That is certainly Hermione
-   Nurse is with her now
-   The birth-pangs are beginning
-   Artemis be with her
-   I pity her – I pity
     All who were born in this house
-   She endures as women must.

(*They speak a formal mantra, but mean it*)

ALL   Artemis, Protectress
Of women in labour
And of all little children
Grant her a safe delivery
And peace to her child.

(*A baby is heard crying*)

What kind of child will this be?   (*)

(*NURSE enters with a new baby*)

NURSE   A boy, but not a pretty one.

His mother is asleep now:
Give us a drink while I suckle it.

CHORUS   Drink this and tell us
What we really want to know.

(*NURSE drinks and suckles the baby*)

NURSE   Ninety-nine…

CHORUS   What?

NURSE   I have now nursed and suckled
Ninety-nine royal babies.

(*She drinks deep*)

CHORUS   Tell us about the one
Aethra spoke about at Delphi.

NURSE   I have never assisted
A delivery in Athens.

CHORUS   We have heard how you once helped deliver
A secret child in Sparta.

NURSE   I'm always where I'm needed.

CHORUS   But you took Helen's child to the mountains
To a shepherd – Did he take it?

NURSE   Some shepherds do,
Some shepherds don't.

CHORUS   What happened to that baby?
– You took it to Helen's sister.

NURSE   O that one? I've forgotten...

CHORUS   'Don't believe you: tell us more.

NURSE   It was just when Clytemnestra
Bore her own first child;
That birth was not an easy one.

CHORUS   You delivered her child too?

NURSE   Of course not, my deliveries
Are always satisfactory.
When I got to there she was sick,
So I suckled both babies
And laid them in the very cot
Where I once laid this old man.

MENELAUS (*Sleepily*) Don't remember.

NURSE   Such a shame:
Cot-death is common.

CHORUS   The baby died? Which one?
Clytemnestra's or Helen's?

NURSE   How can we be certain?
One lives, one dies:
That's the way it goes.

CHORUS   Stick to the point: when you saw
Clytemnestra's baby dead
Did you give her Helen's?

NURSE   Why should I do that?

CHORUS   Did you swap the babies?

NURSE   Such mistakes have been known.

CHORUS   Does she realise what she's saying?
  —   She is saying the Lost One's found
  —   And we know who it was!

NURSE   'If': pooh to 'if'.
         I must go in and change
         Electra's dirty bed-clothes.
         I'm expecting more visitors
         Before the day is out.
         This one's wet already.   (*)

         (*She goes in with the baby*)

CHORUS   Wake up Menelaus!
  —   We've discovered the truth
         Of who your wife's first child was.

MENELAUS (*Half awake*) My wife?

CHORUS   Your star-girl
         Was Iphigenia's mother!

MENELAUS   It is said among the wise
            We are all born from the stars...

CHORUS   Iphigenia's the Lost One:
          She was Helen's child!

MENELAUS   It may be so or not so.

            (*He goes to sleep again*)

CHORUS   Let him be – Are we certain?
  —   Aulis – We remember!
  —   Then why did Clytemnestra
         Kill her husband when he sacrificed
         A girl who wasn't theirs?
  —   She didn't know – She did:
         We were there, don't you remember
         Her strange words at Aulis?
         'Keep it in the family:
         It would be a kind of Justice.'
         Artemis meant Agamemnon
         To sacrifice Hermione
  —   That would have been much better
  —   But if Clytemnestra knew it
         Why kill her husband?

	— Can you tell us, Python-girl, Why she did it?
PYTHONESS	Use your wits. You each have the truth inside you: It is all in one word.
CHORUS	But she loved him, we know that.
PYTHONESS	What destroys love?
CHORUS	Hatred — Cruelty – Indifference...
PYTHONESS	Do better. Every woman Knows the truth: speak it.
CHORUS	Do you mean she was jealous? — Not Clytemnestra – Cassandra? — She had cause there, it was just — If Clytemnestra knew The girl was Helen's daughter And saw how her husband loved her She must have been jealous.
PYTHONESS	Go back in your sources: Helen was fairer still.
CHORUS	But she loved her sister; she said so.
PYTHONESS	She said so to keep secret What she felt inside. It happens to many.
CHORUS	It happened to me — I don't believe a word of it.
PYTHONESS	Then choose your own version As your Poet said you would. Wait till Apollo's back And they have rebuilt Delphi.
CHORUS	How can you tell if they will?
PYTHONESS	Because they always have. In the beginning Delphi Was only made of feathers Held together by bees-wax, So it soon blew away;

(*)

So they tried twisting and binding
A great sheaf of fern-stalks,
And then they tried laurel boughs
And cemented them with honey
Which lasted a little longer.
Thousands of years later
Hephaestus rebuilt it with bronze
And a huge serpent guarded it;
But when he was only a baby
Apollo slew the Python
And set a young girl on the tripod
To utter his truth to the world.
When Mother Earth realised
Apollo was shedding his light
On her and all human-kind
She covered the tripod with mist

(*Tiny droplets fall from the sky*)

And filled us with dreams and imaginings.
She knew it is better
To tell truth disguised.
Apollo was angry
And persuaded his father Zeus
To stop mortals dreaming
Lest they learn more than they should;
So he took away the gift
Half light and half darkness,
That feeds all songs and dreams.
That is why mankind forgets
The truth in the night
And honour now and long for
Apollo in the Light.   (*)

(*An earth tremor and a strange sound. The air
begins to clear*)

CHORUS   I see a light far off
        —   Is it earth-fire or air-fire?
        —   A hearth-fire or a war-fire?
        —   Or the Helen star falling?
        —   Or the pyre of some warrior
                Or another city burning?

PYTHONESS

It's the light of the god:
Apollo has come home.

CHORUS

Look, that tree's in leaf again!
— And the streams are running fresh
— Apollo has come home again!

(*A sound of hammering. The tree blooms. The PYTHONESS puts on a robe*)

PYTHONESS

He has rebuilt the Oracle
As he rebuilt Troy before:
The god-plan is fulfilled.
Now on Dardan plains
A new citadel is rising
While Orestes has brought
The Image home to the West.
All is as the gods will it
Whether for good or ill.

CHORUS

Praised be Zeus and Apollo!

(*CHORUS bang the gong*)

— Wake up, Menelaus!
— Can't you see or sense
The sunlight on your face?
Apollo will show us
The bright truth of all things.   (*)

(*The CHORUS bangs the gong again. HERMIONE enters with her baby*)

MENELAUS

Zeus defend us all
From the truth of Apollo.

HERMIONE

Father, be quiet!
You have woken my baby!

(*The baby starts to howl*)

MENELAUS

O *Talanton, Talantatos...*
Take me home to Sparta:
Someone fetch my chariot!

CHORUS

Go back in the house, Hermione:
You shouldn't be out of bed yet
— You should go in and rest.

HERMIONE   I endured as women must;
           Why do girls make such a fuss?
           Isn't he adorable?
           I have named him Tisamenus.

MENELAUS   Now Orestes your husband
           Is home he should name him.

HERMIONE   He's home?

CHORUS   Safe and sound.

HERMIONE   Then I'm leaving immediately.

CHORUS   But he must see his child.

HERMIONE   I have no wish to see him;
           This is my child, not his.

CHORUS   Surely that day by the river
           He made some contribution?

HERMIONE   The rape-seed was his
           But the womb-fruit is mine.

CHORUS   But where will you go?

HERMIONE   To my father's, of course;
           Someone must rule his house.

MENELAUS   Babies should never travel
           On bad roads in a chariot.

HERMIONE   If my charioteer is sober
           I am not afraid of pot-holes.

MENELAUS   But there's always a risk
           Of collisions at crossroads.

HERMIONE   There is no risk of road-rage
           Unless travellers lose their temper.

MENELAUS   But there's only room for one
           Besides the charioteer.

HERMIONE   Excellent, I'll take it.
           Send my things after me:
           And women, honour Artemis,
           For she has been good to me.
           It is true that Orestes

Has his qualities in bed
But his character is nauseous.
I will prove a better mother
Than those who lived here before me;
This house is not a healthy one.

(She goes)   (*)

CHORUS   But where is Orestes, Pythoness?

PYTHONESS   He has brought the image with him
To Delphi. It is time
To drink of the streams again
And see what's past as I have.

(The CHORUS drink. Music)

Now close your eyes and tell the world
All how it was and is.

(Music changes)

CHORUS   I see a ruined altar
And Orestes kneeling by it...

(Music changes again)

–   A woman in strange robes
Is standing above him...

(Music changes)

–   Electra? – No, some stranger
–   Is raising the sacred flame
To purify the suppliants.

PYTHONESS   All travellers from Tauris
Must be cleansed of pollution.

(Music changes)

CHORUS   I see another woman
By the altar with a fire-brand
–   No, an axe: it's Electra!
–   Now she thrusts the brand
At the stranger girl's eyes
–   But Orestes has seized it
And thrown her on the ground.

468

CHORUS   Now he tells Electra
That the stranger is friendly:
– Now there's weeping – And now laughter
– Now Electra is telling him
He must come back to Mycenae
And kill Aegisthus' children
To win back his Kingdom.

(*Music changes*)

– There's Pylades her husband:
He has come back with Orestes
– He is telling Electra
If she does not go home with him
And bear a child in Phocis
He will beat her – She likes that:
She is silent and obeys him.

PYTHONESS   So ends Electra's story.

(*Music changes*)

CHORUS   But the stranger stands apart
– She is weeping – I feel
As if I have seen her before
– Where? – When? – In the beginning...

PYTHONESS   If you would know the truth of it
You must first speak her name:
All of you, shape the sound.
Honour Apollo and Orestes
For she who is lost is found.

(*CHORUS names IPHIGENIA, some
wonderingly, some dubious. Music climaxes.
Then silence*)

They are both coming home:
They are coming to Mycenae.

CHORUS   If it's true, the gods are great.

PYTHONESS   It is all in the sources;
You should drink of them more often.

(*She goes*)   (*)

CHORUS   We do not believe you, Python-girl,
                Iphigenia is not with him:
                No one comes back from the dead
          –   Theseus did – The results
                Were not entirely happy
          –   If Zeus can make two Helens
                Why not two Iphigenias?
          –   Rejoice, Menelaus:
                The prophecy is fulfilled.

                (*Trumpets sound far off*)

MENELAUS   Fulfilled yet not fulfilled;
                Helen is not home again
                But an Image stuck in space.
                If busy-body gods have brought
                This girl to life again
                What did my brother die for
                And all our brave warriors
                And all those unhappy Trojans?
                Why should poor Clytemnestra
                Kill my brother for a crime
                Which he did not commit?
                And why should Orestes avenge it
                And go mad for obeying an order?
                If this is Zeus' god-plan
                All the world's a chaos.

                (*He goes. Trumpets sound nearer*)

CHORUS   Do you hear the people shouting?
                They are coming to Mycenae
          –   How shall we greet them?
          –   Is Orestes healed from madness?
          –   This could be dangerous
          –   We must warn Erigone;
                Someone go into the house
          –   How can you all believe this?
                We were all there at Aulis;
                We saw the bloody knife;
          –   We saw her father strip her
                In front of all the army.

I heard her words as they hooded her
– Do you really remember them?   (*)

(As the CHORUS girl screams and throws herself on the ground. IPHIGENIA enters, painted and robed as a Taurian Priestess, and watches her as she speaks Euripides' lines from 'Iphigenia In Aulis')

CHORUS

"O my Father, my Father,
I want to live, have pity!
I love this life; there's nothing
Fairer than the day sky
And the golden sun shining.
Do not let me die!"

(IPHIGENIA goes to AGAMEMNON's grave and lays a libation. The CHORUS watch in uncertain silence)

– Here's our truth: be silent.

IPHIGENIA

O my darling in the darkness,
We each did as we had to;
I died for your sake
And my brother has told me
How you died for mine.
I drove you into evil,
You who were the noblest,
The gentlest and the kindest
Of all living men.
Now you lie in Asphodel
But it's you whom the gods
Should have brought to life again.
O all you dead men,
It is I who have doomed you
To your death's day on the plains:
I am to blame
For all the world's sorrow.

CHORUS

Her words are as strange as her robes are
– We must tell her what we know.

(IPHIGENIA rises)

IPHIGENIA	Women of Mycenae,
	It is good to be with you
	Among my own kind again.
CHORUS	It seems so – We are glad
–	If you are whom we're told you are.

(*IPHIGENIA begins to wipe the paint off her face*)

IPHIGENIA	My brother has rescued me
	From a brutal savage land
	Where they made me their priestess
	And practise loathsome rites;
	He's healed now of the madness
	Which the god put on both of us.
CHORUS	Your tale is a strange one.
IPHIGENIA	No, it is simple:
	I died and came to life again.
	Artemis healed me
	And bore me through the air
	To the land of the Taurians.
CHORUS	Through the air like Helen?
–	Or fell as Athene's image did
	From the clouds into Troy?
IPHIGENIA	My brother came and rescued me;
	Then a new star in the heavens
	Guided our black ship homewards.
CHORUS	How can we be sure of this?
IPHIGENIA	Must I show you the scar
	Where Calchas' knife struck me
	Or the marks where my child was cut from me?
CHORUS	What child?
IPHIGENIA	The child that Artemis
	Patroness of child-birth
	Took from me.
CHORUS	You were a virgin
	When they brought you to Aulis.

IPHIGENIA	So I was till Achilles raped me In the goddess' sacred shrine.
CHORUS	What became of the child?
IPHIGENIA	I don't know.
CHORUS	We don't believe you
	– You're an image, as your mother was
	– You too may be made of air
	– Give us proof that we may believe you.
IPHIGENIA	You want proof? Then see me As I was and as I am: And believe that with the gods All things *are* possible!

(*She wipes the rest of the paint off her face
and tears off her robes. She is wearing the
yellow dress she wore at Aulis. It is dirty and
torn and the old blood stains are not quite dry*)

CHORUS	– Praise Apollo! – Praise Artemis!
	– Calchas spoke truly!
	– The Lost One is found!

(*Music*)

IPHIGENIA	Now take me into the house.
CHORUS	There is something you must know
	– We have much to tell you
IPHIGENIA	Not now, my brother's coming. (*)

(*ORESTES enters in armour with SOLDIERS
and ALETES' body. He is carrying his father's
axe*)

CHORUS	Our lord and king, we greet you: You have fulfilled the god's command And have brought your sister home again.
ORESTES	Aletes is dead: I have killed him.

(*Singing again in the house*)

Where is Erigone?

CHORUS	Do not think of her now But kneel beside your sister

	And offer a libation At your father's grave.
ORESTES	This?
CHORUS	Pour this bowl of wine and honey Over our kindly earth.
IPHIGENIA	And when you have offered him Your prayers and your love You must bury forever The axe which destroyed him.
ORESTES	What shall I say to you, General of the war-men? How can I offer you Libations, love or tears? You began a pointless war By murdering my sister And made many thousands suffer As I too have suffered Because of your stupidity At Aulis long ago.
IPHIGENIA	You must not say such things; It was I who made him kill me. Give him love now as I do.
CHORUS	How could you make him kill you If you loved him?
IPHIGENIA	Because I loved him too much As I think he loved me.
ORESTES	What does that mean?
IPHIGENIA	It means what it always means.
ORESTES	I do not understand you.
CHORUS	Maybe it is better so.
IPHIGENIA	Women, bring us wine.
ORESTES	When I've done what I came for.
CHORUS	She has done you no harm: Stay with us, Orestes.

ORESTES	No, I have killed her brother; She will try to avenge it.
CHORUS	Forget her, she's a child.
ORESTES	So was I once.
CHORUS	We remember.
IPHIGENIA	You must rest now: you are home again At home in Mycenae.
ORESTES	She is hiding in the house; I can see it in their faces.
IPHIGENIA	How can you think of her? We are home and I love you.

(She makes him sit and drink. CHORUS begin to disarm him. Music)

	Don't you remember how Mother Told us all who are human Are born to be happy?
ORESTES	But how does our happiness Disappear? What spoils it?
IPHIGENIA	Mine died at the very moment My father undid the clasp On the shoulder of my dress.
ORESTES	When I was little And noble stories moved me I thought I would do nobly When I became a man.
CHORUS	It is right that men should think so.
ORESTES	We are wrong; we assume Because of the stories That we too will be noble But we all lose our way.
CHORUS	Look how the streams are bubbling; Now the ice has cracked They will soon help to heal him — He must first crack the ice That's still frozen inside him.

IPHIGENIA	Have you never been happy?
ORESTES	Yes, when they sent me to Phocis I went up to Parnassus.
CHORUS	And you heard them?
ORESTES	Briefly.
CHORUS	It is said if one hears the Muses One survives.
ORESTES	It is said so; But when the god commanded me To kill my own mother I forgot them for ever; I thought it was Apollo Not I, who was mad.
CHORUS	But at first you did not come.
ORESTES	I only came when the letters came.
IPHIGENIA	The letters?
CHORUS	From Electra — We pity both of you.
ORESTES	It's convenient to say so.
IPHIGENIA	I pity our mother too.
CHORUS	Why should you pity her? Up there she is easy.
IPHIGENIA	Up there?
CHORUS	We must tell her The truth now.

(*ORESTES rises. To SOLDIERS*)

ORESTES	Fetch Erigone.
IPHIGENIA	First let me see That chain round your neck.
ORESTES	It's a nothing.
IPHIGENIA	Let me see it.

(*She takes the chain*)

ORESTES	It belonged to a man Whom I killed at Delphi.
CHORUS	At Delphi?
IPHIGENIA	But I know it!
ORESTES	How can you? I won it a year ago Before I set out for Tauris.
IPHIGENIA	Achilles tied this round my neck When he took me at Aulis.
CHORUS	Someone must have stolen it – All soldiers steal in war camps.
IPHIGENIA	But I had it still on Scyros.
ORESTES	Scyros?
CHORUS	It's the island Where we helped to hide Achilles.
IPHIGENIA	What was the name of the man you killed?
ORESTES	Neoptolemus.
CHORUS	Achilles' son.
IPHIGENIA	But I'm sure I had it on Scyros.
CHORUS	– Then someone must have taken it After your child was born.
ORESTES	What child?
IPHIGENIA	Achilles raped me I gave birth on Scyros.
CHORUS	But what happened to this child?
IPHIGENIA	I think some old man took it: Achilles' father…
CHORUS	Peleus!
ORESTES	Who?
CHORUS	Old Peleus… – He was Pyrrhus' grandfather.
ORESTES	Who was Pyrrhus?
CHORUS	It means 'rage'.

IPHIGENIA	That is how I named my son.
CHORUS	We do not want to know this.

(*ORESTES cries out*)

IPHIGENIA	What is it?
ORESTES	*Talantatos…!* Zeus' game goes on for ever.

(*His madness seizes him again*)

CHORUS	This man is not healed.
IPHIGENIA	Why have my words changed him? These sounds are not language.
CHORUS	The army named your son 'Neoptolemus' – 'New Soldier' – Orestes killed him at Delphi.

(*IPHIGENIA cries out*)

– We pity both of you:
The curse goes on for ever.

IPHIGENIA	Ai, Ai, Apollo… Why did you bring me back To this house which has bred evil Since its founder laid the stones?
CHORUS	Your brother did no evil When he rescued you from Tauris.
IPHIGENIA	He did! He only came there To seize me as an image As a warrior steals a war-prize To adorn his brutal walls. He was tainted in the cradle; Have you all forgotten The poison pus of Telephus?
CHORUS	No, we remember.
IPHIGENIA	Yes! This creature was polluted Before I went to Aulis.
(*To Orestes*)	Since that is how you are Go in and kill your sister!

CHORUS	But the very day you died You hugged him and kissed him; You may be polluted too.
IPHIGENIA	It is true, I am so.
CHORUS	But you have not shed kin-blood.
IPHIGENIA	No, I have done worse; When Artemis took me to Tauris They made me High Priestess And taught me to sacrifice All war-kings and warriors Who came there from the West Because of what they'd done to me. I was glad to and enjoyed it.
CHORUS	Both of you are guilty, Yet both of you are innocent.
IPHIGENIA	None of us are innocent But I alone am to blame Because I loved the man Everyone thought was my father.
CHORUS	You knew the truth?
IPHIGENIA	O yes!
CHORUS	How?
IPHIGENIA	Artemis told me.

(*ORESTES fit grows worse*)

CHORUS	We must take him into the house Or he'll frighten the people.
IPHIGENIA	I will never take this killer-boy Into this house of blood, But live and die a priestess.
CHORUS	Of Artemis?
IPHIGENIA	Not of Artemis.
CHORUS	But she gave you back your life again…
IPHIGENIA	And a second time destroyed me.
CHORUS	Lady, we have heard There's a temple close to Athens

Where the guardian gods are kinder
Than those that rule Olympus.

(*The sea sounds*)

IPHIGENIA

Time to go in again.
When the ice melts, the sea swells:
It has always been so.
Day-sky, I greet you
Once more and bid you farewell.
Why hope it will be otherwise? (*)

(*She goes. ORESTES mumbles here in Greek
from the source plays. The visors of the
SOLDIERS turn into masks of the FURIES. A
buzzing sound in the air*)

CHORUS

Pollution, I smell it:
Keep away from this man
– Look, his hair is snake-locks
– He reeks of the cess-pit
– Slime oozes from his gums
– They are here, I feel them
– Don't name them, never name them
– But they've always been here;
They are older than Zeus,
All engendered by the venom
Of good things turned foul.

– My mother called them the Gentle Ones
But their real names are the Erinyes
– What does that mean? – The Reminders
Of what we've forgotten.
– They have always done their work,
Cruel yet kindly – Kindly?
– Sometimes if we honour them
We may find they can be kind
– What does that mean? – Maybe
Finding a balance.

(*ORESTES screams again*)

– This is pain, not balance
– Gods, heal this man

— How can there be healing
    When pollution is so deep?
— I have heard that the weapon
    Which wounds can sometimes heal
— But if it has been forged
    Inside the man himself
    There can be no healing.

(*ERIGONE comes out of the house. The
CHORUS do not see her yet*

*Note: from here on some of the CHORUS are
individually named*)

[MELPOMENE]   Look at him, he's loathsome:
              Something must be done.

CHORUS   What can we do?

[MELPOMENE]   We can choose
              Our own story's ending!

(*She goes to the axe*)

CHORUS   Leave that to Erigone
              Not us – But she's a child.

[MELPOMENE]   So was he when he killed his mother.

CHORUS   What can we do? We are powerless.

[MELPOMENE]   We had power once in Troy.

CHORUS   We chose wrong and we suffered.

[MELPOMENE]   Yes, and all we've suffered
              Has been at the hands of men:
              Agamemnon, Achilles,
              Odysseus, Neoptolemus.
              Have you forgotten the answer
              To the riddle of the Sphinx?
              'Man': take up the axe.

[CLIO]   Sometimes the answer
              Has also been 'Woman';
              There would have been no war
              If Iphigenia had not forced
              Agamemnon to make the sacrifice.

    — Or if Hecuba for Hesione's sake
       Had not pushed Priam into it
    — Wisest to let him be.

[MELPOMENE]   Wiser? Weak! A woman's courage
       Is greater than a man's.
       If all of you are cowards
       I will use the axe myself
       And end this mad male cycle
       Of blood-shed and revenge.

*(CHORUS begin to move towards ORESTES.
ERIGONE steps in also)*

CHORUS   — Careful; he is stirring.

(ORESTES lifts his head and sees ERIGONE)

ORESTES   Are you watching, Zeus?
       Spare a moment from your feasting
       To look down on these women
       And give them strength to do
       What they're bound to by the laws
       You put on all humans.

       Erigone, go on:
       We share one mother's blood
       And we are both polluted,
       So do not be afraid
       Of the blood-laws of our house:
       Do as we have all done,
       Mixing good and evil
       Until they seem as one.

(ERIGONE lays hands on the axe)

       Give her strength, Apollo,
       To lift the axe and end it.
       Let her live in this house
       As a free and loving woman,
       Sharing some good man's bed
       And let her give milk
       To a better son than I am:
       That would be Justice.

CHORUS	Show us your light, Apollo:
–	Reveal your purpose, Zeus,
	For this house and human-kind! (*)

(ERIGONE tries to lift the axe. The NURSE comes out of the house and strikes the gong. It makes a different sound)

NURSE	Dinner-time, children!
	What are you all playing at?
	Put that down, Erigone,
	It is much too heavy for you.
	Orestes, I'm ashamed of you,
	Letting young girls play with axes;
	Dangerous weapons should only be used
	By those trained to use them.
(To Chorus)	You should all of you know better
	Than to let them be so silly.
CHORUS	We wanted to know the ending.
NURSE	But everybody knows it
	And if they don't, they ought to;
	Zeus himself has taken
	Great pains to get it right.
	Hasn't your Poet told you?
CHORUS	He's not here – We think
	He may be drunk somewhere.
NURSE	Of course he is drunk;
	Poets usually are.
	Go in, Erigone,
	And take off that mourning dress:
	All the best stories
	End with a wedding.

(The NURSE produces a red wedding dress)

CHORUS	How can these two marry?
–	He's got a wife already.
NURSE	Hermione's gone for good.
	In our world, marriage customs
	Have not yet been blurred
	By perverse genetic taboos.

If the gods had been so narrow-minded
There would have been no Olympians
And no human-race.
Many of my babies
Have married their siblings
And it worked out as well
As most human marriages.
Orestes, wash your face
And take off your armour,
Nice girls don't like husbands
Who are smeared with blood and vomit.
Why did I ever try
To teach this boy manners?

CHORUS   She speaks like a god.

NURSE (*To the Soldiers*) Pick up the axe,
And hurl it into the ocean;
Then go home to your wives
And let them refresh you.
Do take off those helmets
Or you will lose your way.

(*SOLDIERS take off their helmets and go*)

The rest of you, go in
And change into something
More fitting for a wedding,
And when the music sounds
The wedding dance shall begin.

(*ORESTES washes at the pool and then kneels
at AGAMEMNON's grave. Music begins*)

CHORUS   O all you gods that are
Or may be or might be
And whether cruel or kind
Or merely indifferent,
Spare a moment as you wipe
The ambrosia from your lips
To look on this house
And all human people.

— Zeus Father, we are told
That you are still all-powerful,

So if it is true that we
Are made in you image,
Grant us a clearness
And perhaps to judge in all
A little more wisely.
—   We search without solving,
—   We seek without finding;
—   We suffer and it dulls us,
We are brief but...

NURSE   We endure.
How could it be otherwise?

(The CHORUS go in)

Why are you weeping, my babie
Tonight you shall lie together
In the bed you both were born n.
(To Erigone)   Now put this lovely dress on
And then all the jewels
Your grandmother wore before her.
Wipe your eyes, no more sniffles,
And then you shall dance for him
According to the custom.
It is how the world began.

ERIGONE   First tell me, if you can
The meaning of my name.

ORESTES   Eris: 'Child of Strife.'

NURSE   That was not why her mother named her:
She was thinking 'Child of Spring'...

ORESTES   'Child of Spring'? Like Persephone?

NURSE   ... Or maybe 'Many Offspring';
As with Persephone
It can go either way.

*(She takes up the POET'S mask from Play 1
and goes in. ORESTES and ERIGONE are left
there alone)*

ERIGONE   Tell me her story.

ORESTES   Her name in the beginning
Was 'Bringer of Death',

So when Hades seized her
A winter world began:
The cattle starved on the plains
And the people starved in the cities
Till Zeus did a deal with Hades
And so won her back from the dead
For a glorious long summer,
And that is how spring-time began...
And they called her 'Pherephaino'

ERIGONE (*To Orestes*) Take me into the house.

(As ORESTES and ERIGONE go in. Music begins gently and the PYTHONESS re-enters)

PYTHONESS But of course Persephone
Had many other names:

(She empties a bag she is carrying on the floor: masks for the CHORUS etc)

Pherephatta, Persophonia,
Prosopine, Proserpina...
So many Persona
For all of you who are human...   (*)

(A buzzing of ant-men as the fire smoulders and spits. The POET enters with the mask of DIONYSOS. The PYTHONESS strikes the gong. The fire blazes)

DIONYSOS Let the wedding dance begin!

(Music. The CHORUS re-enter dancing. Their nymph-like dresses are diaphanous and covered with hanging red ribbons to match ERIGONE as she enters in her wedding dress with ORESTES. She dances the wedding-dance. Then ORESTES leads her into the house. Fireworks and bright music. The Earth wobbles slightly. The CHORUS continue dancing. DIONYSOS strikes the gong and utters a wild cry)

A happy hour for humans!
Brought to you by permission
Of Olympian Apollo
In close association

	With his father, the Thunderer And all the twelve on Olympus!
CHORUS	What's this?
	(*POET takes his mask off. He has a wine-bag* *and a paint-pot*)
POET	Ha! My Muses!
CHORUS	It's our Poet! – Drunk again.
POET	And all the gods are too!
CHORUS	Where have you been?
POET	At a great moot millennial On Olympus: they've resolved To bring in a new god. They had all grown weary Of only drinking nectar, And so with your help They have brought in Dionysos. My old pupil has grown up And has come to refresh the world With this gift from Zeus' own table!
	(*Presents a huge wine bag*)
CHORUS	Is it wine or is it nectar?
POET	It is my own concoction; A little bit of both With a seasoning of moly.
CHORUS	What's that?
POET	Taste and see.
	(*One or two drink*)
CHORUS	Let me taste it! – It's gorgeous.
POET	Careful, no gulping.
	(*As they each drink there are more* *exhalations and fireworks. The earth and sky* *shiver. A little dust shimmer falls from the rock.* *From now on the CHORUS gradually become* *more drunk and reckless, and throw off their* *'ribbons' to look increasingly nymph-like*)

CHORUS	What's that?
POET	Atlas hiccuping; They gave him some wine too And he almost dropped the earth.
[CALLIOPE]	Quiet, all of you! A question: If they've brought in a new god There'll be thirteen on Olympus: That will upset the balance.
[THALIA]	Mine is upset already.
[CALLIOPE]	The balance in heaven Six gods and six goddesses.
POET	One in, one out: That is the rule in heaven.
[CLIO]	Have they thrown out Ares?
POET	They will never throw out Ares; It is true that no one likes him But he is much too useful Both to gods and men.
[CALLIOPE]	But the balance must be kept Between males and females.
CHORUS	– We smell male trickery – Who have they thrown out?
POET	Hestia of the Hearth.
ALL	Hestia?
POET	The gods find her boring. Since she never goes on ventures But lives quietly on Olympus No stories can be told of her; So the gods have decided It is time they should retire her To cherish your human hearth-fires.

(*Music*)

ALL	But if she has no stories?
POET	She is the occasion Of all the world's stories: Light the fire and honour her.

(*)

(The CHORUS light the fire which blazes
briefly as they put their masks on again.
FIRST WOMAN enters as HESTIA)

HESTIA

Where there's a hearth-fire
In a house or in a wilderness
On a ship or in the mountains
On a beach or in the forest,
Then when girls come together
There will always be a story.

[POLYHYMNIA]

Lady, we welcome you:
All honour be to Hestia.

HESTIA

Put more logs on the fire
And let's have some more wine.
Where is young Orestes?

[CALLIOPE]

In bed with Erigone.

HESTIA

That is as it should be.

[CALLIOPE]

Has Apollo healed him?

HESTIA

In so far as any human
Is ever healed he's whole again.

CHORUS

But he and Erigone...?

HESTIA

Will be happy.

CHORUS

        And Hermione?

HESTIA

She too will be happy;
But if she'd stayed there'd have been
More murders in this house.
Mycenae will have peace now
For fifty years precisely:
Orestes will rule justly
And found colonies in Asia
In the lands the West destroyed,
And when he is seventy
He'll retire to Arcadia
And die of a snake-bite.

[CLIO]

And we in the West?
Will we become a country?

HESTIA

That in time will be written.

489

.O]   But will it have a name?

HESTIA   It will have many.

[CLIO]   Tell us.

HESTIA
In time, but first each of you
Shall also have a name
According to your natures.
Drink again my darlings
From your own Poet's wine-bag.

POET
Pick up that helmet, my Muses,
And each take out a pebble
And I'll tell you the name
Apollo has given you.   (*)

(*CHORUS go to the helmet as the POET
takes masks from the PYTHONESS. Music.
One of them steps forward. The PYTHONESS
studies the pebbles. As the CHORUS is
named, the POET puts a mask on each of
them*)

POET (*To Euterpe*)
Now, let's begin with you;
You, who loves music
The god names you 'Euterpe'.

(*EUTERPE plays on the flute and the others
start humming. Another steps forward*)

It is Apollo's pleasure
That you shall lead the singers:
He has named you 'Polyhymnia'.

(*POLYHYMNIA begins to sing and the rest join
in slowly. Another steps forward*)

Apollo knows that you
Love poems of love and passion;
Be it so, 'Erato'.

(*ERATO cries out and leaps with joy. One of
the CHORUS begins to dance*)

HESTIA
No need to peruse your pebble:
Carry on, 'Terpsichore'.

(*TERPSICHORE gradually leads the rest in a
quiet dance*)

POET You who look into the night-sky,
The god has named 'Urania'.

(*URANIA looks up. Singing and dancing
increases*)

Yes, there's the Helen star…
But one will be needed
To shape words to your songs.

(*CALLIOPE presents her pebble*)

You shall mould new tales from old ones
And your name shall be: 'Calliope'.

(*CALLIOPE begins to speak in Greek. Some
of the others pick up her words*)   (*)

HESTIA Now we need one to ensure
That all your tales are true:
It is time to distinguish
True history from a story.

[CLIO] What is history?

POET   You are.

(*CLIO joins the dancing. Two remain sitting
apart*)

THE TWO And us?

HESTIA   You are hard to name:
You're a muddle and a mingle,
But you'd better join the dance.

PYTHONESS Show me your pebbles.

(*They do so nervously*)

'Melpomene' and 'Thalia',
Beloved of Apollo
And especially Dionysos.

[THALIA] But which of us is which?

POET That will be known hereafter.   (*)

(*CHORUS build a great chord of harmony.
They are now transformed into Muse-like
creatures. These masks should be simple, so*)

491

that paint can transform them quickly later.
CALLIOPE takes off her mask. The POET
rises suddenly)

[CALLIOPE]   Where are you going, Poet?

POET   A new story's troubling me;
              I've been studying a map
              Of the journeys of Odysseus:
              They do not cohere.

CHORUS   Odysseus? forget him.
          —   Perhaps the world has changed
              Since your map was made, Poet.

POET   Ha! I think I see him sleeping
              Beneath a pile of leaves
              In the land of the Phaeacians.
              He has had many sorrows
              And they are not yet over.

CHORUS   We are glad.

POET   Those that endure
              Don't always deserve to;
              It is usually the good men
              Who perish, not the bad ones:
              That is the meaning of tragedy.

[MELPOMENE]   What is tragedy?

POET   You are.
              One day I must go into it.

CHORUS   Wait! You shall not go
              Till you've shown us one person
              You have left out of your story
          —   Yes, show us Tantalus!

              (*CHORUS grab him and drag him under the*
              rock)

HESTIA   Your Muses have cast you.

POET   Then give me a drink
              And I'll try to get into it.

              (*The CHORUS beat a drum as for a*
              court-martial. They grow more aggressive.

492

The POET puts on a mask also from the
PYTHONESS' pile)

[CALLIOPE]   Tantalus of Lydia,
We charge you with bringing
A curse on this house.

TANTALUS   It is so, yet not so.

CHORUS   That's a contradiction.

TANTALUS   Yes.

CHORUS   Speak plainly and truly
– Did you cut up your own child
To feed to the gods at a banquet?

TANTALUS   The gap between truth
And metaphor is hazy.

CHORUS   Wasn't a goddess sick
When she swallowed your son's shoulder-
bone?
– Metaphor or fact?

TANTALUS   I meant well but the gods
Misunderstood my motives.

CHORUS   But you stole Zeus' dog
And then the boy Ganymede
And took him to Olympus.

TANTALUS   Zeus loved the boy; that's why
He invited me to dinner.

CHORUS   You were an honoured guest
But you stole from your host's own table.

TANTALUS   The ambrosia was excellent
So I took a second helping.

CHORUS   You hid it in a doggy-bag
And stole a jar of nectar.

TANTALUS   I wanted my friends and children
To share the divine experience.

CHORUS   But Zeus in his cups
Told you all his secrets.

TANTALUS	Such exchanges are normal Among friends after dinner.
CHORUS	But you betrayed his secrets!
TANTALUS	Sooner or later All secrets are betrayed. If they weren't, social intercourse Would soon grow intolerable.
CHORUS	*What were those secrets?*
TANTALUS	We were drunk, I don't remember.
CHORUS	You stole from the gods!
TANTALUS	Who that's human doesn't? Some call it Private Enterprise, Others Emulation.
CHORUS	You made the whole world suffer: — *You, you are to blame.*
TANTALUS	It is true that to mean well Is often a mistake.

(*Thunder. The POET's mask drops visor-like so that it turns into a full mask. His voice changes as he speaks to the audience*)

Ant-mortals, mark me:
You all want to do good
Or at least to think you do
And it always leads to disaster.
Agamemnon, Menelaus,
Electra, Clytemnestra,
Iphigenia, Orestes,
Priam and Hecuba...
As the long Ages pass
The list keeps growing longer.
But Zeus is apt to punish
Those who think they are godlike
By giving them what they ask for.
Attention must be paid
To the moral tale of Midas
Who turned apples into gold
And of others from the stories

You should all know more of.
Yes, you that live on
Through the Long Age of Iron
You are all beneath the rock,
You and you and you;
Your mistake is not to notice.
And yet Zeus put it there
Not just to frighten you
But to put you on your mettle;
That is why he bound me here
Not merely as a Punishment
But as a Reminder.

*(A buzzing of ants, then a distant rumble of
thunder. There is another hint of an earthquake
and the rock tips a little. Then the light
brightens and the POET takes his mask off)*

POET   Atlas totters, but take heart;
                    The rock will not fall
                    Till the Fates cut the ropes.
                    Give me another drink.

CHORUS   Are you sure they won't cut them?

POET   Apollo has made them
                    As drunk as the gods are.
                    Clotho cannot spin tonight,
                    Lachesis cannot use her tape
                    To measure human spans
                    And Atropos' shears are too blunt
                    To cut a human life off;
                    So though mortals totter
                    No-one will die today:
                    Time stands still again!

CHORUS   Where are you going, Poet?

POET   I must pop up to Olympus
                    To congratulate my pupil
                    And interrogate Hermes
                    On the soundness of this map.

CHORUS   We want to go with you
                    And sing to the High Ones.

POET   Then you must close your eyes again
And drink from the streams,
And then it must go as it will.   (*)

(HESTIA picks up an instrument and begins to play as the CHORUS go the streams. The POET, begins to climb the tree)

Epilogue
ZEUS

ELSEWHERE

CAST

First Woman	NURSE/ HESTIA
Second Woman	PYTHONESS
Third Woman	HERSELF
Fourth Woman	WITH CHORUS

Third Man	ODYSSEUS

CHORUS
Herein cast as:

CALLIOPE	(Epic Poetry, Story-telling)
CLIO	(History)
URANIA	(Astronomy)
ERATO	(Personal and Erotic Lyric)
MELPOMENE	(Tragedy)
THALIA	(Comedy)
POLYHYMNIA	(Hymns in honour of the gods)
EUTERPE	(Pipe and Musical Instruments)
TERPSICHORE	(Choral Dance and Song)

(The ambience changes back to the prologue)

HESTIA	Take your masks off, children.

CHORUS

Where are we? – There's the streams
Where Zeus once lay with Memory
– The oracle of Trophonios…
I remember… – But these streams
Look *otherwise*: are you sure
They're the same ones? – Where are we?

HESTIA

Wespero… Hesperides…

PYTHONESS

The garden of the Evening,
The garden of the West…

CHORUS

But where *is* Hesperides?

HESTIA

On the edge of the great ocean
Very near to the isle of Leuce.
When Zeus married Hera
Mother Earth gave her an apple
To make her womb fruitful,
So the Queen of Heaven planted it
And there grew a great apple-tree
And all its fruits were golden.

(The Tree begins to glow and the streams trickle again)

The rock-springs of Hesperides
Are brim and bright with nectar
And the soil is rich with ambrosia;
All living things are fertile there
In an eternal spring.

CHORUS

Can gold grow on apple-trees?

HESTIA

Of course, if the soil's right
And the right streams run through it;
Some call it Gaia's garden.
Of course the tree is old now
And the garden is not kept
As well kept as it used to be;
Some say the soil's thinned and eroded
And will soon sink in the ocean.

CHORUS   But we're back in the Golden World...

PYTHONESS   No, we are in the Fifth Age
                   Where men have lost their way
            —   But not women – No, not women.

                   (*The CHORUS drink of the streams and
                   slowly begin to change as if bewildered with
                   wonder*)

                   Not so long ago Heracles
                   Paid it a visit.

HESTIA   Yes,
                   It has always attracted pirates;
                   That is why it was guarded
                   By Atlas' own daughters,
                   Three nymphs named the Hesperides.

PYTHONESS   They are gone now; they were caught
                   Pilfering the apples.

CHORUS   But where *is* it?

HESTIA   Where the horses
                   Of the sun rest every night.

CHORUS   In the West?

HESTIA   In the West.

CHORUS   Not tonight when time stands still
                   But the sun is still moving:
                   The leaves of that tree are golden;
                   Won't it soon be evening?

PYTHONESS   *Wespero* means 'evening'.

CHORUS   *Wespero*...

                   (*They think about it and the music changes
                   again*)

            —   Time stands still by firelight...
            —   I heard once that Time
                   Depends on the Laws of Nature.

[CALLIOPE]   No, Zeus himself once changed them;
                   It was in the time of Atreus.
                   Zeus stopped the sun's chariot horses

	At high noon and turned them round So all the stars made a U-turn And the sun set in Asia.
[CLIO]	But if the sun sets in the West How can it rise in the East? – And what does it do in the night-time?
[CALLIOPE]	It sleeps.
[ERATO]	I think it makes love.
CHORUS	As Zeus does – Zeus be praised – When I look at a hearth-fire There is no such thing as Time… No beginning and no ending.
PYTHONESS	Do you know what 'Zeus' really means?
[CALLIOPE]	It's his name, that's all.
PYTHONESS	It means 'sky' or 'day-sky'. *Deiwos… Dyer… Deiwos…* That's how in the very beginning Zeus' name was first sounded.
CHORUS	It's night now, so forget him.
	(Quiet singing)
HESTIA	Yet the day-sky is changeable And Zeus' name will last In human tongues no longer Than each day that is forgotten: *'Deiwos'* will fade into *'Teiwas'*, *'Tiw'* will die on Tuesday – As *'Woden'* will on Wednesday; *'Thor'* will fade by Thursday…
[CALLIOPE]	No, a god lasts for ever and ever!
	(Music changes)
PYTHONESS	*N-mr-to… M-brotos…* Before the Age of the West 'Ambrosia' did not mean immortal: It only meant 'not mortal' Or perhaps 'postponing death': All the gods know that…

HESTIA	That is why they drink so much,
	Humans too should be careful
	When they drink from a poet's wine-bag. (*)

(They all drink deep. Another flash of light far off and a deep hooting sound. THIRD WOMAN enters in everyday clothes)

THIRD WOMAN	Is your play not over yet?
	You must change or you'll miss the boat.
CHORUS	We are Muses now! – We're immortal!

(They put on their masks and become wilder and more reckless)

[CALLIOPE] –	Where have you been?
THIRD WOMAN	To Dodona.
HESTIA	The Oracle of Zeus...
CHORUS	Did you find it? – Did you see him?
THIRD WOMAN	All I found was a petrified oak-tree.
HESTIA	What did you learn there?
THIRD WOMAN	More than they have.
CHORUS	Sit down and shut up
–	We are talking about the gods.
THIRD WOMAN	You? God-talk? Girl-talk;
	Get up and get dressed.
CHORUS	Not till we've finished the wine-bag.
	They begin to sing again
THIRD WOMAN	*God*...do any of you
	Either know or think you know
	What you mean when you speak of the gods?
	Do you really believe
	One word the Poet's told you?
CHORUS	How can you say that
	When we have drunk their nectar?
THIRD WOMAN	Why believe in the words
	Of a poet, a priest or a prophet?
CHORUS	Because they speak gods' words.

THIRD WOMAN   But god's priests may twist them:
               And how can you assume
               A god speaks our language?
               How do you even know
               If gods speak words at all?
               Time to go home.

               (*An ancient apple rolls from behind the tree,
               but they do not notice. A strange deep sound
               like a foghorn is heard far off. A rope falls loose
               from the rock above. Music ceases*)

CHORUS   What's that?

THIRD WOMAN   It's the Boatman.

CHORUS   If we don't all change at once
               We shall miss the last boat
           —   Not till we've finished the wine-bag
           —   We don't know where our clothes are.

THIRD WOMAN   You are very silly girls:
               They are all over there.

               (*She goes and fetches some*)

               If you don't put proper clothes on
               You won't be allowed on the boat.

               (*THIRD WOMAN dumps a pile of their own
               clothes in front of them*)

[THALIA]   The Boatman will let me on!

THIRD WOMAN   It is not the same boatman:
               This one is ugly and surly.

[CALLIOPE]   Better put them on then.

CHORUS (*To Erato*) You can't go home like that.

[ERATO]   First let us finish the wine-bag.

[MELPOMENE]   I am never leaving this place.

THIRD WOMAN   At least put your shoes on.

[ERATO]   Muses never wear them.

               (*She passes the wine-bag to THALIA and
               MELPOMENE*)

THIRD WOMAN   You two, get dressed at once!

[THALIA]	But I feel soft as swan-down: Has anyone seen a swan?
[ERATO]	Try the bull-rushes, gorgeous.
[THALIA]	Don't need clothes where I'm going.
	(*She starts to undress as she goes*)
[MELPOMENE]	Urg…I am feeling peculiar.
HESTIA	Don't be sick in the streams.
THIRD WOMAN	Get it over behind the bull-rushes.
[MELPOMENE]	O Zeus, I feel terrible!
	(*She rushes out. The fog-horn sounds again. The rest begin changing*)
CHORUS	Where's my dress? – Where are my sandals?
–	That's mine! – No it isn't!
–	She's mixed them all up.
HESTIA	Leave your masks; they may be needed In some other play.
	(*The foghorn sounds again. MELPOMENE runs back, followed by THALIA*)
[THALIA]	Look what Zeus gave me: catch!
[MELPOMENE]	The swan had me, not her! I am feeling much better.
	(*MELPOMENE catches the apple and throws it to another girl. CHORUS girl throws it back to MELPOMENE*)
CHORUS	Catch!
THIRD WOMAN	Stop this!
CHORUS	Catch!
[ERATO]	Let me see it!
[MELPOMENE]	Catch!
	(*MELPOMENE throws it at ERATO, who catches it*)
[ERATO]	Oh, it's a golden apple!
CHORUS	Look up there – It's the one! (*)

(*The tree begins to glow with golden apples and gold dust falls*)

HESTIA   *Wespero... Hesperides...*

(*Silence. The CHORUS look up in awe*)

CHORUS   Now I believe that all
Is true that the Poet told us
  – We are back in the Golden Age
  – We will feast with the gods tonight!

THIRD WOMAN   No, The Boatman is waiting.

[MELPOMENE]   Why don't we climb up and pick some?

PYTHONESS   Let Tantalus remind you
That the gods punish those
Who steal their private property.

HESTIA   All human makings
Begin with a kind of stealing.
Poets and prophets...

[ERATO]   And pretty girls like us!

[MELPOMENE]   If each of us takes one
It will make us immortal!

(*She drinks again from the wine-bag*)

CHORUS   We'd like to – But we daren't
  – Hera wouldn't like it.

[MELPOMENE]   Dionysos would!

[THALIA] (*Drinking*) He has blessed us: let's enjoy it!

(*MELPOMENE, THALIA and ERATO put on grotesque masks and begin to sing and dance obscenely. A rope falls loose from above*)

HESTIA   Muses, like their music,
Have grown rather noisier
Than they used to be in the old days.

[THALIA]   We're not Muses, we're Maenads!

[MELPOMENE]   Now I feel the god inside me!

(*The rope falls towards the ground*)

[ERATO]   You could climb up this rope
And they could swing it sideways.

HESTIA	For climbing trees and mountains The proper dress is fawn-skin.
[ERATO]	Thalia, up the tree-trunk; Melpomene, the ropes!
CHORUS	If it swings too much we'll hold it!
THIRD WOMAN	The ropes weren't meant to swing on!
[MELPOMENE]	If they can hold the rock up They can hold up Melpomene.
CHORUS	Careful, you'll anger the gods.
THIRD WOMAN	You must stop this!
HESTIA	Why? Each must be as they are.
[MELPOMENE]	One more drink and follow me! (*)

(*The boat-horn sounds louder as the three of them begin to climb. The rest pass round the wine-bag. A ragged man appears, almost naked and wetter than ever*)

[CALLIOPE]	Wait! There's a man in the bull-rushes!
CHORUS	It's Odysseus, spying on us While all of us were changing!
ODYSSEUS	It is just as Athene told me: Nausicaa of Phaeacia Is playing ball with her maidens! I know you will treat me kindly.
CHORUS	But how will you treat us?
ODYSSEUS	Take me to your father: He will give me a ship.
CHORUS	Go away – It is typical Of dirty old men and sea-dogs To snoop where girls are dressing.
ODYSSEUS	Do you think I want a woman After three years with Circe And seven with Calypso? I want my Penelope But Poseidon keeps wrecking my ship.

CHORUS	– Back in the sea, sailor-man
	– You stole the Palladium
	– You branded us and whipped us.
CHORUS	Odysseus, piss off.
ODYSSEUS	I fear that in this country They speak an uncouth language. Save me once more, Athene! (*)

(He disappears as the sea sounds)

CHORUS	Forget him, look up there! – Let's all be Maenads too!

(The rest of the CHORUS put on masks and begin to dance round the tree)

[MELPOMENE] (*Swinging*)	Look, I'm on my air-horse!
[THALIA] (*Above*)	Ouch!
CHORUS	What's the matter?
[THALIA]	There's a twig caught in my knickers.

(Detritus begins to fall from above)

[MELPOMENE]	Oh, I'm feeling air-sick.
[THALIA]	Look, do you see what I see?
[ERATO]	I can't see anything; Your feet are in my face.
[THALIA]	It's the genitals of some god!
HESTIA	It's Heracles…still climbing Trees in the Hesperides…
CHORUS	Heracles: let's see him!
[THALIA]	Ooh, I've got him!
CHORUS	Who?
POET (*Above*)	Leave my text alone!

(Pages of writing fall from the Tree, while other detritus and dust keeps dropping from above)

HESTIA	Pick them up: no litter Is allowed in Hera's garden.

CHORUS	Time for testicles, not text!
[MELPOMENE]	My hair's caught: help, I'm unhappy!
POET (*Above*)	Stop fiddling, woman!
[MELPOMENE]	Stars and rock and dust Are falling from the sky!

(*Garments fall from above. The rock quivers, and there are increasing rumbles in earth and sky*)

HESTIA	Sometimes when Atlas totters Mother Earth has qualms.
[MELPOMENE]	Help us, we're falling!
THIRD WOMAN	It's the rock, not you!
PYTHONESS	Sky-quake and fire-blasts!
(*To Audience*)	See how Poseidon's horses Flood the forests and the plains! Mark the tale of the Apple-Tree, The pleasure and the pain: What has happened before Is happening again... (*)

(*Cosmic commotion begins: thunder, lightning, fireworks etc. The Fire leaps high as more detritus and dust fall*

THE ROCK FALLS to head-height

A mist descends: as the dust settles it clears. The CHORUS have disappeared. The SECOND and THIRD WOMAN are standing naked, holding the towels they used at the opening of the cycle, now burned and dirty, to cover themselves. The FIRST WOMAN still sits by the remains of the fire, dressed as she was at the beginning. The wind blows and the sea sounds. Then silence. The POET stands as CHARON beneath the rock, masked and ancient)

CHARON	The ferry boat is full But I will be back: Zeus' plan is fulfilled.

(He takes his mask off)

THIRD WOMAN   But the rock has not quite fallen.

POET   Not yet, but it will.

(He goes)

FIRST WOMAN   So you two missed the boat?

SECOND WOMAN   We missed it, but the rest
                Went with the Boatman.

THIRD WOMAN   All gone... Nothing... Silence...

SECOND WOMAN   All the birds in the world are dead.

THIRD WOMAN   All the pretty girls are gone...

(Silence)

                I can still hear a baby weeping.

FIRST WOMAN   Put more logs on the fire.

(FOURTH WOMAN, in the remnants of ERIGONE's wedding-dress, comes out of the cave carrying a real baby)

                Ah, here comes my hundredth baby.

SECOND WOMAN   What is its name?

FOURTH WOMAN   I have named him 'Penthilus'.

SECOND WOMAN   What does that mean?

FIRST WOMAN   It means 'Assuager of Grief'...

(FOURTH WOMAN suckles the baby. The wind rises and sea sounds. ODYSSEUS crawls in, even wetter, a survivor)

ODYSSEUS   Save me from Poseidon!

FIRST WOMAN   You must do that for yourself.

ODYSSEUS   Is this Ithaca?

FIRST WOMAN   Not yet,
                But Penelope is waiting.

SECOND WOMAN   Finish your own story!

(He disappears into the sea. Storm rises and falls)

THIRD WOMAN   Sh, the child is sleeping.

FIRST WOMAN   When he wakes you must teach him language.

FOURTH WOMAN   O I have, he has already
                            Spoken his first word!

                            (*She cuddles the child*)

                            Gheue...gheue...ghuto...

SECOND WOMAN That's baby-talk, not language.

FIRST WOMAN   Have you forgotten already
                            What you learned beneath the earth?

SECOND WOMAN Yes, forgotten.

FIRST WOMAN   That is the first word
                            Which every baby speaks...

THIRD WOMAN   What word?

FOURTH WOMAN   *Gheue...ghuto...*

FIRST WOMAN   That is how in the beginning
                            The name of 'god' began.

SECOND WOMAN That?

                            (*ERIGONE sheds her dress and becomes a
                            modern girl again*)

FOURTH WOMAN (*Gurgling*) *Gheue...ghuto...*

SECOND WOMAN I seem to remember now:
                            In the beginning 'god' only
                            Meant 'Him or her whom we call on'...

HESTIA   It is said so among the wise.

FOURTH WOMAN But when he learns to speak
                            Which god shall my baby honour?

FIRST WOMAN   If he's wise he'll honour all of them.

THIRD WOMAN   We've all forgotten their names.

FIRST WOMAN   Then it's time to go in
                            And tell the child the stories.

                            (*The three WOMEN take the baby back into
                            the cave murmuring Gheue etc. The FIRST
                            WOMAN lies on her back and looks skyward.
                            A bird chirrups far off*)

Zeus, have they forgotten you?
Are you sad? Are you lonely?
Come down to your Mnemosyne
And she will refresh you.

(*Bird chirrups again. She speaks to the
audience*)

In the very beginning
Or perhaps a little after
A black dove was seen
Flying north from Egypt;
It flew and it flew and it flew
Till it came to an oak-tree
Ancient, gnarled and twisted
In the mountains of the north-lands.
It perched there and rested
Till it chirped and it twittered
And began to proclaim
The Oracle of Zeus.

(*Sounds of bird-song. The MUSES begin
singing far off*)

Soon feathers were fluttering
All over the young world
And on Dodona's tree-tops
A thousand birds were perching
All singing the mind of Zeus!
It is said (though it is not certain)
That the fishes in the sea-deeps
Sang softly too as they danced;
And on every branch of the oak-tree
There hung rusty bits of bronze
Left there by some ancient race:
It is told if you listen long enough
To the chirrups and the clankings
Sometimes if you're lucky
You will learn the mind of Zeus...

(*Much bird song and clanking. Feathers fall,
the streams bubble and all the MUSES sing*)

The End

POSSIBLE CURTAIN-CALL SONG

FOURTH WOMAN   Sing me the truth of things,
THIRD WOMAN   What's past and what's to come.
SECOND WOMAN   The First Things and the Then Things
FIRST WOMAN   Sing it, all or some.

ALL   The When Things and the Then Things
               The First things and the Last;
PYTHONESS   If you want to know the future
               You must go into the past.

CHORUS   Sing us the truth of it,
               The maybe and the might;
POET   And sing the things that do not fit
               If you want to get it right.

ALL   The How Things and the Now Things
               And the next things and the next;
POET   If you sing it true and sound it well
               It may grow into a text.

THIRD WOMAN   The High Things and the Why Things,
FOURTH WOMAN   The right things and the wrong
[THALIA]   The fixed things and the mixed things:
[MELPOMENE]   And the things that don't belong.

ALL   Sing it in the day-sky,
               Sing it in the night.
               Atlas, hold the earth up
               And Apollo show us light!

               (*The rock lifts as more ropes fall. The
               CHORUS swing on them*)